That's Not Fair!

A Teacher's Guide to Activism with Young Children

by Ann Pelo and Fran Davidson

Redleaf Press

Published by: Redleaf Press
                a division of Resources for Child Caring
                450 North Syndicate, Suite 5
                St. Paul, MN 55104-4125

Distributed by: Gryphon House
                Mailing Address:
                P.O. Box 207
                Beltsville, MD 20704-0207

Library of Congress Cataloging-in-Publication Data

Pelo, Ann, 1965–
    That's not fair! : a teacher's guide to activism with young children / by
Ann Pelo and Fran Davidson.
                    p. cm.
    Includes index.
    ISBN 1-884834-74-4
1. Multicultural education—United States. 2. Toleration—Study and
teaching—United States (Early childhood). 3. Discrimination—Study
and teaching—United States (Early childhood). I. Davidson, Fran, 1940– II. Title.

LC1099.3 .D393 2000
370.117-dc21
                                                        99-055729

To my parents, Carol and Ken, who prepared me for the journey and who continue to inspire and guide me, and to Margie, mentor and friend, who invites me to keep journeying.

ANN

To Barbara R. Hartsfield (April 10, 1933– January 28, 1999), "warrior woman" and tireless advocate for all children. I valued her friendship, her wisdom, and her fearless determination to live life to its fullest.

FRAN

Contents

Acknowledgments   vii

Foreword   ix

Introduction   xi

Chapter 1:
   Gathering Knowledge for the Journey:
   Guidebooks and Road Maps   1

Chapter 2:
   Preparing the Travelers:
   Fostering Dispositions for
   Activism in Young Children   21

Chapter 3:
   The Journey Begins:
   An Activism Project Emerges   45

Chapter 4:
   Travelers' Aid:
   Planning and Provisioning for
   an Activism Project   71

Chapter 5:
   Traveling Companions:
   Involving Families in
   Activism Projects   105

Chapter 6:
   The Journey Ends:
   Concluding an Activism Project   127

Chapter 7:
   Rest Stops and Other Oases:
   Finding Support   141

Resources   151

Acknowledgments

This book grew out of a series of workshops that we did with our friend and colleague, Kim Francisco, about our experiences with anti-bias activism and young children. As we met one morning to plan for an upcoming conference, Ann exclaimed, "We always have more to say than one workshop can hold. Let's write a book!" It seemed like a straightforward proposal, something we could do in short order after all those workshops together.

Hah. This book has been a journey for both of us. Along the way, Kim disembarked; the timing wasn't right for her and her family. We have missed her voice and her spirit.

On this book-writing journey, we've been both delighted with our adventures and footsore, eager to discover what waited for us around the next bend and daunted by unexpected detours. We had few maps, but made our way step by step, learning from each other and drawing on the support of many people.

Thanks to the families and staff at Hilltop Children's Center, especially Susan Alexander, Megan Arnim, Lisa Chambers, Sarah Felstiner, and Leslie Howle, for their generous accommodation of the writing process and their warm and nurturing spirits. Denise Benitez, Susie Eisman, Liz Kennedy, Nancy Lang, Danica Langaynor, Melissa Parson, John Pelo, Bonnie Robbins, Amy Stephens Cubbage, and Kathy Wilson-Fey offered sustenance—emotional, spiritual, and physical—on this long journey.

Thanks to the families and teachers of Madrona Cooperative Preschool who worked so long and hard to keep a dream alive. The school is no more, but the dream will endure in the hearts and minds of many. Special thanks to Roslyn Adams, Naomi Barry, Janine Chu, Mallory Clark, Karry Fefer, Joanne Graham, Lorraine Hoshide, Charlotte Jahn, Garry Owens, Bev Sims, Yuriko Ueda, Sara Yamasaki, Laurie Rotecki, and many more, for their wisdom and for their determination in the face of challenge and adversity to bring anti-bias curriculum to all of the Madrona families. Thanks to Denny, Shannon, Daran, Amy, Jake, Ben, and baby girl Davidson, and Peggy Mercer, who were there for every step; and to the many colleagues and friends who along the way offered encouragement and reassurances for the journey. Special thanks to Wei Li-Chen, who made the journey doable with her unwavering support and understanding.

Judy Fjell, Bonnie Lockhart, Ruth Pelham, and Nancy Schimmel willingly leaped into the project with a deadline near at hand and shared the power and beauty of their music with us. Julie Bisson opened her treasure-filled library of children's books to us. Beth Wallace guided us on this journey, sometimes nudging us forward, sometimes helping us find the road, always encouraging us to keep traveling.

We are indebted to the work of Louise Derman-Sparks and the Anti-Bias Task Force, who paved the way for anti-bias activism work with young children. When we were lost, their work was our road map.

Thank you, Stella. You brought lightness into our heaviest moments.

Foreword

When educators today discuss equity and how we can promote it within schools, it is common to hear phrases such as *community building* and *power sharing,* which embody lofty goals. But far less common are conversations about active experiments to achieve them—particularly strategies designed for very young children. Even the thought of children as activists in the social change process is a rare one in these broad discussions.

Since the publication of *Anti-Bias Curriculum: Tools for Empowering Young Children* (Louise Derman-Sparks and the ABC Task Force. Washington, DC: National Association for the Education of Young Children, 1989), early childhood care and education teachers are engaging more and more in helping young children learn about fairness and social justice. But I suspect that most teachers' first attempts at anti-bias curriculum activities boil down to helping children share with and be nice to people who are less endowed, or less privileged, or less accepted than they are. Where this is true, the enduring lesson learned is probably benevolence. Although benevolence is an important and desirable virtue, it is also, in essence, a single quality of character rather than a general, all-pervasive lens through which a person sees the world. And as the authors of *Anti-Bias Curriculum* tell us, the movement toward social justice may well benefit by the participation of people of good character, but it takes *social action* to make things change.

It is difficult to find material for teachers of young children that is grounded in this social-action point of view or that extends the lessons of anti-bias curriculum in this direction. That is why this book is important. For I firmly believe that we must continue to enrich the repertoire of anti-bias teaching strategies that lead us to fundamentally transform our societal relationships with one another and what they yield, not just temporarily shift sentiments and resources from one place to the next.

But why is it necessary to do activism with young children? Why can't we just teach children about the positive consequences of acting against unfairness and injustice? Because in order to foster their disposition to take action against injustice, we want them to experience how it feels to engage in group social action, and in so doing, to nurture their sense of themselves as change-makers. We want them to experience the power of working for change.

Why are some people more than a little uncomfortable with children in the role of change-makers? Because it suggests that we are placing the responsibility on children to change society, and absolving adults from this burden—shifting it off to children, if you will. However, as the authors of this book suggest, the adults choosing this kind of work with young children have a responsibility to be activists themselves. Modeling activism in one's own life creates the context for children to operate as change-makers. Instead of shifting the burden to children, which would be unfair and inappropriate, we are encouraging them to respond with action to the unfairness they already experience and witness.

In order to do activism with young children well, we must thoroughly understand what we want children to learn about activism before we engage them in this work. We must understand it, in contrast to benevolence, as an *engagement in group activity* to change some condition rather than an individual quality of character. I remember a similar feeling of understanding something very profound when, while in graduate school, I figured out what Erik Erikson really meant when he described the first socio-emotional task of childhood. Prior to my revelation, I had thought that developing a sense of trust versus mistrust meant that the child learns she can trust the world to meet her needs. But after reading carefully and rethinking and reflecting, I began to understand that a sense of trust develops as the child learns *she can trust herself* to get what she needs in the world. It is as much a sense of assurance about her own efficacy as it is confidence in the world around her. It strikes me as being a very powerful moment in the developmental cycle of any human being.

In much the same way, I feel the potential power in the moment we help children come to realize their own efficacy as activists who work *together* to create change. That is, to learn that "I can participate in making change happen" must help build self-esteem, empathy, and the ability to take another's perspective, yes. But it does more. It gives you the chance to feel the power of working with others to achieve some change. The power of joining with a group to fight for a just cause. The power of contributing to making the whole greater than the sum of its parts.

What Ann Pelo and Fran Davidson share through writing about their experiences here has much to offer, to each of us as individuals and early childhood educators, and to the change process in our society as a whole. Join them in nurturing young children's disposition to act against unfairness, and watch the world change!

CAROL BRUNSON DAY

Introduction

This book grows out of two European American women's experiences with young children and anti-bias activism. We had both been teaching young children for years, doing similar work in very different settings, when we were introduced to one another in 1993 by Margie Carter, a teacher educator in Seattle who knew that we were both passionate about working with young children to strengthen their identities as activists. We began to meet to talk about our activism work with young children, eager to share our stories. Out of our conversations came some shared notions: children naturally notice unfairness and have strong feelings about it; with adult support, children can think critically about unfairness and can generate creative solutions to address injustice. We also began to identify key dispositions that lead children to speak out for fairness. Inspired by our conversations and eager to share our developing understandings, we began to present workshops at local conferences.

As other people learned of our work, they introduced us to teachers and parents who also felt pulled to do anti-bias work with children. Among the people we met was Kim Francisco. As the mother of African American children, she recognized the importance of anti-bias activism both for her children as they identified and confronted bias and for teachers of children of color. Kim began to lead workshops with us, sharing her perspective as a parent that it is immoral to ignore or dismiss children's experiences and observations of unfairness.

The workshops we led together strengthened our beliefs, sharpened our thinking, and enriched our understanding about anti-bias activism. Our work with children has benefited from the learning we've experienced together.

We've come to activism through different doorways that reflect our life stories, our reflection, and our work. Our experiences don't represent the diversity that exists in early childhood education. We hope that other people will add their voices to this dialogue about young children and anti-bias activism, and that other experiences and perspectives will be highlighted.

We want to share how we came to believe that it is not only appropriate but critically important to engage with young children in anti-bias activism, so that you understand the context in which we work and write. Throughout this book, you'll encounter stories about our experiences with young children in very different settings. Despite these differences, there is a unifying thread: a shared commitment to act for justice for and with young children.

Ann's story

I came to activism in high school in Spokane, when I met a mentor who built on the predisposition to do good and to serve others that had been carefully fostered by my progressive white middle-class parents. My mother works for the Catholic church as a pastoral assistant. When I was a child, we were surrounded by free-thinking, passionate priests, nuns, and lay people who sought to create authentic faith communities distinct from the institutional Catholic church. My father taught history and politics for thirty-seven years in a high school serving one of the poorest legislative districts in Washington state. Growing up, I heard him talk with compassion about the kids he taught and coached, and with anger about the forces holding their families under siege.

Despite a family orientation that decried the injustices of the dominant culture, we were still a part of it. I grew up privileged by color and class, and certainly the unconscious rules of my culture were to accept my privilege without question. I didn't have to think of myself in terms of race or class, because mine were the givens in mainstream America.

My commitment to peace and justice work led me into work with young children. After my college experiences with a range of justice and social change movements—working with adults, then teens, then preadolescents—I wanted in on the ground floor, where attitudes form and become cemented. I wanted to help shape children's values and to coach them about how to oppose injustice. I didn't know about developmentally appropriate practices or educational principles, but I had vast experience with forming activist groups, with organizing protests, and with rallying people for justice. I had been hired as many of us in the field have been: I'd worked with kids in various settings—mostly school-age recreation programs—and was friendly and willing to learn. I was on the doorstep when the program needed a staff person. I had no particular training or experience with preschoolers, but I had a big heart.

My understanding of anti-bias teaching and activism has deepened and changed as I've taught and learned. I've spent several years deeply engaged in learning about the philosophy of the schools in Reggio Emilia, Italy, and about emergent curriculum as it's practiced in the United States. These have been powerful influences on my teaching and have shaped how I understand anti-bias work with children. Now, my anti-bias work is anchored in my commitment to shape children's values about themselves, community, and relationships.

My experiences with children have been primarily with white and privileged children. I've come to articulate my work in this way: to help the children in my classroom develop dispositions to use their power and privilege for justice. I want them to internalize a disposition to critical thinking and opposition to injustice, guessing that their position in our society now—in white, middle- and upper-income families—will not change radically as they grow into adulthood.

I'm more like the families at the center where I work than unlike them. The kids have, in many ways, the childhood that I had. That shared culture provides a common ground on which to build.

Hilltop Children's Center

Since 1992, I've been teaching four- and five-year-old children at Hilltop Children's Center in Seattle. Hilltop is a full-day child care center. There are about seventy children enrolled at Hilltop, ranging in age from three to ten years old; most of the children are preschoolers.

The families and staff at Hilltop reflect the dominant culture of the urban neighborhood in which our center is located. The majority of the families and staff are European American, with only a handful of exceptions. The parents at Hilltop are mainly professionals, working full time in law offices, architecture firms, computer software companies, and other high-income fields. They are typically politically liberal, religiously unaffiliated, and culturally hip.

All of us involved with Hilltop take pride in staying on the cutting edge of the child care field; our program has been featured in journal articles and in videos. At the heart of our program is a commitment to child-centered learning, to social problem solving and critical thinking, and to an emergent approach to curriculum. At Hilltop, we view curriculum as everything that happens during our time together with the children. We believe that each moment offers an opportunity to explore relationships and to create a community that nurtures children, teachers, and families; each moment holds a question to pursue, a hypothesis to investigate, or a discovery to celebrate. For many years, we did not have a collective understanding of anti-bias work and how to integrate it into our program; each teacher brought her passions (or her lack of passion) about anti-bias issues to the classroom, and each teaching team found its own way to integrate anti-bias work and activism into the life of the classroom. We are only now beginning to talk together as a staff about issues of diversity and anti-bias work, exploring what a centerwide commitment to anti-bias work might mean for our program and reflecting on ways to involve parents in creating a school as dedicated to anti-bias work as we are to emergent curriculum.

Fran's story

How did I come to do this work, which I think of as anti-racist work for adults and anti-bias work for kids? My favorite story about this comes from my friendship with Kim Francisco, who is African American. After we had known each other for several months, and after we'd had many passionate conversations about ourselves, our children, other people, and the "isms," Kim said to me, "How come you know about this, Fran? How come you can talk about anti-bias work this way?" And Kim says she's always remembered my response: "Why, I sat in the front row with the oppressor!"

In the community just outside of Vancouver, British Columbia, where I grew up during the 1940s and 1950s, people worked hard to maintain a white, middle-class, Anglo-Saxon, Protestant enclave. Outsiders who were white but did not meet the other criteria changed their names and denied their roots in order to "melt in." People of color from China, Japan, and India lived on the outskirts of town, in the industrial areas where my father's business was located. Many were farmers who eked out a living selling their produce from baskets at the side of the road. They were the objects of racist name-calling and stereotypes. Jews, Catholics, and anybody whose last name ended with -ich or -insky also got called names; however, the daughters and sons of white immigrants came to the schools I attended and the parks I played in. Not so for children of color. To this day, I've not been able to figure out if or where they went to school.

When my older sister started college, she brought another view of the world to the four kids in my family. On the campus of the University of

British Columbia she joined the International Club. She met people of color from all over the world who could talk about British and American imperialism.

When it was my turn to attend college, I, too, participated in events at the International Club. This was my first exposure to multiculturalism, and my first model of inclusion. I was brought up in a world that was intent on keeping people separated by race, class, and gender, and on keeping the power and resources concentrated in the hands of a few white men. The folks in the International Club, on the other hand, were intent on dismantling those hierarchies and putting an end to exploitation and oppression, particularly in their countries of origin.

The meaning anti-bias work has for me today is rooted in the lessons from my past. Keeping people out, keeping people segregated, keeping people marginalized, keeping people oppressed and without dreams or hope—I learned about this at the feet of my elders. And as former Harvard University law professor Derrick Bell has said, it will be the undoing of us all. Multicultural inclusion, cultural democracy, cultural pluralism—all of these terms have meaning for me. They imply a struggle and movement toward equity and justice for all; they also imply dismantling hierarchies of power and privilege. For me this means listening to the wisdom of people of color, learning how to be collaborative, and experiencing the creativity and strength that swells from groups of diverse people working together to undo unfairness.

Madrona Cooperative Preschool

Between 1982 and 1997, I worked at Madrona Cooperative Preschool, first as a teacher, then as a parent educator. I think we got closest to creating a fair and just community at Madrona in 1990, my eighth year there as a teacher. Sadly, Madrona closed its doors in the spring of 1998.

Madrona Cooperative Preschool, located in the inner city of Seattle, had a legacy of multicultural perspectives and struggles spanning more than twenty-five years. Cultural, ethnic, racial, and socioeconomic diversity could be found among the families attending the preschool. In addition, some of the children had special needs, and in later years there was a deliberate effort to recruit families with gay and lesbian parents.

The paid staff at Madrona consisted of one or two teachers and the parent educator. Because Madrona was a parent cooperative, four parents helped in the classroom each day. Kids came to preschool for three hours each day.

Assembling snapshots from Madrona's twenty-five years would reveal these demographics:

- Consistently around 50% of the children were of color, mostly of Asian and African descent. Included in this number were biracial/bicultural children. Filipino children were a strong presence in the Asian cultural group. Many of the children from minority cultures were also bilingual.

- Many different religious practices were represented among the families, mainly Buddhist, Jewish, Catholic, and liberal Protestant.

- There was a range of socioeconomic conditions among the families. Almost 40% of the school population received tuition scholarships. Two homeless families also participated in the co-op.

- The paid staff was mostly white women.
- Fathers participated in all aspects of the co-op, including working in the classroom, serving on the board, and planning curriculum, although not in equal numbers with mothers.

Up until 1987, parents and staff talked about the curriculum at Madrona as "multicultural." The following points reveal something of how that curriculum looked: ethnic foods were served at snack time; ethnic music, dance, and folk tales were included, as were dress-up clothes that included ethnic costumes; dolls with different skin colors, some dressed in ethnic costumes; art projects that came from ethnic traditions; ethnic cooking projects; field trips to experience cultural/ethnic events in the community; family potlucks with a focus on ethnic foods and entertainment; posters on the walls depicting "children around the world" in ethnic costume; and songs, numbers, colors, and salutations in the different home languages of co-op families and staff. The intent was to highlight the rich interplay of the different ethnicities and cultures. Most parents contributed with pleasure and pride, and most children delighted in noticing and celebrating the differences and similarities.

In 1987, I learned of the about-to-be-published *Anti-Bias Curriculum: Tools for Empowering Young Children*. I recognized it as the next step for the co-op: adding "confronting unfairness" to "becoming comfortable with differences."

The introduction of the anti-bias curriculum turned out to be a catalyst for conversations that had been neglected in the more benign interpretation of the multicultural curriculum at Madrona. As the school became more firmly rooted in an anti-bias approach, we revisited our philosophy, policy, and practice. Board members were sensitized to the need to include multiple perspectives in their decision-making processes; anti-bias principles informed the methods of hiring, enrollment, recruitment, and fundraising; and every fall new families had to be oriented to the meaning and interpretation of the anti-bias approach at Madrona Cooperative Preschool.

Bringing anti-bias work into the classroom began with taking a look at the existing multicultural curriculum and ridding it of its "tourist" aspects. The sights, sounds, smells, and celebrations of different ethnic groups, so very much enjoyed by the families, continued to be woven into the daily life of the school. That didn't change. But the anti-bias curriculum introduced an approach to thinking and talking about differences that went beyond the senses and celebrating. It called upon adults and children to take a look at the issues of unfairness and injustice that accompany some differences, and to consider why this is so.

That's Not Fair: A Teacher's Guide to Activism with Young Children

Our experiences have shaped this book. Our lives and our work with children provide the lens through which we examine anti-bias activism. We offer you these stories about our lives and our teaching to put this book in a context. Knowing our histories and our teaching experiences will help you better understand our insights about anti-bias activism.

As you read this book, you'll encounter stories about children's activism. These stories took place at Hilltop and at Madrona. They are rooted in those particular contexts and grew out of the unique communities of children and families in those schools. We offer these stories as examples of what's possible when children are supported as change-makers, not as formulas to follow or themes to try in your classroom. We encourage you to reflect on the particular context and the unique community of children and families in which you teach, just as we reflect here about the contexts in which we work. We believe that teachers do their best work when they are aware of their personal journeys as teachers, and attuned to the unique people, places, and times that create the context for their teaching.

Throughout the book, you'll find songs written for young children about fairness and activism. We've enjoyed singing with children about justice and peace, following a long tradition in which music both grows from and shapes movements for justice and peace. Together with Nancy, Bonnie, Ruth, and Judy—the songwriters who offered their songs to us—we invite you to sing these songs with the children you teach as a playful yet potent way to strengthen children's identities as activists. You can hear Nancy's songs on her Web site at www.sisterschoice.com. Just click on the button that reads *Songs from That's Not Fair!*

When I Feel Mad

Words and Music
© 1991 by Bonnie Lockhart

Chapter 1

Gathering Knowledge for the Journey: Guidebooks and Road Maps

If we teach children to recognize injustice, then we must also teach them that people can create positive change by working together. . . . Through activism activities, children build the confidence and skills for becoming adults who assert, in the face of injustice, "I have the responsibility to deal with it, I know how to deal with it, I will deal with it."

—Louise Derman-Sparks and
the Anti-Bias Curriculum Task Force

"Activism with kids? Now that's a stretch." "Why would anyone want to do that? We have enough to do in our classrooms already!" "These early years are for playing and having fun, not solving the ills of the world!" "That's for adults, and they shouldn't be forcing their political issues down the throats of young children! I'd say *that's* what's not fair!"

These are some of the responses we've received during our workshops on activism with young children. However, our experiences working within an anti-bias framework and responding to the emergent themes in children's play have convinced us that children do indeed want to be change-makers. As children go about their work of noticing differences, they also recognize the inequity inherent in some of those differences and want to do something about it. They want to be activists!

The anti-bias approach as a foundation for activism

Early childhood education changed dramatically when the groundbreaking book *Anti-Bias Curriculum: Tools for Empowering Young Children* was published in 1989 (Louise Derman-Sparks and the ABC Task Force. Washington, DC: National Association for the Education of Young Children). *Anti-Bias Curriculum* shone a spotlight on the social and cultural context in which children grow and learn. It provided a foundation for understanding how children acquire bias and offered teachers of young children strategies for countering this developing bias. The book sparked a movement in early childhood education to support children's cultural identities and to teach children to resist bias.

Anti-bias education moves beyond the limits of multicultural curriculum, which acknowledges and celebrates cultural differences and similarities. Teachers who use an anti-bias approach to curriculum recognize the importance of celebrating cultural differences, and they also believe that it's essential to help young children understand and confront the social and cultural biases facing them. As children work to make sense of their world by noticing and naming similarities and differences, they also begin to attach societal biases to these similarities and differences. Anti-bias curriculum invites children to notice, name, and actively respond to bias. Teachers who use anti-bias curriculum strategies encourage children to challenge injustice and inequity, even as they celebrate differences and similarities.

Very young children, perhaps as young as six months old, notice skin color differences (Phyllis Katz, interviewed in the video *Prejudice: A Big Word for Little Kids,* produced by Patty Johnson at KSTP-TV, St. Paul, Minnesota). By the time children are three years old, they begin to absorb social biases about skin color, responding positively to light skin and negatively to dark skin (Katz, ibid.). When children are four and five years old, they begin to enforce stereotypical gender-appropriate behavior in their play: Girls ought to play house, boys ought to play with cars (*Anti-Bias Curriculum: Tools for Empowering Young Children,* Louise Derman-Sparks and the ABC Task Force, National Alliance for the Education of Young Children, 1989). Preschool-aged children also soak up societal biases about gay and lesbian people, people with disabilities, and people who speak with accents, among others. Misinformation, stereotypes, and omissions in books, TV programming, and videos influence children's understanding of their world.

Consider this scenario: A boy and a girl sit together in the middle of a pile of small blocks. While the boy chooses the green blocks to build with, the girl picks out all of the pink ones, commenting, "I like pink and you like green. Pink is a girl color." They begin to build towers side by side. Their shared delight in their work ends when the boy impulsively demolishes the towers, sending the girl into howls of rage. She's even angrier when her building companion comments, "You're a crybaby. Girls always cry." These children are refining their knowledge of themselves and of each other. As they notice similarities and differences ("I like pink and you like green"), their understanding is infused with biased cultural values ("pink is a girl color" and "girls always cry").

Shortly after the publication of *Anti-Bias Curriculum,* Louise Derman-Sparks identified four goals for anti-bias education. These goals have been widely disseminated, and have been published most recently in *In Our Own Way* (Cecelia Alvarado et al. St. Paul: Redleaf Press, 1999) and *Start Seeing Diversity* (Ellen Wolpert for the Committee for Boston Public Housing. St. Paul: Redleaf Press, 1999).

When teachers consistently keep anti-bias goals at the center of classroom life, both adults and children get better at recognizing social injustice and understanding its origins. The goals provide a useful framework for thinking about children's development in light of anti-bias issues and for creating a curriculum that supports dispositions for activism.

As part of their daily work with children, teachers notice details about their development: whether or not a child is walking, or that they love to draw, or that their speech is hard to understand, or that they can count by threes, or that they hate to get dirty and never play in the water table. In the same way, teachers who are using the four anti-bias goals as a framework notice the ways in which children show a strong sense of who they are, or their comfort or discomfort with differences, or their ability to speak up in the face of

The Four Goals of Anti-Bias Education
developed by Louise Derman-Sparks

Goal One: Nurture each child's construction of a knowledgeable, confident self-identity and group identity.

Goal Two: Promote each child's comfortable, empathetic interaction with people from diverse backgrounds.

Goal Three: Foster each child's critical thinking about bias.

Goal Four: Cultivate each child's ability to stand up for herself or himself and for others in the face of bias.

unfairness. There are a lot of ways to create systems to use the four goals in your classroom planning. Here are some examples.

Some teachers use the goals as a way of thinking about individual children's development and learning. For example, below is a story about Trevor, a four-year-old in Claire's class. What do Claire's observations tell her about Trevor's development in terms of the four anti-bias goals?

> Trevor was the first to welcome Wendy, who has an unsteady gait, into the classroom, always saving her a place at the snack table as she moved slowly across the room. Now Claire observed him hovering near the play of several imaginative girls, drawn to their ever-changing "rescue" dramas, yet being pulled back into the Lego play of his buddies by their admonishments that "dress-up is girl stuff."

Teachers can also make sure they reflect the goals in the activities they plan for all of the children. Sometimes, as in this case, teachers plan this way in response to their observations of developing biases in the children.

> After observing the tension that Trevor experienced between traditional girl and boy play, Claire decided to plan curriculum around the issues of gender bias and gender role limitations. She started by using some pointed and yet open-ended questions to learn more about the kids' understandings of gender identity. She began to stock the reading corner with books depicting boys and girls, men and women working together and making choices outside of traditional gender roles. And she began thinking about field trips the group could take to visit men and women working at nontraditional jobs.

Some teachers create posters representing the goals and hang them in the classroom to remind themselves of the everyday appropriateness of the goals. Sometimes teachers use the anti-bias goals to inform their regular classroom themes. For example, a teacher considering a harvest theme for fall might think about ways to give children the opportunity to reflect on the ways several different cultures celebrate the harvest, ask parents to share their harvest customs with the class, or ask questions and hold discussions to help children explore the tension between the abundance of the harvest and the scarcity that many people experience. In considering any theme, teachers can think about how to strengthen and support children's understanding of themselves, how to incorporate differences, and how to help children think critically about stereotyping and unfairness. Regular attention to these questions supports children's development of the dispositions crucial to activism and prepares them for the emergence of an activism project.

Other practices for weaving the anti-bias goals into the daily life of the classroom include telling stories and singing songs that highlight the anti-bias goals. The resources at the end of this book includes a list of anti-bias books and music for children. Thinking games like those featured in Carolyn Pope Edwards's book *Promoting Social and Moral Development in Young Children* (New York: Teachers College Press, 1986) invite children to wrestle with questions of difference and similarity, fairness and unfairness. Here's a story about Ann using a thinking game in her classroom to promote the children's ability to think critically about questions of unfairness.

One fall, a small group of children in Ann's class became embroiled in a debate about how many crackers kids ought to eat for snack after nap. The debate raged at the snack table over several days, and kids weighed in with passionate opinions. After about three days of controversy, Ann decided to create a thinking game about this fairness issue. The next time the class gathered for a meeting, she brought out some puppets and acted out a story.

"I'm hungry," said one of the puppets. "I didn't eat much lunch and I'm really hungry for lots of crackers."

Another puppet responded. "You have to just have three, like me. You can't eat a lot of crackers."

The first puppet explained, "But I didn't like the lunch today and so I didn't eat it and I'm awfully hungry. I have to eat crackers or I'll be too hungry to play."

"But it's not fair for you to eat more crackers than me."

"You're not as hungry as I am, so you don't need as many crackers."

Ann stopped the puppet show and turned to the kids. "What's fair here? Should kids all have the same amount of crackers, or should kids eat as many crackers as they're hungry for?"

The children were silent for a moment, then leaped into a loud and energetic conversation.

"Kids should all have the same amount. Some kids feel sad that they don't have as many crackers as their friends."

"It's not fair if a kid is hungry and they don't get enough crackers."

"But one person can't eat all the crackers. It's not fair for the kids who didn't have any snack."

"Mommies and daddies bring snacks when they pick kids up, so a kid could just wait and eat that snack, and just have the same amount of crackers as everyone else."

The conversation continued for quite a while. The children thought deeply about this problem, as they explored a range of perspectives and became more articulate about their own points of view. The thinking game helped the children sort out the fairness and unfairness issues, solidifying their dispositions to pay attention to other people's ideas and feelings, to speak out about unfairness, and to work together to solve problems.

Goal One: Nurture each child's construction of a knowledgeable, confident self-identity and group identity

Many teachers feel comfortable with this goal because they are familiar with strategies that build self-esteem. However, this goal challenges teachers to stretch beyond conventional self-esteem building and to consider the issue of culture in the healthy development of children. Teachers working on this goal explore the meaning and implications of children's cultural identities. They support the development of a strong and healthy cultural identity in children from nondominant cultures, paying attention to bias that gets in the way of a healthy identity. Teachers also support the development of a strong and healthy identity in children from the dominant culture by challenging the conditions that contribute to their false sense of superiority.

Teachers can begin to work on this goal by examining the images of children, families, community workers, and cultural heroes reflected in classroom books, puzzles, games, posters, and photos. Do they reflect the families, cultures, and communities of the children? Do the images of people of color reflect healthy, happy people at work and play, rather than just dressed in costume? Do they reflect the diversity present in our communities and in the country in nonstereotypic and nontrivial ways? Appropriate and accurate images speak loudly to children and families, affirming that all people share equal and valued status in the classroom.

Goal Two: Promote each child's comfortable, empathetic interaction with people from diverse backgrounds

This goal takes into account what teachers already know about children's cognitive, social, and emotional development. Children make sense of their experiences by noticing and classifying what is the same and what is different.

Teachers working on the second anti-bias goal with children encourage and model positive responses to differences. They help children develop the cognitive awareness, emotional disposition, and behavioral skills that they need to comfortably negotiate differences and to understand the common humanity that all people share. Teachers call attention to differences in positive and relaxed ways; for example, a teacher may point out textural differences in the clothing that children wear or she may draw attention to the different kinds of families in the school. Teachers respond with openness to children's observations of differences: "You're right, you have skin that is a lighter color than his skin." "She uses a wheelchair because her legs don't work for walking." "His voice sounds like that because he can't hear, and not hearing changes how people talk." Teachers seek out ways for children to encounter differences, stocking their classrooms with books, fabrics, music, and materials that represent a range of cultures and experiences.

Goal Three: Foster each child's critical thinking about bias

When children feel confident about themselves and comfortable with other people and their differences, they can begin thinking about the bigger scheme of things. They can begin to identify names, images, and behaviors that are unkind, untrue, or unfair. They can begin to think critically about bias and injustice.

Teachers sometimes call children who are at this stage of anti-bias development the "unfairness police." Teachers can appreciate this attention to unfairness as a sign that children are developing a healthy concern for themselves, for people in their immediate circle, and for people they encounter in books, stories, and real life.

Teachers working on the third anti-bias goal take every opportunity to help children reflect on their observations of unfairness. Teachers may paraphrase children's comments about unfairness: "Yes, it really is unfair that he ate all the snack crackers. Let's figure out why he might have done that." They may ask open-ended questions: "Why do you think she said that to the woman on the bus?" Teachers may weave together the ideas of several children: "Jana thinks the boy is crying because he got his pants wet and so does Jerome. But Carlos thinks it's because no one will play with him. What do you think, Daisha?" Teachers acknowledge children's feelings and thoughts about unfairness and build a foundation for children to take action against the bias they identify.

Goal Four: Cultivate each child's ability to stand up for herself or himself and for others in the face of bias

This goal builds on the first three; a confident identity, empathy for others, and critical thinking are necessary prerequisites for confronting bias. Children who grow up comfortable with who they are and with the differences they encounter in others, who recognize that all people feel anger, disappointment, pain, and joy, and who think critically about unfairness are likely to want to take action to remedy injustices.

In response to this goal, teachers build on children's observations of unfairness by encouraging children to reflect on their feelings and to think critically about an issue. For example, a teacher who overhears children in the dramatic play area discussing what to do about a shortage of play foods uses that opportunity to initiate a conversation about people's real-life experiences of not having enough food and what people can do to help with that problem. This leads to a trip to a food bank, lots of questions for the people running it, and a list of foods the children could gather. Later, the children play "food bank" in the drama area, collecting and distributing food to their playmates, pretending to be hungry and to be helpers, and making lists of foods that everybody needs to eat.

This book is about the fourth anti-bias goal: nurturing young children as activists.

What is anti-bias activism?

Children wrestle with unfairness daily, whether it's a part of the teacher's lesson plans or not. Children notice unfairness because children notice differences. That's how they make sense out of their world. I have one doll. You have three. And that difference isn't fair to me. I get to live in a warm, cozy house. You're living on the cold street. And that difference isn't fair to you. A big leap, yes, but one that young children make eagerly when their teachers encourage them to pay attention to their feelings and experiences and to the feelings and experiences of other people. Anti-bias activism provides young children with a way of challenging the biases they see in their own lives and in the lives of others. Anti-bias activism happens in programs where teachers wholeheartedly promote action rather than indifference or resignation as a response to injustice.

In teachers' daily work with young children, they focus much of their time and effort on social interactions and social development—helping children learn how to interact with respect and kindness, how to understand and respond to one another's feelings and ideas, how to resolve conflicts, how to divide materials fairly. Teachers help children sort out how to share a new toy, for example, or how to make more space at the art table. They coach children about words to use when they are angry or sad or have a problem to resolve: "Tell her that you feel mad when she takes your playdough." "Say, 'I don't want you to knock down my block tower.'" They work to teach children how to respond when they are treated unfairly or hurtfully and when they see someone else treated unfairly or hurtfully. When teachers do this, they are laying the foundation for children to stand up to unfair, biased, or discriminatory behavior.

This daily work with children about equity and fairness leads naturally to activism around larger social and environmental issues. Children naturally notice and ask about the homeless woman they see in the neighborhood park, the man in a wheelchair they see having difficulty getting across the street, the plastic bandage that matches some children's skin colors but not others', the differences in decor in the boys' and the girls' bathrooms. These observations create opportunities for teachers to explore what children do know and support them in their desire to address inequity.

What are the characteristics of young children's activism?

Young children's activism is different from adults' activism. Often, children's activism is simple and direct. It may be as straightforward as confronting a peer about a biased comment: "You called my friend 'Squinty Eyes' and that's not fair. Her eyes are shaped that way because her mom and her dad are from China and that's how people's eyes look in China. 'Squinty Eyes' is a mean word."

Children's activism typically has a clear, tangible focus: helping people who are hungry or changing the layout of the classroom to accommodate people in wheelchairs, or writing a letter to point out the stereotyped images of American Indians on the box of log-shaped blocks. Children's activism is not aimed at abstract systems and social structures, but at particular experiences of unfairness.

The activism of young children often contains elements that adults consider fanciful: collecting coins to give to homeless people "so that they can buy houses," for example. Children do not see all the subtleties and complexities that adults see. They are not weighed down by the intricate systems of oppression, power, and resistance. They are not intimidated by the size and historical weight of injustices. Children leap in to name and remedy unfairness with a desire to help and confidence in their efficacy, unburdened by worries about what's realistic.

The children's experience of acting against unfairness, of exerting themselves to make a difference in their community, is as much about developing the disposition to be change-makers as it is about achieving specific goals related to the project. It is doubtful that the children's distribution of coins to homeless people will change much in those people's lives. It is very likely, though, that the children's distribution of coins will change how they think of themselves.

What is the value of activism for children?

Many teachers who consider anti-bias activism with young children hesitate because they see the danger of adults using children to address their own concerns. Many people also want to preserve the image of childhood as a time free from worries about injustice in the world or other "political" issues. But children are quick to notice injustice and eager to remedy it. Anti-bias activism is a natural outgrowth of children's awareness of what's fair and what's not fair, a natural response to their readiness to act for fairness. Activism is an important validation of children's observations and experiences.

Anti-bias activism has other intrinsic benefits for young children. Activism projects

- nurture self-esteem and empowerment
- develop empathy and appreciation for differences
- facilitate critical thinking and problem solving
- provide a mental model of survival for children at risk from bias
- provide a model of equity and justice for privileged, dominant culture children
- contribute to community-building

In addition, like all child-centered project work, activism projects contribute to children's learning in a range of academic areas. As children craft letters and signs to ask people to pick up litter in a neighborhood park, for example, they are building a foundation for literacy. And as they count the coins they've collected for people who are homeless, or notice that there are six boy characters and only one girl character in a Winnie-the-Pooh story, children are strengthening their math skills. As children sketch a school building with ramps for people who use wheelchairs or sew new dolls for the drama area that reflect the diversity of kids in the classroom, they are expanding their creative representation abilities. Anti-bias activism projects support children's preacademic learning.

Let's follow the story of Joannie and her class of four year olds and examine what they gain from their concern for the safety of an elderly neighbor.

Activism nurtures children's self-esteem

Children's self-acceptance, their sense of power and control, competence and moral virtue are nurtured and strengthened when they engage in anti-bias activism. When teachers listen respectfully to children's feelings and ideas about bias, they communicate to children that their feelings and thoughts are valued. When teachers affirm to young children that they can tackle real-life problems, children take on unfairness issues with the creativity, determination, and tenacity of seasoned activists. Activism is an empowering process for young children; it calls on them to flex their social, emotional, intellectual, and sometimes even their physical muscles. They work together to solve complex problems, make forays out into the adult community, ask questions, and declare their feelings. Children understand and feel proud that their activism is meaningful, real-life work about doing good in the world. Activism projects create many opportunities for children to experience the satisfaction that comes from working collaboratively as change-makers.

Some of the kids in Joannie's four-year-olds class were worried that Mr. Beasley, an elderly neighbor who moved slowly with a cane, might be hit by a car as he tried to cross the street near his home. "There isn't even a crosswalk," remarked one child, who had been talking about this at home.

"What if a big ol' truck comes roaring down the street? Then he would be dead," said another.

"He can't even run, you know," a third child observed.

Joannie, who also had concerns for the children's safety in this neighborhood of seemingly indifferent drivers, initiated a conversation about traffic safety when they were out for a walk one day. She asked questions such as, "How do you think drivers know when to go fast and when to slow down?" and "How do you keep yourself safe when you're walking near traffic?" She wanted to stimulate the children's thinking and to find out what the kids already knew. Back at school they made a list of traffic safety rules. They also generated an action list of ideas for improving conditions, especially for elderly people, which, at this point, was the real concern of the children.

Activism develops empathy and appreciation for differences

Activism projects grow from children's feelings about unfairness. They are built on children's empathetic responses to the needs of different people.

Sometimes an activism project will take children to places outside of the neighborhoods and communities familiar to them and to places where they are likely to encounter differences among people as well as issues of unfairness.

When teachers provide opportunities for children to process their feelings and thoughts about bias and the impact it has on people, they foster in children an appreciation for differences and a deepening sense of empathy. For example, when the children in Joannie's class expressed their anger and fear about Mr. Beasley's dangerous street crossing, they found respect and support for these feelings, as well as for their thinking about the circumstances that had created this serious problem. This response on the teacher's part supports the children's developing empathy for Mr. Beasley and for other people in unfair situations.

> The children and Joannie worked together to compose a letter to send to the mayor, outlining the traffic safety issues they had identified on their street. "Dear Mr. Mayor," it read, "Our school is near an unsafe street. Cars and trucks and buses and motorcycles and even taxis go really fast on our street. There aren't any crosswalks or stop signs or flashing lights. Also, we couldn't find a speed-limit sign, and we looked everywhere, even on the ground. Mr. Beasley, who is old and our neighbor, could get knocked down. And so could we. Sometimes we trip on the bumpy sidewalk when we are running. Mr. Beasley can't run, but he still could trip and fall when he is walking. Please help us to make our street safe for Mr. Beasley and the other old people and for us and for our teacher Joannie."
>
> Having given their final approval to the letter, the children were anxious to get it into the mailbox. They counted the days as they waited for a reply. And when they received a response, Joannie read aloud the letter that affirmed their concerns and made note of their suggestions. The children listened carefully and proudly. One child said, "I think the mayor thinks we are really, really smart, and nice too."

Activism facilitates critical thinking and problem solving

Activism projects grow from children's observations of unfairness; they are not preplanned curriculum units carefully scripted by teachers. For children, this means that their work is quite real and meaningful. They wrestle with ideas and experiences, name a range of feelings, ask questions, and explore answers. They follow their passions rather than teacher-prescribed activities. They draw on their critical and creative thinking skills as they chart a course to address unfairness.

> With the children focused on Mr. Beasley and his safety, Joannie encouraged the children to share their thoughts and feelings about aging by asking open-ended questions: What happens to our bodies as we get older? What things can old people do? How do different communities take care of their aging citizens? The kids told lots of stories about their grandparents and invited some of their grandparents to visit the school. These visits challenged the stereotypes that some children have about older people. Joannie planned a trip to a neighborhood nursing home. Before their visit, a social worker visited the school and described what the children would see and do at the nursing home. Meanwhile, some of the children became interested in helping older people who lived in the

 school's neighborhood. They dictated a list of their ideas to Joannie: "Things we can do to help: pick up litter, sweep sidewalks, do errands, be crossing guards." Joannie respectfully considered each of them, offering them to the group for discussion.

Activism provides a mental model of survival for children at risk for bias

Children of color and other marginalized children (poor children, children with lesbian and gay parents, and children with disabilities, for example) are at risk for internalizing cultural biases that tell them that their place is on the sidelines of society, out of sight and out of the way of people with power, privilege, and ability. When these children participate in anti-bias activism, they develop a mental model for survival in a society that does not value them. As Louise Derman-Sparks writes in *Anti-Bias Curriculum*, "For children to feel good and confident about themselves, they need to be able to say, 'That's not fair,' or 'I don't like that,' if they are the target of prejudice or discrimination" (77).

For children of color, anti-bias activism offers a way of understanding their experiences in a racist culture and practice with confronting racism. As children of color move from their homes and preschools to enter the world of elementary education, they are at risk for experiencing racism at the hands of other kids and teachers. They will experience racism embedded in the educational system (see, for example, *Savage Inequalities: Children in America's Schools,* by Jonathan Kozol. New York: Crown Publishers, 1991). With anti-bias activism, teachers affirm children's feelings, acknowledge the unfairness they see and experience, and encourage them to confront bias. Children learn to recognize racist images in books and the media. They become familiar with a legacy of opposition to oppression. Experience with activism communicates to children of color and other marginalized children that pain and anger are legitimate feelings in the face of racist words and deeds, and it is important to take action in the face of injustice—that you are not alone as you do this; your peers and teachers will support you.

Anti-bias activism offers the same benefit to children who experience injustice because they are poor, or the children of lesbian or gay parents, or disabled, or female. When teachers foster in children the skills to think critically and to take action in response to unfairness, they give them a lifelong model for survival. By taking action, children resist internalizing the bias directed at them. They begin to acquire the skills that will allow them to actively and collaboratively confront injustice for the rest of their lives.

> Joannie assembled books from the school's collection that featured elderly people, some of them grandparents. While sharing them with the children, the group made the discovery that none of the books featured people who looked like the African American and Asian American children in the class. Following a resounding outcry of "That's not fair!" they brainstormed what to do about this. Already accustomed to taking action, they easily filled the chalkboard with creative ideas: update their collection with books from the library or from home; write letters to the people who write books about this omission; write letters to the people who buy books—librarians, bookstore owners, teachers, and parents—asking them to favor books that feature a variety of ethnic groups; and finally, make their own books featuring their grandparents and the elderly people they know. The process of generating this list allowed children the opportunity to talk about their feelings, to think critically about the problem, and to begin to take action.
>
> Rebecca remarked, "If I was the boss of the whole city, or even of the whole world, I'd tell the people who make books that they have to do it—that they have to have pictures of families with two moms, and two dads, and even one mom. And they have to have pictures of my friend Danny, who is Deaf and who knows how to play, too."

Activism is a mental model of equity and justice for privileged, dominant-culture children

Like their marginalized peers, dominant-culture children are put at risk by bias that goes unchallenged. The risk for privileged children is absorbing feelings of superiority and entitlement. These economically and culturally advantaged children are surrounded by images and experiences that not only affirm their existence and importance, but also promise that if they "set their mind to it" they can do and have anything they want. Role models who occupy powerful positions in the popular culture are abundant for these children. Often, children who are white and middle- or upper-class live apart from people of color and other disadvantaged groups. They may not encounter people whose lives are different from theirs, and the only images of happy and successful people they see in books, TV shows, and videos may well be white. These kids may conclude that people who look different from them and live differently from them are less important, less central, or simply less successful than they are.

Anti-bias curriculum, with its emphasis on celebrating diversity while at the same time confronting unfairness, brings to these children a more balanced picture of what the world is really like. As they learn about people who are different from them, European American upper- and middle-class children come to know about the people who are not reflected in their daily experiences and about the similarities and differences of many groups of people. Anti-bias activism helps children to develop a healthy and realistic assessment of their own cultural identities, coupled with a developing sense of empathy for those treated unfairly because they are judged different from the norm.

Anti-bias activism invites privileged children to recognize unfairness and to act on it, joining together with other privileged children and with children who are marginalized. It invites them to stand up for the rights of all people to be treated kindly and with justice. It invites them to use their privilege to bring about justice.

> When a young boy from a wealthy family criticized Mr. Beasley for "not driving a nice big car like my grandpa does when he goes to the doctor and stuff" and another child made fun of his clothing, Joannie decided to address issues of financial privilege head-on. She played a game of "store" with the children, giving some kids a lot of pretend money and some kids only one or two pieces of pretend money. When the kids with just a little money ran out, they got mad and sad that they couldn't play anymore, while the kids with lots of money could still buy things at Joannie's store. Joannie stopped the game for a conversation about the children's feelings. She pointed out that the kids with lots of money might choose to share their money or buy things for the kids without money. She wanted the children to experience some of the dynamics of wealth and poverty, and to wrestle with the moral issues of privilege.

Activism contributes to community-building

Anti-bias activism work with young children contributes to a feeling of community among the families in a classroom group. By focusing children, families, and teachers on issues of fairness, activism brings people together to think about real problems, and to share their wisdom and expertise in search of solutions. Families and teachers may share their feelings about and experiences with unfairness and bias. They come to know one another in new ways as they talk about these real and complicated issues.

> The children's concern for Mr. Beasley's safety on the streets helped Joannie and the children's families articulate their concerns about how the traffic conditions affected the children. They recognized that these city kids would soon be walking or taking public transportation to many of their destinations, and that they would need to be street smart. The parents were grateful when Joannie told them that she would be teaching and enforcing safe practices when they were out walking in the neighborhood, and parents agreed to reinforce these safety rules away from school.
> During all the conversations about traffic and transportation, the children and Joannie learned that Jerry, one of the kids in the class, came to school on a bus with his grandmother each day. Children in the class exclaimed that it

wasn't fair that his grandmother had to travel by bus every day. They took this news and their feelings home to their parents. Some parents worked out a car-pool to help with Jerry's transportation. In the course of the planning, several other carpools formed, as parents learned about the intricacies of one another's schedules and transportation arrangements.

And finally, because the children's concern for Mr. Beasley developed into a concern for other elderly residents in the community, three families chose to adopt an elderly neighbor and to take on more serious issues like house and yard maintenance and transportation to appointments and to the grocery store.

Am I ready to engage in anti-bias activism with children?

Many doorways lead teachers to anti-bias activism with young children. Some teachers are drawn to this work because of their life experiences. Teachers of color, or teachers who come from other marginalized groups, may have experienced the ways in which activism contributed to their cultural survival. Teachers who have experienced privilege may also see social justice as central to their survival and want to work for equity.

Teachers' goals for children's learning may lead them to anti-bias activism. Some teachers engage in this work because they want to extend the social, moral, and cultural learning of children in their programs. Other teachers may arrive at anti-bias activism because of their commitment to creating a curriculum about the issues that emerge from the children's play. Parents' goals for their children may open the door for anti-bias activism, as well. Some parents have asked teachers to focus their programs around anti-bias issues.

However they may have arrived at anti-bias activism, teachers who do this work with children share some common ideas. Anti-bias activism grows out of

- our concern that every child will grow up in a world that is fair and equitable for all people
- our commitment to children's whole growth and development
- our respect for children's ability to recognize and challenge unjust acts and deeds
- our passion for and our practices of taking action to address social and environmental injustice
- our deepened understanding of the anti-bias goals and principles and how they liberate the children and families we work with and ourselves

These ideas provide the foundation for our work with children. As you think about your interest in supporting young children as change-makers, ask yourself the questions posed in the following exercises.

What is the role of activism in my own life?

Many teachers who engage in activism can describe the role of activism in their own lives. They have thought carefully about the value of activism for adults, considering when and why it is appropriate for adults to take a stand. They are aware that adults have many different perspectives about activism and a range of comfort levels with it.

What are my expectations for young children's activism?

Adult activism looks quite different from children's activism. Teachers understand that young children's activism is not a way to promote an adult political or social agenda. Instead, they believe it encourages children to view themselves as change-makers. For example, a teacher who hears children comment on the litter in the playground encourages them to pursue an activism project about cleaning up the neighborhood. She wants children to know that when they see a community problem, they can do something about it. During the project, she keeps her focus on strengthening children's awareness of themselves as activists rather than on teaching children that littering is bad.

This is a subtle but important difference. Activism work with young children is about children acting as change-makers rather than adults imparting social and political lessons. This work requires teachers to be always vigilant about not allowing their adult passions to overwhelm children's activism. If teachers are not scrupulous about this, children do not learn that they can make change; they only learn that their teacher feels strongly about a particular issue. Teachers can get involved with adult activist organizations to work on issues they care about, but the work in the classroom with children ought to stay focused on children's pursuits.

What is my experience with anti-bias curriculum?

Teachers who engage in activism with young children understand the basic principles of anti-bias education. They may have read the pivotal book *Anti-Bias Curriculum: Tools for Empowering Young Children.* They may have attended workshops or taken classes about anti-bias work with children. Before stepping into activism with children, some teachers reflect on how anti-bias curriculum fits into their teaching context. For example, a teacher who works in a program that primarily serves children of color may emphasize the elements of the anti-bias curriculum that build children's knowledge about and pride in themselves. A teacher who works in a program that primarily serves white, middle-class children may emphasize experiences of diversity to counter a white-centered view.

?

To think about:
Reflect on your knowledge of and experience with anti-bias curriculum. What are your strengths? Are there aspects of anti-bias work that you want to learn more about? What would help you become more skillful?

To do:
Review *Anti-Bias Curriculum: Tools for Empowering Young Children* by Louise Derman-Sparks and the Anti-Bias Task Force. Pay particular attention to chapter 9, "Activism with Young Children."

Make a list of words that describe the group of children you currently work with. What anti-bias issues and goals do you think are most important to emphasize with this group of children? Why?

How do I already build curriculum from children's interests?

Teachers who undertake activism with young children are ready to pay close attention to children and their interests and to build those interests into the curriculum. They understand that children use play to explore ideas,

questions, and experiences, and so they observe children at play to learn about what children are thinking and feeling. They recognize that the learning that engages children most is rooted in children's lives—they learn about children's thinking and feeling as the basis for curriculum. For example, a teacher who observed children playing house day after day noticed that the children debated daily about who should be in a family: a mom and a dad? one mom alone? two dads? She decided to focus her curriculum on families so that she could support the children's exploration of who makes a family. She responded to the issue that children were exploring in their play by shining a spotlight on it with her curriculum planning.

To think about:
How do you include themes from children's play in your curriculum planning?

To do:
Practice observing children's play and naming the themes of their play. If the play you observe were made into a movie, what would its title be?

How do I currently work with parents and other teachers?

Teachers who practice activism with young children regard themselves as collaborators with parents and colleagues. They are comfortable talking with parents and colleagues about child development, anti-bias teaching, and the issues that children explore in their play. They value the insights and understandings that other adults offer about young children's learning and seek out conversations with them to stimulate their thinking and planning. They recognize that parents know their children well, and they use parents as resources to help them understand the children in their group.

To think about:
How would you describe your relationships with the parents in your program? In what ways do you collaborate with parents?

How do you keep parents informed about what is happening in the classroom? Will this approach change at all when you begin to engage the children in activism?

To do:
Educate! In the next few weeks, begin to talk about your interest in anti-bias activism with families in your program. Share your thinking and questions about anti-bias activism with them, and ask them for their thoughts.

Who will support my activism work with young children?

Teachers who engage in activism with young children realize that they need a support system. They know they need to talk about the issues that arise when children notice unfairness, and they want someone to listen and offer insights, encouragement, and suggestions. They seek out people who believe that activism with children is important and appropriate, and who recognize that it brings up unusual challenges for teachers. They may rely on a partner or spouse, a coteacher, a licenser, a parent or teacher educator, or a director for this support. They don't venture into this work without a support system.

To think about:

What kind of support do you already have for your work with young children?

Who do you know who would support your work as you encourage young children to act as change-makers?

To do:

Begin to talk with your coteachers and program administrators about children acting as change-makers. Share your thinking and ask them to share their thinking. From these conversations, try to identify people who will support you as you begin the work of anti-bias activism with young children.

What's ahead in this book

In order to do activism work with children, teachers need to think about these things:

- How to plan learning experiences that lay the foundation for activism projects
- How to watch for anti-bias issues emerging in the classroom
- How to build an activism project around emerging anti-bias issues
- How to know when to bring a project to a close
- How to include families in activism projects
- How to build support for themselves

Each of the following chapters focuses on one of these issues. We explore them from several perspectives, reflecting on our teaching experiences and the different communities in which we work and live.

Playing Winnie-the-Pooh

Words and music
© 1999 by Nancy Schimmel

A girl went by some boys she knew, Saw they were play-ing Win-nie-the-Pooh, She stopped and asked if she could play, But the boys said, "Sor-ry, not to-day, 'Cause there are no girls in Pooh." Chris-to-pher Ro-bin! Pig-let! Roo! Does an-y-one here know what to do? It is-n't fair, but you know it's true, There are no girls in Pooh.

The boys said, "You could play a boy,
You could use this Tigger toy."
But she said, "No, it's not the same,
I could be a girl and play your game
If there were girls in Pooh."

　　Christopher Robin! Piglet! Roo!
　　Does anyone here know what to do?
　　It isn't fair, but you know it's true,
　　There are no girls in Pooh.

Then the Pooh toy said, in a growly way,
"If I had a sister, you could play!"
And the other boys said, "Helpful bear!
You found a way to make it fair!"
And now there's girls in Pooh.

　　Christopher Robin! Piglet! Roo!
　　Come meet the sister of Winnie-the-Pooh
　　She made us think about what to do
　　To get some girls in Pooh.

Chapter 2

Preparing the Travelers: Fostering Dispositions for Activism in Young Children

In *Helping Others Learn to Teach* (Urbana, IL: ERIC Clearinghouse on Elementary and Early Childhood Education, 1979), Lilian Katz defines *dispositions* as "relatively stable habits of mind" or "tendencies to respond to one's experiences or to given situations in certain ways." Although Katz was talking about adults, the concept applies to children as well. Children's dispositions—the ways that children think of themselves and others and the ways they tend to react to problems, difference, and unfairness—can either launch them into action as change-makers or encourage them to be passive in the face of injustice.

One of the most important tasks for teachers who hope to grow activism projects in their classrooms is to foster change-making dispositions in children. Young children's dispositions are being formed by the experiences they have every day. Teachers have a profound influence as young children develop dispositions that will carry them through their lives. They can encourage the growth of certain dispositions and discourage the growth of others by how they arrange the environment, what sorts of materials and activities they provide for children, how they respond to children's pursuits and struggles, and how they plan curriculum. There are five dispositions that are critical for change-makers. Below, Fran reflects on how she came to identify dispositions for activism in one of the children in her class at Madrona.

Fran: Like many children at Madrona, Eula expressed what I called "organizational" or "participatory" dispositions when she arrived at the co-op as a three year old. I didn't initially name her displays of leadership and authority so positively; I perceived her as "bossy." She seemed to spend an awful lot of time telling other children what to do and how to do it. I often found myself being the mouthpiece for another child's ideas, admonishing her: "Eula, listen to what your friends have to say about that."

But slowly, over time, I began to piece together a pattern: Eula had really good ideas, sometimes a vision of sorts, that she proposed, often in the face of chaos or disruption. Her ideas were action plans, and the kids welcomed them and even came to depend on them. I was the only person uncomfortable with her "bossiness"; her peers welcomed and respected her leadership. As I observed the group more closely, I began to see an aspect of Eula's leadership that I missed: Once she had proposed her plan or solution, she would drop back and listen to the other children. She seemed to understand the adult concept of participatory decision making. She spoke, but so did others. And I think that's why the kids didn't find her "bossy."

I didn't realize at first why Eula was the sort of leader that she was. I guess I assumed it was just her nature. It took time for me to realize that these patterns and tendencies were being shaped within a family and community that placed a high value on action as a response to injustice.

Dispositions for activism

As Fran came to know Eula and her family, she understood that Eula was developing the dispositions for activism. The following story about Eula and the postholes illustrates the ways in which Eula brought these dispositions to her work and play at Madrona.

When Eula arrived at school one morning, she made a point of telling Fran how strong she was, and how tired, from digging post holes. Her dad, Tyree, laughed, explaining that over the weekend, everyone in their neighborhood had rallied to replace a rotting fence that the wind had finally laid to rest. The fence belonged to an elderly widow who depended on her neighbors' help to remain in her home. Tyree said, "Everyone is expected to pitch in—even the kids. My kids know this already, and for the most part they don't complain. There's a lot of satisfaction for everyone in working together to accomplish something."

After hearing from Eula and Tyree about their fence-building, Fran decided to add some props to the play area to extend Eula's experience of helping build the fence and to invite her to practice her new skills. She put a couple of sharp spades near the tired fence surrounding the outdoor play area, thinking that Eula might want to continue digging postholes with her friends.

Later Fran encountered Eula absorbed in digging during outdoor time. She didn't stop as her teacher stood by admiring her work. She was proud of her ability to work hard and accomplish her goal. And soon her determination attracted other children.

Molly: "Why are you doing it? Can I do it, too?"

Eula: "Don't you even know about postholes? You've got to dig and dig and dig and dig—you don't do anything else. Here, dig!"

Eula adjusted her rhythm to include Molly, and the two worked silently for the next five minutes. Soon Sean, a good buddy of Eula's, rolled up on a tricycle.

Sean: "Get a bike, Eula!"

Eula: "Can't you see I'm doing something?"

Sean: "I want to do it too."

Molly: "You can't. It's just for girls. Right, Eula?"

Eula: "No, it's not. It's not fair for just girls to do it. My brother and my dad and my uncle Damien dig postholes. Everybody gots to. It's too hard work. Go get a really sharp shovel from Fran."

Molly stopped working, looked at Eula, and watched Sean approach Fran for a shovel. As the three began to dig, Fran hovered nearby, worried that these sharply pointed tools might injure someone as they came together in a tight circle. But she needn't have worried. When Molly came perilously close to stabbing Sean, Eula comforted him and demonstrated proper spade-handling techniques. Soon all three were digging furiously, clashing shovels, and laughing in delight at what had become an intimate gathering of friends.

Later, when Fran called the three together to point out the danger of leaving the holes open, Eula listened attentively before collaborating with her teacher and the other kids on a solution. And she was instrumental in keeping the other two kids focused on their responsibilities, saying things like, "You know, we have to work some more. Workers don't just stop. They work and work and work."

As she dug holes with Molly and Sean, Eula demonstrated habitual patterns of thought and action, the same ones that give rise to the cry "That's not fair!" and the readiness to do something about it. Although they take different forms in different settings, the following five dispositions in young children form a foundation for their ability to act for fairness.

- **Children notice and accept differences.** In this story, Eula's acceptance of and comfort with differences is reflected in her friendships. Eula, an African American girl, welcomes both Molly (European American) and Sean (African American) into her play, while quickly shunning Molly's attempt at gender discrimination.

- **Children include one another in their play; they are willing collaborators.** Eula began her work alone, practicing her new digging skills, but she soon made room for Molly and then Sean in her work. She taught them important information about digging postholes, so that they could join in her work with knowledge and skill.

- **Children pay attention to other people's ideas, feelings, and needs.** Eula paid attention to her friends' needs and feelings. She comforted Sean after his close call with Molly's shovel. She noticed that Molly needed help figuring out how to use a spade, and she offered instruction about safe shoveling techniques.

- **Children speak out about fairness and unfairness.** Eula confronted Molly's attempted exclusion of Sean.

- **Children take responsibility for solving problems, offering their ideas and action.** Eula took responsibility for addressing the danger of open postholes on the playground, collaborating with Fran, Molly, and Sean to implement a safety plan. She contributed suggestions about how to ensure her classmates' safety and rallied her friends to action.

Supporting dispositions toward activism

Teachers can support children's development of the five critical dispositions for activism both generally and specifically. General support can be offered in the ways they set up their classroom and plan the daily schedule. Specific support can be provided by interacting with children and planning curriculum designed to support children in noticing and accepting differences, including one another in play, noticing one another's feelings and ideas, speaking out against unfairness, and taking initiative to solve problems.

Supporting dispositions through planning the program

There are three general ways teachers can support the development of dispositions toward activism:

- Allow plenty of time for play.
- Replace teacher-made rules with negotiation.
- Set aside time to observe and reflect on children's play.

Allow plenty of time for play

Play should be a key element in every child's day. Through their play, children actively seek to explore and understand themselves, their friends, their culture, their experiences. With their play, they are asking questions, constructing knowledge, practicing elements of their home cultures, and extending and deepening their understandings. Providing time for children's play gives them the message that the activities they initiate are important and nurtures their disposition to offer their ideas and actions to solve a problem.

When teachers open long stretches of uninterrupted time (as much as an hour or two) for play and conversation, children discover ways to extend ideas, work through conflicts, and practice collaboration. When play is at the center of a program, children have many opportunities to interact with each other, noticing one another's feelings, listening to one another's ideas, learning to take one another's perspectives. They practice critical thinking and problem solving as they negotiate the course of their play. The learning that unfolds from play builds children's empathy, their ability to take another person's perspective, and their skills with critical thinking and collaborative planning.

There are many ways in which early childhood programs can prioritize play. Teachers may set up activity areas and balance teacher-planned curriculum work with time for "free play." During this time children are invited to choose from activities like dress-up play, sand and water play, blocks, puzzles, playdough, drawing and painting, and reading, establishing their own play scripts and following their own agendas. In other programs, teachers may plan the curriculum around the developmental themes and pursuits that they observe in children's play, creating opportunities for children to revisit and refine their understandings through a variety of encounters with an idea.

The following story from Hilltop illustrates the ways that children's play supports the habits of thinking and doing that are essential for activism. In their play, the children are building dispositions that they will later draw on to launch an activism project. The children propose ideas and listen to others, rethink their own and empathize with one another's positions, hypothesize solutions to a problem and consider a number of alternate solutions, and conduct experiments to see what works best.

Ian, Jeffrey, Adrianne, and Carl were together in the block area. They had built a castle out of wooden unit blocks, then tumbled it, laughing and shrieking. They had begun to put the blocks away on the shelves when Ian made a discovery. "Look at this teeter-totter!" he exclaimed, standing on a long rectangular block that had fallen on top of a cylindrical block. The block tilted and tipped from side to side, and Ian moved with it, delighted.

Carl began to investigate the mechanical workings of the teeter-totter. "Hey, you guys, watch this!" he commanded, and set a square block on the low end of the teeter-totter. Then, with a huge grin, he leaped onto the high end of the teeter-totter, flinging the block high into the air, to the amazement and delight of the other children.

When Carl catapulted the wood block into the air, Ann stepped in, alarmed, and asked the children to explain their new game. She knew that she did not want kids flinging solid wood blocks into the air to come raining down, but she really liked the spirit of joyful discovery that their game held. The children's game really wasn't a problem. It was not disrupting other children's play, and it was engaging and provocative and could be played safely. She decided not to stop the game right away, but to coach the kids to develop a safer way to play with the catapult. She told them that she would feel more comfortable with the catapult if they launched something soft into the air.

In no time, the kids were off searching the room like bloodhounds. Carl called out, "How about fabric pieces?" He grabbed several small squares of fabric from the drama area and brought them over. Adrianne arrived back at the blocks with a basket of corks. Jeffrey brought a handful of Lego plastic building blocks, and Ian optimistically carried over a container of playdough. Ann stepped aside as the children showed one another their finds.

"Not playdough! It would get stuck on the ceiling! That would be a huge mess!" laughed Adrianne. "I think only corks would work."

Carl agreed about the playdough: "Playdough is not a good idea. But not only corks work, Adrianne. Fabric is much better. Corks might still hurt someone."

Jeffrey thought the Lego blocks would be great. He gently held one against Carl's face: "See, it doesn't hurt at all. Legos really are soft."

The four children decided to try the Lego blocks, the fabric, and the corks on the catapult to see which was the "coolest" thing to send flying. Together, they figured out how to set up the catapult with the props on it. They argued and debated and critiqued one another's ideas as they worked. Which prop worked best? Should each kid use her or his own prop on the catapult, or should they choose one that everyone would use? How would they share the catapult? Would they take turns? Would each kid build her or his own catapult? Who should do the job of retrieving the flung props? Ann cringed inwardly at some of the suggestions and cheered inside at others, but she only entered the debate once, to say firmly that she felt comfortable with one catapult only, that four at a time would be too many.

The kids took turns using the catapult with the corks. They divided up the jobs to be done. One child was the "jumper," catapulting the corks all over the block area. The other kids retrieved the corks and set them up on the catapult, then stood back for the next jump. They decided it would be fair for each kid to jump two times in a row. Each time the catapult was set up, all four debated how many corks should go on it and which way the corks should be set up. It was an elaborate game, with a lot of collaboration and debate. The game lasted for about an hour, until it was time to clean up for lunch.

This story isn't about activism, but it is an example of the child-initiated approach to learning that makes activism a very real possibility in early childhood classrooms. As the children developed the catapult game, they proposed ideas and debated their merits, listened to one another's thinking, and tried to understand their friends' perspectives about what would make the game most fun and most fair. Through their play with blocks and corks, these children were honing the dispositions that activists need: the ability to empathize, to take another person's perspective, to think carefully about a problem, and to communicate ideas and listen to other people's ideas.

When play is a central element of children's days, teachers have many opportunities to study their play and learn about their passions, understandings, and misunderstandings and to identify the anti-bias issues that are important to children. In a more teacher-led program, adults may develop and lead an activism project in much the same way they develop and present other curriculum activities. The danger, of course, is that an activism project developed *without input from children* will reflect adult concerns and may fail to engage the children's passions, curiosity, or understanding. Activism projects that are given to children as "assignments" are inappropriate. Activism should grow out of children's developing understanding of themselves and their community. Children must have a real voice in shaping activism projects in order for the projects to be appropriate to their development.

Replace teacher-made rules with negotiation

Many teachers rely on rules to maintain order and fairness. However, in classrooms with many predetermined rules, teachers and children can spend a lot of their time enforcing and testing the rules. Long lists of rules can get in the way of children's creative and critical thinking. They can inspire rigid, dependent, manipulative, and antagonistic behavior as children focus on obeying and enforcing rules or on sliding past them.

One way of addressing this problem is to keep teacher-made rules to a minimum, to use them mostly to address issues of health and safety. As the need arises, children and adults can work together to generate classroom agreements about shared spaces and the materials and equipment in them, strengthening children's dispositions to speak out about fairness and unfairness and to take responsibility for solving problems. The process of debating classroom agreements can feel tedious for teachers who like to move swiftly through a list of daily activities. But when teachers want to support children's growth as people who can generate fair and inclusive solutions to problems, then conversations about how to share space and resolve conflicts become an important part of the curriculum. Indeed, this is the work of recognizing what is fair and not fair and doing something about it. This is activism work.

In some classrooms, for example, when two children want to use one toy, there is no rule about sharing to fall back on. Instead, teachers coach the children to talk about whether they want to find a way to play together or whether they'd rather make a plan about taking turns with the toy. In their conversation, the children are asked to consider each other's ideas, feelings, and needs to explore what is fair and unfair and to offer their ideas for solving the problem. When both children feel satisfied with a plan about the toy, they move on with their play.

For children who are members of nondominant cultures, the notion of creating and challenging rules may initially be uncomfortable. It may run counter to explicit messages they've received from their families that it is dangerous to question rules. Ann and Fran's colleague Kim, who is African American, remembers her mother teaching her that it was essential to her survival that she know, understand, and follow the rules of the dominant culture. As a parent, her perspective is somewhat different. She now encourages her children to know and understand cultural rules so that they can effectively challenge them. It's important to her that her children are able to identify and challenge unfair rules, and she views that as essential learning for her children's survival as people of color.

Set aside time to observe and reflect on children's play

Observing children at play gives teachers a window into their hearts and minds. Looking through this window, teachers can begin to see hot topics, big issues, flags about biases and stereotypes. As teachers watch and listen to children at play, they learn about children's interests, understandings, misunderstandings, and musings. This information then becomes the basis for activism projects that build on children's questions and passions. Read the story below for an example of a conversation that Ann overheard one day at Hilltop. What information about children's understandings and interests is contained in the conversation? How could you imagine following up on it in the classroom?

> Taylor, Anthony, and David stood side by side at the sand table, gazing across the table at Julia. "You have to be a boy, Julia," explained Taylor.
>
> "Yeah," said David, "There are only boys in Winnie-the-Pooh. I'm Pooh, Taylor's Tigger, and Anthony's Piglet. You can be Owl or Eeyore or Christopher Robin."
>
> The three boys had been playing a lively game about Winnie-the-Pooh in the sand table, using tiny animal figures as characters. Julia was eager to join their game, but reluctant to take on the persona of a boy. "I really want to be a girl. Are there any girls that I can be?" she asked.
>
> "There's only Kanga," answered Anthony. "She's a kangaroo, and we don't have any toy kangaroos to play with. We have an Eeyore and an Owl and a boy. You can be one of those."
>
> "No! That's not fair! I only want to be a girl."
>
> "There are no girls in Winnie-the-Pooh for real, Julia. I know because I read the story with my mom," David asserted.
>
> "I could pretend to be a different character, a new one that's a girl," offered Julia.

Taylor was open to this idea. "You could make up a girl, like Tigger's sister could be in the game."

Anthony objected: "Tigger doesn't have a sister!"

"We could just pretend that he does, okay?" said Julia.

"Yeah," said David. "It's just for pretend, not for real. For real, there's only boys. For pretend, Julia can be a sister."

Anthony conceded, and the kids looked through the bin of plastic animals for another tiger to take the role of Tigger's sister.

This conversation has the potential to launch an activism project about gender inclusion because the children are thinking and debating about the issue. They are personally invested in the issue. They didn't immediately move their conversation into consideration of activism, but they laid the groundwork for it by thinking about the absence of female characters in the Pooh stories and by caring about whether that absence is fair or not. They created a doorway into activism. Because she was listening to the children's conversation and reflecting on what it told her about their concerns, Ann was ready to follow up with them later.

When teachers listen carefully to children's play, they learn about what children are thinking and feeling, what experiences and issues they're struggling to understand, and what children know about a range of topics. The insight and information that teachers gain about children allows them to develop activism projects that are responsive to children's real concerns about injustice, rather than crafting activism projects that reflect adult passions and that are removed from children's thinking and feeling. Here's Ann's story about how the kids with the catapult became activists later in the year.

The children at Hilltop who created the catapult game joined with other classmates later in the year to initiate a schoolwide project to collect coins for homeless people. Their project was launched during a casual conversation in which one child, Julia, told the story of her encounter with a homeless person outside a neighborhood grocery store. Her story became fodder for children's play. They began to include homeless characters in their pretend games and to build houses for homeless people in the block area.

As Ann listened to children's conversations, she began to see a theme. Kids were concerned that homeless people were hungry and didn't have dry places to sleep in the rainy Seattle winter. They understood that homeless people didn't have money to buy food and houses, and they wanted to give them money. They weren't interested in homeless shelters, as adults might be, or jobs for homeless people, or the government's responsibility to help. They saw people who needed food and houses, and they wanted to give them money to buy those essentials. They thought of themselves as people who could take on the problem of unfairness and work to solve it.

As the children included homelessness in their play, they got better at articulating their understanding of the issue, and Ann became clearer about their concerns. Often during this project, she caught herself wanting to direct the children toward learning about homeless shelters or support agencies; however, the children's play continually brought her back to their passion about giving money to those who have little.

Throughout this activism project, Ann's observations of the children's play and their inclusion of homelessness in it kept her in touch with the children's real concerns. The child-centered nature of the program allowed for (indeed, demanded) this attention on Ann's part.

Supporting specific dispositions

In addition to supporting children's dispositions toward activism in the general organization of the program, teachers can support each disposition specifically through their interactions with children and through planned activities.

Children notice and are comfortable with differences

Young children explore the world with all their senses, tasting, touching, smelling, looking up close at an object to investigate it. They are curious, seeking to understand all that they encounter. In their exploration, children notice the ways in which things are similar or different. Sometimes they just notice ("That man has a big tummy"). Sometimes children attach judgments to what they notice ("That man is fat. He looks funny").

As you read the next story, notice how the children explore differences in skin color and share their understandings of what those differences mean in our society.

Two children arranged their classroom's multiracial collection of dolls on a long line of chairs. "These kids are riding on the bus," explained Jamie, one of the children, to the teacher watching their game.

The other child, Amber, addressed the dolls: "Now, you kids have to stay in your seats. No walking around on the bus. It's too dangerous."

Jamie asked Amber, "What if the kids don't like where they're sitting?"

Amber: "Well, they can't move, because they'll fall down and hurt their heads. My mom told me that when we were on the bus."

Jamie: "Let's put all the brown kids at the back of the bus. That's how it used to be. My grandma told me that when she was a little girl, she had to sit at the back of the bus because she has brown skin."

Amber: "That's not fair!" She gestured towards the line of dolls. "Kids can just sit wherever they want to, like this black boy is right at the front of the bus! Kids with brown skin and kids with white skin all get to sit anywhere."

Jamie: "I have brown skin and I don't have to go to the back of the bus. But my grandma with brown skin used to."

Amber: "I have white skin. I don't have to go to the back of the bus either."

Jamie: "Did your grandma have to when she was a little girl?"

That's Not Fair! A Teacher's Guide to Activism with Young Children

Jamie and Amber were investigating the meaning of skin color differences. The teacher had a choice: She might decide to honor this exploration of difference and discrimination, intervening to affirm that when their grandmothers were young, there were unfair laws in our country that required African American people to sit at the back of buses, and that many people worked hard to change those laws. This approach, which acknowledges skin color differences, would strengthen these children's disposition to notice and feel comfortable with differences. Or she might try to smooth over the children's conversation about difference, commenting that, "The color of people's skin doesn't matter. We are all equal and we can sit anywhere we want to on a bus. We shouldn't pay any attention to people's skin color." This approach would communicate that kids shouldn't pay attention to differences and would tend to undermine any disposition toward activism.

Although teachers encourage children to notice differences and similarities in objects—encouraging children to sort colors and shapes, for example—they sometimes feel uncomfortable when children point out differences and similarities in people. They worry that noticing a difference is inevitably linked to evaluating a difference, that the man with a big tummy will always be labeled funny-looking. Teachers want to teach children not to judge people in biased and unkind ways. But sometimes this leads them to promote a way of seeing the world that ignores differences. Their desire to avoid discrimination is communicated to children as a desire to ignore differences.

Children will continue to notice differences and similarities, whether adults want them to or not. In fact, this is a key disposition for young activists. We want children to notice differences and to accept them comfortably. Often, unfairness issues are rooted in discrimination because of differences. Children who notice differences and who are comfortable with them can identify discrimination more clearly and can explore the unfairness that arises from biased understandings of difference. This is the beginning of activism.

Another reason to encourage children to notice differences and to accept them comfortably is that children who are comfortable with differences are willing to collaborate on a project with a range of people. For example, a group of children at Hilltop decided to take action about homelessness. In the course of their work, they spent a lot of time with two homeless people, Anitra Freeman and Dr. Wes Browning. The children certainly noticed the differences between them and their two homeless friends, asking Dr. Wes one day, "Why do you always wear the same clothes every day?" and commenting to Anitra, "You live in a shelter and we live in houses." However, because they were comfortable with difference, the children readily accepted these two companions in their project, focusing on the unfairness of homelessness rather than on the differences.

Teachers support the disposition to notice and accept differences when they talk honestly and directly with children about differences: "That man does have a big tummy. He probably would feel sad if he heard people calling him funny-looking, though." "Her skin is darker than your skin because it has more melanin—that's something in our bodies that colors our skin."

To foster the disposition to notice and feel comfortable with differences, teachers can do the following:

- Make art materials such as playdough, paper, felt, crayons, markers, and paint available in a range of brown "skin-color" shades, and use a variety of music, books, and posters to stimulate and extend children's thinking about a range of cultural groups.

- Ask families to share artifacts and tools that reflect their ethnic identities. This often sparks discussions about difference and similarity and creates opportunities for conversations about culturally specific events and history, including struggles and heroes.

- Designate a place for children and adults to display things that are important to them, communicating that each person in the classroom is honored and that together they can create new knowledge and understanding about their group and get better at noticing individual differences.

- In programs serving primarily white children, infuse the classroom with images and stories of people who are not represented in the program. Avoid trivializing these cultures or making them exotic. It is important for children who have their roots in the dominant culture to look outside that culture and see real people. Books that feature people of color involved in regular sorts of kid adventures, face-matching games that include a range of people, and brown-hued playdough are examples of appropriate ways that teachers can introduce diversity into the classrooms of white children.

- Represent other kinds of diversity in the classroom. Images and stories about lesbian and gay people, people from a range of social classes, people with disabilities leading active and productive lives, elderly people, people with a range of body sizes, and women and men in nontraditional roles belong in early childhood classrooms where teachers hope to strengthen children's dispositions to notice differences and similarities and to pay attention to other people's ideas, feelings, and needs.

- Call attention to differences among children that arise during everyday activities in the classroom. For example, a teacher might say, "Look! Katie is using mostly green and blue on her painting, and Kazuo is using mostly black and red. Such different choices for their paintings!" or "Jenny's choosing to lie down to listen to the story today and Ben is sitting cross-legged."

- Out on neighborhood walks or visits to the park, play a game of finding autumn leaves that are different and the same—or pebbles, trees, birds, cars, clouds, traffic signs. . . .

- Invite children to try a range of new experiences, eating unfamiliar foods, for example, or exploring words in an another language. Call attention to the connections between these new experiences and children's more familiar world: "*Jambo* is another way to say hello—it's a word in a language called Swahili." "This fruit looks different than the fruits you're used to eating, but it sure tastes sweet—sweet like a peach!"

- Use persona dolls, puppets, or flannelboard stories to bring important differences into the classroom that are absent: for example, a Muslim family celebrating Ramadan, or a family with gay parents.

- Take polls that represent the range of experiences among the children and graph the results. Consider getting information on favorite ice cream flavors, names for pets, number of siblings, holidays each family celebrates.

- Regularly critique the classroom's picture books for omissions or stereotypes.
- Invite people to visit the classroom who are comfortable describing a "difference" in their lives, for example, a friend who works in a non-traditional job.

Children include one another in their play

As children grow from toddlers to preschoolers, they become increasingly interested in playing games with rather than just alongside other children. Young children are drawn to their friends' games, asking, "Can I play?" Children may easily welcome another child into their game, or they may resist. Their responses to these situations reflect the strength of their disposition to include others.

How do the children's dispositions toward inclusion show in this common scenario from an early childhood classroom?

Two children, Max and Tessa, were building a rocket with blocks. They played loudly and with energy, talking together about their plans to blast off in their rocket once it was built. Their game attracted Ella, who came to the edge of the block area and asked, "Can I play?"

Tessa looked up from the blocks and said, "No, we're building this just for two people. There's not room for three kids in this rocket." She returned to her building.

Ella, undeterred, replied, "It's not fair for just two kids to go in that rocket. I really want to be in your game. I don't like it when you just say no to me."

Max put down his block and looked at Tessa, then at Ella. "We are two astronauts going to outer space," he said.

Ella retorted, "Three people can be astronauts, you know. There can be a captain and a map-reader and a passenger."

Tessa said, "There's not room for three people, only two."

"I know how to build big rockets. I can help you build it," Ella said.

"Well, Tessa, what if we make it bigger? Then three people could fit in it," Max said.

Tessa began to shake her head, then changed her mind. "Okay, let's all three be astronauts. You can play with us, Ella." She started to rearrange one of the rocket's walls: "First, we need to make this bigger so three kids can fit. Here's what to do. . . ."

The three kids reconstructed the rocket so that there was room for all of them. Once they began building together, they became a team and their initial difficulties were forgotten.

Tessa's initial resistance to Ella's request to join the rocket construction was overcome as she listened to Ella and Max. Ella described her feelings about being left out. Max and Ella both proposed ways to change the rocket game by adding a passenger to the rocket's flight roster and making the rocket bigger. All three kids demonstrated their willingness to collaborate to make the game inclusive.

The disposition to include others and to willingly collaborate is important for young activists because activism rarely happens alone. Activism requires that children think together about a problem, propose and reflect on a range of possible responses to unfairness, and collaborate to address it. Just as Ella, Max, and Tessa negotiated a way for all three of them to build a rocket, children with the disposition to include and collaborate with others are able to come together to stand up for fairness.

To support children's disposition towards including one another, teachers can do the following:

- Coach children about ways to include their friends. They may suggest new ways to ask about joining a game: "How can I be in this game?" "What character can I be?" "What job can I do?" These questions require consideration beyond a yes-or-no answer and invite children to think in concrete ways about how to include another person in a game.

- Call attention to children's feelings. For example, "Ella says she doesn't like it when you say she can't be in your game. Ella, do you feel sad?"

- Help children think about ways to include others in their game. For example, "Does this rocket need a passenger?" "I wonder whether she could build a space station for you to visit in your rocket." "Let's make a plan about how three kids can use these blocks."

- Intentionally nudge children to "rediscover" one another. For example, when singing together, encourage children to build new relationships by announcing a guideline such as, "Find a friend whose hair is shorter than yours to dance with." Or during snack or small group activity times, arrange for children to sit with people that they don't usually play with (for example, by using name cards or place mats).

- Present the class with a challenge, inviting them to work together to solve a problem. Examples include moving all the blocks to a different storage area or making a path through the newly planted spring garden.

- During the early part of the year, ask the children to generate a list of ideas about what it means to be a friend. Check into the list throughout the year. Share your own observations of them being friends with one another, and ask the children to share their own observations, as well.

- Group the children together in twos or threes and ask them to figure out a game to play with one another. Establish rules like "every person in the group has to say yes to a game before you can start playing."

- Avoid placing limits on the number of children who can play in an area at one time (for example, "Three children in the block area"). Instead, encourage children to talk with one another about how to use a space together: "Five kids want to build here; how can we make space for that many builders?" "Let's figure out a way that all of you can use some playdough." "How could we find a way for you all to feel comfortable in the book corner?"

Teachers sometimes try to encourage a disposition toward inclusion by instituting rules: "No excluding" or "Children have to share." Rules like these, while well-intentioned, can shut down children's thinking about inclusion, fairness, and feelings. In response to them, children merely invoke rules or listen to teacher injunctions rather than thinking and talking carefully with one another.

Children pay attention to other people's ideas, feelings, and needs

As kids create games, take turns with toys, have arguments, and share space, they encounter a range of feelings, ideas, and needs. They may pay attention to the emotions and ideas that they encounter, or they may ignore them, holding tightly to their own experiences and reactions. Imagine this scenario:

Four children painted together around a table. Lauren and Toshi negotiated as they painted.

Lauren: "I'm painting my house. I have to use yellow paint, because my house is yellow."

Toshi: "You can have the yellow paint after me. I've got to have it first, because I'm painting the sun, and it's yellow, you know. And I'm going to paint yellow flowers. I'm going to take a long time with the yellow. You've got to wait."

Lauren: "I don't want to wait for a long time. I only want to wait for a little time. Maybe I can have the first turn and you can have the yellow after me."

Toshi: "Well, I don't want the second turn."

Lauren: "I've got to paint my house yellow. I have an idea! You paint the sun and then I paint my house and then you paint the flowers. That way, we just have short waits."

Toshi: "Short waits are more fair than long waits. I don't want a long wait and you don't want a long wait."

Lauren: "Yeah, so we should just pass the paint around. First you, then me, then you."

Toshi: "Okay, I'll paint the sun and then it's your turn to paint your house. When you're done, you give me the yellow again, okay?"

Lauren: "Okay. We can both use the paint."

As Toshi and Lauren negotiated turns with the yellow paint, Kendra and Evan worked on their paintings.

Kendra: "My ocean is the beautifullest. See how pretty it is?"

Evan: "Well, I don't care, because I'm just painting about sledding."

Kendra: "You're mean to say that. Mine is beautiful."

Evan: "I don't even want to listen to you."

Kendra: "I'm using all the blue paint and you can't use any."

Evan: "I don't even need blue paint for my picture anyway."

How were these conversations different from each other? Lauren and Toshi listened to each other, acknowledging each other's feelings and needs, considering several proposals for taking turns with the yellow paint, and finally settling on a solution that satisfied them both. Kendra and Evan, though, barreled ahead with their separate viewpoints, disregarding the other person's work and feelings. They might have talked about blue oceans and sledding or about the colors of paint they each needed; instead, they didn't so much interact as negate each other. The conversation between Lauren and Toshi reflected their dispositions to pay attention to other people's feelings, ideas, and needs. That disposition was not as well reflected in Kendra and Evan's conversation.

The disposition to pay attention to other people's ideas, feelings, and needs is important for child activists, because issues that lead to activism projects are often about injustices that hurt people or about people's needs not being met. Children who pay attention to other people's feelings and needs can identify these injustices. For example, children might notice that a classmate's shoes are worn out and learn that his family doesn't have extra money to buy new shoes. They might decide to offer their extra shoes to help. Or they might object to a TV ad claiming that "boys will love this new toy," recognizing that "girls can like that toy, too, and they'll feel sad to be left out."

In addition, this disposition provides a foundation for the collaborative work of activism projects. Lauren and Toshi, in the scenario above, are able to come up with a plan about taking turns with the yellow paint because they pay attention to each other's feelings, ideas, and needs. They can move their conversation forward, acknowledging their feelings and needs and then considering possible action plans before eventually settling on a plan that is agreeable to both of them. In just this way, children who are ready to take on activism are able to listen to other people's ideas and feelings, discuss strategies and hone action plans to address unfairness.

Teachers can support the growth of this disposition by doing the following:

- Create plenty of space for children to come together and play in the classroom, and avoid rules that limit the number of children in a space.

- Provide open-ended space and open-ended materials that encourage children to discuss, negotiate, and make decisions together about how to play.

- Coach children to notice other people's feelings and ideas. During conversations among children, teachers can coach: "Let's each take a turn telling an idea." "Look at her face—what do you suppose she's feeling?" "We'll know the problem is solved when everyone feels happy about the plan." "Each person in the game gets to help make up the rules." "He's hurt—ask him how you might help."

- Invite discussions about storybook characters' feelings and needs and about ideas that the children have about what a character might do and why.

- Use puppets and dolls to play out dramas in which characters both do and don't pay attention to one another, provoking conversations about the implications of both approaches.

- Give names to feelings, so that children develop an ample vocabulary of emotions. Games like "Moods and Emotions" or "Feelings and Faces" (both available from Lakeshore Learning Materials) help children recognize feelings and expand their vocabulary of words that describe emotions. That old childhood standby, "When You're Happy and You Know It," can be reworked with new verses that address current issues in the classroom, providing children with ways to think and talk about them. For example, you might sing, "When your friend feels lonely, invite her to play," to help children think about welcoming a new child into play. Or to deal with name-calling, "When someone calls you a mean name, say 'That's not okay.'"

- Play miming games with children in which they hone their skills at identifying the ways in which people express their feelings. For example, at a circle or meeting time, a teacher creates a story with feelings for children to name and act out: "When Jonah walked into his dark kitchen, he felt _____. What did he look like when he was feeling that way?" Children may want to create their own stories about feelings for their friends to act out.

Children speak out about fairness and unfairness

"That's not fair!" is a common refrain in early childhood classrooms. Four- and five-year-old children are quick to identify unfairness as they move through their days with other children: "It's not fair that he's taking a long turn with that truck," "It's not fair that she has more crackers than me," "It's not fair that she gets to go home early," "It's not fair that he always gets to sit by you," "It's not fair that her skirt twirls better than mine." Indeed, teachers hear this cry so often that they may begin to screen it out or shrug it off as a stage that kids move through, hoping it passes quickly.

However, this predilection to name unfairness is at the heart of an important disposition for activism. With adult support, children who think about fairness and unfairness in their everyday lives can expand their thinking to explore fairness and unfairness for other people.

Here's an example:

> Lou and Alex carefully lined up the play food along the top of the shelf in the drama area. "Let's get our store ready so we can sell food," Lou said to Alex. They arranged boxes and cans in neat rows, chatting as they worked about how much the food cost. When they finish setting up their grocery store, they went to find some bags for customers to use to carry their groceries home. As soon as they had left the drama area, Mac and Kyler left their nearby block structure and rushed over to the shelf. They each grabbed an armful of food and ran back to their block house. Lou and Alex hurried back to the drama area as Mac and Kyler disappeared into their house. "Hey! Give us our food back!" Lou yelled.
>
> "That's not fair! You can't just steal our food!" Alex exclaimed.
>
> Amy, their teacher, walked over to the drama area, stopping along the way to collect Mac and Kyler. "Let's have a meeting about what happened," she said. "I saw Lou and Alex get food ready for a grocery store, and I saw Mac and Kyler take some food into their house."
>
> She had barely finished talking when Mac declared, "Well, it's not fair they have all the food. We don't have any food in our game. We need food."
>
> Lou disagreed. "It is fair for us to have the food because we're making a grocery store. We need all the food to sell. It's not fair for you to take our food."
>
> Kyler argued, "But we don't have any food and we're in a house and we have to have food in our house or we'll be hungry."
>
> Amy intervened. "Lou and Alex want to use food in their store, and Mac and Kyler want to use food in their house. It's not fair for Mac and Kyler to take food out of the game that Lou and Alex are playing, and it's not fair for Lou and Alex to use all the food when Mac and Kyler need some. There are two things that are unfair. How can we solve this problem?"

Lou and Alex were quick to identify stealing as unfair, just as Mac and Kyler quickly named their shortage of food unfair. Amy supported the children's analyses and laid the foundation for negotiation around these conflicting views of fairness.

Activism is about taking a stand against unfairness. Teachers who want to encourage children to become activists need to support children when they speak out about unfairness on both small and large scales. Teachers do this when they acknowledge the injustices that children notice—however trivial they may seem to adult ears—rather than minimizing children's concerns or modeling resignation by saying things like, "Well, life's not fair." When teachers talk with children about the unfairness that they identify, they affirm that it's important to notice unfairness and to act to change it. Amy might have stepped into the children's conflict about food and directed Mac and Kyler to return the stolen food, reminding them that they shouldn't take other children's toys, without engaging the children in a discussion of the unfairness that they experienced. She would have fixed the problem, but she would also have communicated to the children that issues of unfairness are not particularly important.

Teachers can strengthen children's disposition to speak out about fairness and unfairness by doing the following:

- Talk with children about the unfairness they name in their daily classroom experiences.

- Tell stories about people who have identified injustice and acted to change it.

- Present children with hypothetical problems to consider. Is it fair for a kid who didn't have breakfast to have more crackers at snack than a kid who did eat breakfast? Would it be fair or unfair for teachers to make a rule that only boys could play in the art area? What are the fair and unfair things about a kid taking a long turn with a toy? These problems ask children to consider multiple perspectives and to pay attention to people's feelings and needs. They invite children to perceive themselves as people who notice what's fair and what's unfair and to think carefully about how situations that are unfair can be resolved. They lay the foundation for children to take a stand against unfairness.

- Rearrange spaces and "close" spaces to challenge children to think about issues of inclusion, exclusion, and fairness. A teacher might decide to close the block area to boys for a day when the girls complain that the boys "use all the best blocks and don't share." Or a teacher might respond to children's complaints that the classroom is "filled up with games" by working with children to create a new quiet area. These changes may provoke questions about individual and group rights, sparking conversations that strengthen children's ability to think critically, consider many perspectives, and contribute to solving problems.

- Add things to the environment that provoke investigation and debate among the children. For example, a teacher who observes kids pretending that their legs don't work may decide to add a wheelchair to the drama area. At Hilltop one year, many of the children in Ann's class were playing basketball any chance they could get, so she brought in several posters of women's basketball teams. She was interested to see how the children would integrate the photos of women playing basketball with the dominant cultural image that basketball is a game for boys and men.

Children take responsibility for solving problems, offering their ideas and action

Children encounter many challenges each day. How will they share the play-dough? What will keep their block tower from tumbling again? How might they respond to their sobbing friend who is sad to leave her dad? Children can meet these challenges with passivity or with action. They might wait for a teacher to divide the playdough, or they might debate about how to share it. They might storm away from the block area when their tower falls, or they might start building again, trying a slightly different stacking technique. They might watch their friend cry from a distance, or they might engulf her in a hug. Children with the disposition to take responsibility for solving problems meet challenges with action.

Here's an example of this disposition:

Jeanne often took her class to a park near their school. The kids loved this park. There was an elaborate climber, an area with trees that the kids called "the forest," and a grassy field. One day, as they left the park, one of the children, Lucy, stumbled on a rough spot of the sidewalk and fell. She scraped both knees quite badly. Her knees bled and she cried hard. The other children gathered around her as Jeanne sat with the sobbing girl on her lap. They were quiet, somberly acknowledging that their friend was hurt. One child, Peter, spoke up: "Lucy, I fell down one time on the sidewalk at my apartment and my knee bleeded. But now it's all better. See?" He pulled up one pant leg and displayed a healthy knee.

His words of consolation inspired other children: "Lucy, I'm sad that you're hurt." "I hate that sidewalk!" "You can be my partner back to school." "You can sleep with my stuffed animal at nap, Lucy." The children offered comfort in heartfelt ways. Then Irene declared, "The sidewalk's all broken; that's why Lucy fell down. We've got to fix this sidewalk so kids don't get hurt."

Irene's declaration rallied the other children. "Yeah, if the sidewalk stays broken, more and more kids might get hurt like Lucy did," Peter exclaimed.

"We've got to make a sign that says, 'Don't walk on this broken sidewalk,'" Sandra suggested. "Then no one else will get hurt."

"Well, if people don't walk on the sidewalk, they might walk in the street and get killed by a car," Enrico objected.

"Yeah, but they could watch to make sure there's no cars, you know," Sandra amended.

"I know! What if we just put a new sidewalk right here, on top of the old broken sidewalk. We could make it smooth," Irene proposed.

Lucy perked up during this conversation. She offered an experience: "Once I saw a sidewalk get made and there was a cement truck there and workers with smoothing things to make the sidewalk smooth."

Jeanne had been listening carefully to the children's conversation while bandaging Lucy's knees. Now she added some information to expand the children's thinking. "Taking care of the sidewalks is the job of city workers, like the people you saw, Lucy. I wonder how we could get their help with this sidewalk problem."

The children absorbed this information and used it in their brainstorming. "We could show them the broken sidewalk." "Lucy, you better tell them about your hurt knees." "I know! Let's write them a letter." "No, we should just call them. What's their phone number?" "We better have a meeting with them and learn how to fix sidewalks so that we can fix this one."

Jeanne pulled a piece of paper out of the first aid backpack that she carried with her and began to write down the children's ideas. She explained, "I'm going to make a list of these good ideas about taking care of this sidewalk problem. We can think together about what we should do first about this problem. I'm awfully glad you're ready to help fix this dangerous sidewalk."

The disposition to take responsibility for solving problems was strongly developed in the children in Jeanne's class. Jeanne reinforced this disposition by allowing the children time to consider Lucy's accident and how they might respond. She might have told the children, "I'll take care of Lucy, and I'll call the city to report this sidewalk." Or she might have told the kids, "It's not our job to fix sidewalks. It's our job to pay attention to where we're walking, so we don't fall." These responses would have shut down the children's eager readiness to take action, communicating to them that it's not their responsibility to solve problems. Instead, Jeanne invited the children to take responsibility, offering information so that they could think about real possibilities for action and writing down their ideas.

When teachers support children's efforts to solve problems, they communicate to children that they are competent and responsible. By contrast, when they take over children's problems, teachers communicate that "you should wait for someone to fix your problem" or "you aren't capable of figuring out what to do."

The disposition to take responsibility for solving problems is vital for young (and old!) activists. It inspires people to take action in the face of injustice rather than remain indifferent or passive, waiting for someone else to do something. This disposition leads to children saying, "That's unfair and I want to make it more fair. I'm going to do something!"

Teachers can support the development of the disposition to take responsibility for solving problems by doing the following:

- Coach children gently about ways to solve conflicts and resolve problems rather than fixing problems for children or stepping into conflicts to mete out justice. A teacher who witnesses two children battling over how to divide the playdough might say, "You kids have a problem to solve. How can each kid have enough playdough? Let's talk about ideas for solving this problem," rather than dividing it into two equal parts for them. A teacher who sees a block tower tumble down several times because it's stacked unevenly might say, "I notice that your tower keeps falling down and I wondered if you wanted to think together about why that happens," rather than "You kids need to stack the blocks up right on top of each other."

- When appropriate, encourage children to seek out other children when a problem arises rather than turning to an adult for help: "Owen knows a lot about building with Legos; will you ask him for help with your problem?" "Abby and Ellen once had an argument about this same problem during a dress-up game. Let's ask Abby and Ellen to tell us how they solved their problem." This invites children to see themselves as resources for each other and to identify themselves as people ready to offer ideas and suggestions for solving a problem.

■ Ask the children to help generate solutions to classroom challenges: "At lunch every day, we seem to run out of fruit while kids are still hungry. What should we do about this problem?" "We don't seem to have enough room for all the clay sculptures to dry. How could we rearrange our art shelves to make more room?" "Our group likes to use the gym equipment at the same time as the kids next door, but it's too crowded when we're all there together. Do you have any ideas about how we could change our schedule so that we don't use the gym equipment at the same time as the other kids?"

Ring Around the Cedar Tree

Words and music
© 1999 by Nancy Schimmel

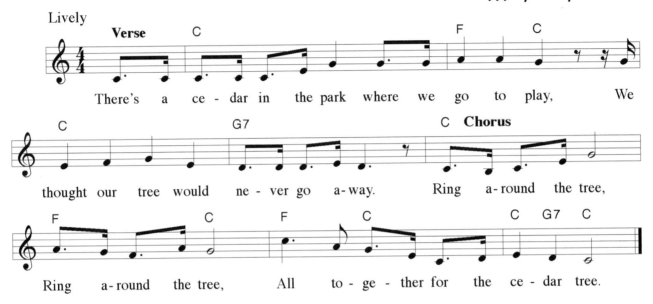

There's a cedar in the park where we go to play, We thought our tree would never go away.	Kids in a ring, "tree" in the center

Chorus:
    Ring around the tree,
    Ring around the tree,
    All together for the cedar tree.
	Circle hold hands and move to right

We always ate our lunch in the shade of the tree, Underneath the branches was our place to be.	Circle move in to tree Move out again
Our teacher named his/her dog for our friend in the park, Cedar the dog has a different kind of bark.	Tree choose teacher, bring into ring Teacher choose dog, bring into ring
A mom/dad told the teacher oh! oh! oh! The city says our cedar has to go.	Dog choose parent
A mom/dad told the teacher, the teacher told us, We started in to yell and we started in to fuss:	Teacher mime telling circle Circle sing chorus loud
The teacher told us and we asked why? Why does our cedar tree have to die?	
The roots break the pavement and people might trip. We started thinking, zip, zip, zip.	Circle trip and fall Get up
We thought and we thought and finally We said "Move the pavement farther from the tree!"	Mime thinking Mime moving pavement
Who shall we write to? Who shall we call? Who can say our tree doesn't have to fall?	Kids in circle turn to each other, mime asking
Where is the mayor? Here is she/he. Come to the park and save our tree!	Parent choose mayor
So the kids and moms and dads and the teachers in a ring, We all saved the tree and now we sing:	All go back to the ring except tree and dog, dog will Become tree for next round

Chapter 3

The Journey Begins: An Activism Project Emerges

In the previous chapter, we talked about a teacher's role in laying a classroom foundation on which activism projects can be built. Teachers arrange their classroom space and schedule to support the children's dispositions for activism. They weave the anti-bias goals into curriculum and make play a priority. They create a context in which activism projects can emerge.

And, eventually, something happens. Teachers notice a hot topic bubbling in the children's play that may develop into an activism project. Perhaps teachers hear children declare, "That's not fair," and they listen carefully, curious and excited about what may follow. Teachers and children may encounter something outside of the children's experience during a field trip and launch into a discussion of fairness and unfairness. Or maybe teachers decide to spark a project to extend children's thinking or to challenge their misunderstandings. One way or another, big issues enter the classroom, and teachers and children find themselves at the beginning of an activism project.

How do activism projects arrive in early childhood classrooms?

There are three main ways that issues that may lead to activism projects can enter an early childhood classroom. Activism projects may grow out of children's and adults' experience at school, children's and adults' experience outside of school, and adults intentionally raising particular issues. Each of these can provide a doorway through which issues of unfairness enter early childhood classrooms.

Activism projects introduced by experiences at school

Sometimes activism projects grow out of an experience that children have at school. Their shared understanding of unfairness provides fertile ground for an activism project. Here's a story about an event at Madrona that sparked discussion about fairness.

Out for a walk in the neighborhood one afternoon in early spring, Fran and the children stopped at a playground before returning to school. They were there only a minute or two when one of the children, Garrett, spotted two men embracing on a bench nearby. Perched on top of the climber, he pointed at them, shouting, "Ooo-eee! Look at those guys—they're hugging." Several children below on the ground were staring at the two men, pointing and giggling.

Helen was not. Her look of anger soon turned to tears. Fran quickly decided to ignore the other children for the moment. Squatting down next to Helen, Fran put a gentle hand on her shoulder and said, "Tell me what's going on, Helen." Resolutely, Helen explained that the two men sitting on the bench were friends of her family and that they lived in the same building that she lived in with her two moms. "I'm very mad because the kids laughed at my friends. That isn't even nice and it isn't even fair." Helen and Fran talked for some time about whether her two friends had heard the laughter and what she would say to them when she saw them next. They also talked about how Helen would let her class-mates know that they were unfair to her friends.

Back at school, when the children had gathered informally on the rug to await parents and carpools, Helen told Fran she was ready to talk to the kids. In a clear voice, she began: "You were laughing at my friends at the park, and I'm mad at you." A girl sitting next to her said, "No, I didn't do it." Several others joined the chorus of naysayers. Garrett piped in with, "But they were hugging and stuff, and they aren't supposed to."

Unable to contain herself any longer, Helen rose to her feet and spoke firmly and deliberately. "Two men can like each other and two women can like each other and so can one man and one woman. My two mommies like each other, so there." With that done, Helen crumbled into Fran's lap.

In this story, the impetus for Helen's activism came from the children's experience during the school day. All the children witnessed the gay couple's embrace on the park bench, they all heard Garrett's mocking call, and they all listened to Helen's strong words. While this can't really be called an activism project, certainly Helen's confronting her classmates' unfair behavior falls in the category of activism defined as "standing up for oneself and others in the face of bias."

Activism projects introduced by experiences outside the classroom

A child, parent, or visitor may bring a potential project into the classroom by relating an encounter with unfairness, telling a story, summing up a conversation, or describing a TV show or movie. For example, a mom may arrive at school with her leg in a brace after knee surgery and describe the frustration she felt when she tried to navigate the stairs in the neighborhood bakery. Or a child may run breathless into the classroom, eager to recount his dad's angry phone conversation with a social worker about food stamps. Or a licenser may come to observe a classroom during an annual licensing visit and catch the children's attention with her comment that "you sure have lots of beautiful pictures of people with dark skin in your classroom; not many schools include such lovely pictures of people with dark skin." Each of these situations presents teachers with an opportunity to cultivate an activism project.

One morning in Jane's class, Danielle first sculpted and then drew an elaborate machine. When Jane asked her to describe the machine, Danielle explained, "It's a turtle-killing machine. It's from the olden days. People killed turtles a lot in the olden days." Danielle's response was unsettling for Jane. Why was Danielle thinking about killing turtles? What was important or intriguing to her about killing turtles? How should she respond to this provocative statement? Jane decided to meet the issue head-on.

"You know, turtle killing wasn't just in the olden days," Jane commented. "People still kill turtles and other animals. Some kinds of animals have been killed so much that they're 'endangered.' That means that there aren't very many of those kinds of animals left in the world."

Danielle listened intently. She nodded. "I know about endangered animals. Sea turtles are endangered because of turtle-killing machines. We don't kill turtles in our city, but my mom told me about other people killing turtles."

By now, a group of children had gathered around Danielle and Jane, curious about this conversation about killing and turtles. One child asked Danielle, "Does your mom kill turtles?"

Danielle emphatically shook her head. "No, my mom would never kill turtles. My mom's teaching me about not killing animals. I don't even want to eat animals, so they don't get killed."

Jane commented that many people work hard to stop animals from being killed. Before she could explain more, a child jumped on the idea. "We've got to be like that. We've got to be people who stop animals from being killed."

"Yeah," said another child. "We've got to stop mean people who want to kill turtles."

Danielle had ignited a passion in her classmates. Jane could feel the children's growing excitement and took a deep breath to steady herself as she thought about what ought to come next for these young activists.

When an issue resonates deeply with a group of children, they take hold of it and shape it, developing a shared understanding of the issue, a common language with which they can talk about it. In the story about Danielle and the turtle-killing machines, Jane's initial work was to create a shared understanding of the issue, a foundation from which the children could launch their action. As soon as they heard Danielle's description of turtle killing, kids were creating individual understandings of the issue. Danielle wanted to protect animals by not eating them, another child was talking about stopping animals from being killed, and a third child was thinking about "mean people" who kill turtles. Before the group could initiate an activism project around this issue, they first needed to develop an understanding of the issue, thinking together about turtles and killing and endangered species, discussing what part of the issue most concerns them, and then deciding from there the steps that they would take in response to the issue.

Sometimes a project arrives in the classroom that needs little initial explanation. The children leap aboard with a shared understanding from the outset. Perhaps the issue unfolds on a TV show or in a movie that many of the kids have seen, or in the neighborhood in which many of the children live. In cases like this, there is already a shared foundation for action, once an issue is raised.

The five- and six-year-old children in Melissa and Barbara's class went nearly every day to a playground near their school. The playground was mostly cement, with a climber built over wood chips. The only tree in the playground was an old cedar tree, growing in an opening cut out of the cement. The children loved the tree. They sat under it and ate frozen treats when the weather was hot, gathered its fallen branches for classroom decorations, and held a party for their families under the tree. Barbara even named her dog Cedar, which delighted the children.

One summer day, one of the parents arrived at school with big news. At a neighborhood meeting, Jamie had heard an announcement that the city park department was planning to cut down the cedar tree. The park's grounds crew was concerned about the cracks and buckling in the cement surrounding the tree, caused by the tree's roots. Jamie's news spread through the classroom. The children, aghast, stopped playing and gathered around Jamie and Melissa. "We've got to have a meeting about this!" one child exclaimed. "We've got to tell the people not to cut down our cedar tree!"

Over the next weeks, the children worked with Melissa and Barbara to write letters demanding that the tree not be cut down, explaining that they loved the tree, that the tree gave them shade, and that they would be terribly sad if the tree were cut down. The children drew pictures of the tree and of themselves protecting it. Jamie collected the children's letters and drawings and presented them to the park department, along with a neighborhood petition that she had circulated calling for the tree to be declared a local treasure, protected from being cut down.

The park department decided not to cut down the cedar tree. The children continue to gather under the tree during the summer and to gather its fallen branches during the winter. The tree stands as a testament to the children's determined activism.

A parent brought the issue of the cedar tree to Melissa and Barbara's classroom. Melissa and Barbara didn't live in the neighborhood; they relied on families to keep them abreast of community news. The kids and teachers might not have learned about the planned removal of the tree without the news Jamie gleaned at a neighborhood meeting. They might have arrived at the park one day to find their beloved cedar tree gone. As it happened, Jamie alerted the kids in time, and their shared passion provided a foundation for quick action.

Activism projects from teacher provocations

Sometimes teachers intentionally call attention to a particular issue, with the goal of stimulating thought and action. They may plan a provocative event, add a prop to the classroom, initiate a conversation, invite a visitor, plan a field trip, tell a story, or read a book, hoping to raise an issue that might otherwise not come up. Teachers may broadcast a change in the physical environment or daily schedule: "I'm going to hang the outdoor brooms here in case we need to clean up any litter on the playground." "We won't be having story time today because Father Tim is coming to talk with us about the refugee center." Any of these actions fit into the category of teacher *provocations,* a word borrowed from the Reggio Emilia schools in Italy and used to described actions teachers take to *provoke* thought and discussion among children.

Sometimes teachers plan a provocative event in response to an event that the children experience or an overheard conversation among children. Here's an example of a way that Fran responded to bias she saw cropping up among the children in her class at Madrona one year.

Body-type differences generate a lot of interest and curiosity in young children. When Jessie's uncle, who was almost seven feet tall, visited the classroom at Madrona one day, there was a lot of gawking and some laughter, especially when he dipped his head and shoulders to pass through the doorways. The next day Fran read from the children's book *Why Does That Man Have Such a Big Nose?* She and the kids began to generate a list of the different body characteristics they found among themselves and in their families. This quite naturally led to a discussion of height and Jessie's uncle and the advantages of being tall. And short. And in-between.

Over the next few days there was a flurry of measuring activities. A couple of kids measured the height and the breadth of the gym to see if *Tyrannosaurus rex* and his pals could fit inside, and one child set up a station to measure anyone and everyone who entered the classroom. Two kids brought in basketball posters, and teachers and kids talked about both men and women being "tall basketball players."

Later, on a field trip to a downtown office building, some of the children protested being "squished" by a "big fat old lady" on the elevator. On the way back to school, Fran noticed giggles and whispers when a large man got on the bus. She decided to invite her friend Lois to school as a guest expert.

Lois is an early childhood practitioner who is a very large woman. She is comfortable talking with children about body-size differences and their implications. Lois has pictures and stories. She asks provocative questions and invites honest responses. Before she left Madrona that day, she had the children thinking and talking about the many situations that challenge tall and short people, large and small people. The initial murmurings of "it isn't fair" grew clearer and more focused. The children thought that no one should make fun of someone because of how they look, and people need to think about ways to make travel more comfortable for people of all sizes and shapes.

"I know what we have to do," exclaimed Stacey. "We have to tell the people who make buses and cars and taxis to make them higher so that Jessie's uncle and some other tall people won't be bumping their heads all the time." Stacey seemed incredulous that no one had thought of that. Not to be outdone, Jessie added, "Trains and airplanes and helicopters too!" For Jonathan it was doors: "We've got to have wide doors so Lois won't ever get stuck!"

Fran invited Lois to visit in response to children's mockery of people they encountered on a field trip. She wanted to provoke the children in her class to reconsider their initial response to people with big bodies. She didn't know whether her provocation would lead to an activism project, but she planned to stay alert for possible next steps. She had opened up an opportunity for activism. She wanted the children to think carefully about the unfair treatment faced by large people, treatment in which they'd originally participated. The children at Madrona were already engaged with the issue before Lois visited. Lois's visit served to shift their perspective, challenging them to understand body size in new ways and inviting them to act for fairness instead of for unfairness. Fran's provocation hit the mark.

Teachers sometimes decide to provoke children's thoughts about an issue before there's any signal from kids that they're thinking about it at all. Teachers may want to introduce an issue that might not otherwise arise; for example, in a classroom serving only typically developing children, a teacher may provoke children's thinking about the challenges faced by children with physical disabilities by planning a field trip to a park built especially for children who use wheelchairs and crutches. Or a teacher might decide to stimulate children's thinking about hunger issues by telling the story of the trick-or-treater who came to her house at Halloween asking for money for children without food instead of demanding candy for herself. Ann sometimes initiates consideration of issues in her classroom through the use of story, as in this example.

Ann reads from "chapter books" to the children before nap each day—books like *Charlotte's Web, My Father's Dragon,* and *The Animal Family.* Each year she reads *The Trumpet of the Swan,* by E. B. White. She reads this book because it brings up big issues, issues that provoke debate, discussion and, often, activism projects.

The book's main character is a swan who cannot speak. The first part of the book focuses on her efforts to find ways to communicate. Ann appreciates the descriptions of the swan's fears, frustrations, and victories as she experiences being silent in a world of speakers and as she creates a language that others can understand. The story is gripping and provocative, sparking many conversations with children about disabilities and the ways in which they are or aren't accommodated (or not) in our world.

The second part of the book focuses on the swan's courtship and mating. When Ann reads the book, she changes the gender of the main character from a male to a female swan. When the main character is a female, her courtship of another female swan becomes the story of two women falling in love. This invariably provokes conversation among the children about women marrying women and men marrying men. It's important to Ann that children feel comfortable with people who are lesbian and gay. She wants children to expect to encounter people who are lesbian and gay and to feel relaxed and at ease with them. When Ann reads this book, the kids already care deeply about Louise the swan by the time she begins to court Serena, her true love. They can't easily dismiss her or ignore her, because they are invested in her life and her happiness. So the classroom conversations about Louise marrying Serena are grounded in affection for Louise. The kids have all been cheering her on throughout the book, and they continue cheering for her as she courts Serena.

When Ann reads *The Trumpet of the Swan,* she can't guarantee that an activism project will happen. But she can lay the foundation for a project by reading about disability and about women who love other women. She can make visible the lives of lesbian and gay people and of people who have disabilities, so that the children can identify situations in which these people are left out or treated unfairly.

Teachers' provocations may or may not lead to activism projects. If the teacher raises an issue that engages children, teachers and children can explore it together, thinking critically about it and deciding together on an activist response. Children might not be hooked by an issue that teachers raise. In that case, teachers can remind themselves that it's valuable to introduce an issue, and, although an activism project doesn't immediately unfold, the groundwork is laid for possible future activism. Teachers' efforts are about opening a door for a potential project, rather than forcing the children to take up an issue.

Many issues enter the classroom without growing into activism projects

Not every issue that arises in young children's classrooms grows into an activism project. Sometimes it's enough—for the kids and for teachers—to acknowledge an issue and then let it go. An issue may not contain enough possibilities for children's action, or it may belong more appropriately in the adult world than in the culture of children.

A child in Ann's class recently commented that "there's people trying to make a law that says girls can't do important jobs." As she listened to him, Ann realized that he was talking about an anti-affirmative action initiative that was being hotly contested in Seattle at the time. He was indignant about the unfairness of the proposed law. Clearly, his parents had talked with him about their opposition to repealing affirmative action provisions. Ann heard and acknowledged his protest that the law was not fair, sharing with him her belief that the proposed law was wrong. But she decided not to pursue a conversation with her whole group about this issue, believing that legislative battles about affirmative action do not hold many entry points for young children.

Similarly, Fran recalls a year when a parent approached her with the suggestion that the children get involved in the campaign of a popular community politician. He told Fran, "After all, she wants what we want for families and kids. All that the kids would have to do is ring the doorbell and say, 'Councilwoman Clark cares about kids!' We could get some parents and maybe siblings to come along. It would be a great experience for the kids. They would feel powerful and important. We do it with our kids all the time."

Fran felt torn about how to respond to this. The man's daughter was always energized after she had been out campaigning with her family. It seemed to be a very empowering experience for her. And there was potential for building strong relationships in the community with this project. But Fran had some doubts too. How might this endorsement be perceived by families both at the preschool and in the neighborhood who did not back Councilwoman Clark's politics? Furthermore, was this adult idea really appropriate for children to carry out? Was this a violation of childhood? Indeed, was this about community building or about coercion? Fran decided not to pursue this project. Her doubts about whether it was really appropriate for young children outweighed the possible benefits.

There are also times when it just doesn't feel right to embark on an idea, because a group is winding down from an intense experience or is still working on outstanding issues from another project. Fran remembers a year at Madrona when she felt overwhelmed as issues about collecting food for refugee families, cleaning up the neighborhood, and helping people who are homeless all arrived in the classroom at the same time. She was reeling, trying to fit all the projects into the daily life of the classroom. She finally realized that she had to choose a project that most engaged the children and pursue that, rather than try to fit all the possible issues into the curriculum.

Some issues don't catch fire; they seem to have only limited possibilities for exploration, or just don't attract the children's interest. For example, Ann was deeply moved one year by *The Last Free Bird,* a children's book about the consequences of pollution. She read the book to the kids in her class several times, hoping to inspire action. The children certainly understood the basic message of the book—that pollution is bad and makes animals sick—but they weren't particularly vocal about the unfairness of this. Ann nudged them into writing letters to corporate polluters (gas companies, an airplane manufacturer), but, once they'd sent the letters, the issue died. Now it seems to Ann that the issue was too abstract for the kids and not particularly engaging for them at the time. The kids wrote the letters with her mostly because they saw that it was important to her that they do this. They were kindly indulgent but eager to get back to their own concerns.

When possibilities for activism arrive in an early childhood classroom, teachers can determine whether or not to pursue them by asking themselves the questions in the following box.

Steps for cultivating an activism project

It's useful for teachers to move slowly when a potential activism project enters their classroom. The first step is to spend time listening to and observing the children, gathering information about how the children understand and feel about an issue. Then teachers can make time to acknowledge children's feelings about an issue by inviting them to talk, draw, sculpt, and play about their feelings. After plenty of time exploring feelings, teachers can help children think critically about the issue. This step of critical thinking leads children to consider possible responses to an issue. Only then—after listening and observing, acknowledging feelings, and encouraging critical thinking—should teachers facilitate action.

When teachers follow these steps, they help children move from asking questions to solving problems, from indignation to understanding and action. When teachers acknowledge children's feelings and support critical thinking before taking action, they teach children to act responsibly, consider people's feelings and perspectives and ideas, and notice how their actions might affect other people. And when teachers move slowly into consideration of an issue with children, they keep potential activism projects anchored in children's understandings and passions.

In the story that follows, watch Fran as she monitors the children's energetic response when they find broken glass in their school parking lot. She wants to keep the kids safe, while encouraging them to share their feelings and move toward a thoughtful plan of action.

Steps for Cultivating an Activism Project

- Listen and observe.
- Acknowledge feelings.
- Support critical thinking.
- Facilitate action.

It was a chilly afternoon in the fall; the children were all dressed in what Stu called their "bigger coats." Molly rushed onto the playground, her cheeks flushed by the weather—and her excitement! "Quick, guys," she called out to everyone. "Get the brooms. There's a big mess out there, and Eula's mom can't even park the car!" Almost everyone dropped what they were doing to run to the fence and view the "mess."

What they saw was broken glass scattered around the three available parking spaces. "I already knowed it," said Larry. "That's why we came in the other door." Eula was standing in one of the spaces, hands on her hips. "So where's the broom, Molly?"

Moving up to the fence, Fran saw Eula's mom, Bev, waiting in her car, and Eula, ready to take action. Eula had sized up the situation, probably with input from her mom, and had taken charge, sending Molly for a broom. The momentum was growing, and Fran wanted to encourage the kids' impulse to address the problem. On the other hand, the broken glass made safety an issue. Quickly sorting through her feelings and thoughts, Fran made a decision. "Okay, kids, we've got a job to do, but first let's think about some safety rules. We have to think about handling sharp glass—and about traffic."

While Bev and Fran took on traffic duty, about seven children with a motley collection of brooms and dustbins meticulously swept up all the glass. Whew! No cut hands, and everyone safe and accounted for.

The kids were delighted with their work, letting out hoots and hollers as Eula's mom parked her car in one of the glass-free spots. Later, during the Check-In meeting, David commented, "People shouldn't break glass." Children shared anecdotes about cut fingers and flat tires. They already knew a lot about the consequences of broken glass lying around.

Eula: "Yeah, who are those guys making all that mess?"

David: "I think they're basketball players. They come in the night. My dad says so."

Eula: "Well, they don't have to smash stuff. There's a trash place, you know."

Graham: "Maybe they didn't see it."

Molly: "Yeah. We've got to make a sign, guys. A big sign."

The children were quick to take action. Some children checked the parking lot to make sure there really was a receptacle for trash. Sure enough, a garbage can was there, but it was almost full. The class decided that Father Tim, the parish priest who was in charge of the building and grounds, should know about the glass, the signs, and the almost-full trash can. "I know, let's write him a letter," suggested Corey, who was never far from paper and pencils those days.

In the end, the children delivered a letter to Father Tim and created two large signs, one for the trash can and one for the fence.

Father Tim responded with a hand-delivered letter of his own. Fran read it aloud at the Big Idea meeting and then summarized: "He's really glad you cleaned up the glass, and that you reminded him that the trash can was getting full. He wants to see your signs before you hang them up. And he's going to come to our Check-In meeting on Monday."

Corey grinned with delight. "Now we have to send him *another* letter."

When kids get support to understand their feelings and are nudged to be critical thinkers around what they experience, then they are likely to want to do something—to take action. The kids at Madrona were aghast and angry to find broken glass in their parking lot. They were eager to solve the immediate problem by sweeping up the glass and willing to think about why the glass was there. Eagerly, they plunged into action, sharing their confidence, creativity, and skills.

Fran was busy, too, anticipating outcomes and solving problems. From the moment Molly invited the other children to participate in the clean-up of the broken glass, Fran was alert to the fact that the project Molly had proposed required the combined management skills of a traffic safety officer, a coach, a mediator, and a project supervisor. As she drifted between feeling all aflutter and relatively calm, Fran was carefully watching what the children were doing, listening for the meaning behind their words, letting them know that their feelings were important, making time and space for thinking, and paving the way for their action.

Step One: Listen and observe

Activism projects are often conceived in children's play. Teachers can miss these gestating projects unless they carefully attend to children's play and the issues it raises. Teachers are collecting information about the children when they make notes about what they hear them talking about, when they save children's drawings, when they make audiotapes of a drama game or a passionate conversation over playdough, and when they write down stories that children dictate. They learn about the issues that children are considering and about their feelings, understandings, and misunderstandings about those issues. They have records to study and to share with coteachers and parents as they work to discern potential activism projects.

Taking notes

One of the easiest ways to capture children's conversations and interactions is to spend a few minutes taking notes. Ann uses this technique to record significant phrases and capture the flow of the game. Taking notes helps her focus on the children's play and communicates to the children that their play is important enough that an adult wants to write about it. Her notes give her a way to revisit children's play during quieter hours of the day. She reads her notes during nap time and pays attention to nuances, themes, and recurring ideas in children's play in a way that she can't as the play is unfolding. Her notes give her a starting place for thinking and planning about emerging activism projects.

Deb Curtis and Margie Carter (authors of *Training Teachers* and *Reflecting Children's Lives*) have developed these questions to help teachers reflect on the play that they observe:

- What is the essence of this experience for the children?
- What questions are they trying to answer?
- What experiences, knowledge, and skills are they drawing on?
- What misunderstandings does their play reflect?
- What is most important about this for the children?
- What might the children want from me?

Here's an example of how Ann used taking notes to help herself ask, and then answer, these questions. This is what she jotted down as she watched children during dramatic play one day:

Kids scatter scarves, seashells, and rocks on the floor—S. says, "We have to make it look like a cat house."

S. is mom, J. is dad, L. is baby kitty.

Kitty eats seashells.

Mom chastises her: "No, no, kitty. That's trash and it will make you sick. Don't put the trash in your mouth."

Gives kitty real food: "Eat this. This will make you healthy."

Later, kitty tries to eat some rocks—dad stops her: "Kitty, remember what your mommy told you? That's called pollution and it gets people sick."

Kitty: "I'm a kitty, not a people. I don't get sick from pollution." She eats the rest of the rocks and Mom and Dad shoo her away.

Kitty runs away from Mom and Dad and gets lost: "Help! I'm lost! Mommy!"

Mommy and Daddy find kitty, take her home: "Kitty, don't run away from us or you'll keep getting lost."

Kitty goes to bed, wakes up, eats more seashells.

Mom scolds her: "I'm trying to teach you about pollution. It makes you very sick and dead."

T. joins the game—he's a puppy.

Kitty shows the puppy the rocks, whispering, "Eat those rocks, puppy! Let's sneak to eat rocks!"

Puppy says, "Pretend that we get sick from eating these pollutions." Gobbles rocks, keels over onto his back, coughing and choking.

Mom and Dad rush over, pat him on the back, help him sit up, give him medicine: "This will get you healthy again. No more eating that pollution! Pollution is very bad for your body! Bad kitty! Bad puppy!"

Puppy is healthy again, begins to wrestle with kitty.

When Ann read her notes later that day, she noticed for the first time the themes of safety and danger, of mishap and rescue—themes she had missed when she was watching the game unfold. Here are some notes she made as she studied her earlier writing:

The kitty and puppy <u>eat</u> pollution: "don't put trash in your mouth"—that's their way of experiencing pollution.

Kids seem to understand that eating pollution makes a person "sick and dead." They debate whether animals get sick from pollution too. They don't explain why animals might or might not get sick, though. Why are they focused on <u>eating</u> pollution? Do they know about other forms of pollution (i.e., air, water)?

Mom and Dad keep rescuing children: stop them from eating pollution, find kitty when she runs away, give medicine to puppy. Generally, Mom and Dad do caretaking ("eat this to get healthy") and teaching/punishing.

Themes of obedience and disobedience: kitty runs away, eats pollution when told not to, encourages puppy to "sneak" pollution—power over adults? Challenging adults' authority? Setting up situations in which adults will need to take care of them?

Kids seem to be drawing on understanding and experience with adult/child roles. Are they trying to figure out something about pollution or something about authority and adults' and kids' roles? Was this game more about safety and danger, generally, or about pollution specifically? Does L. really think that pollution doesn't make animals sick, or was that just for the sake of the game?

As Ann thought about the game and tried to answer questions about its meaning for kids, she realized that she needed more information. She could see the experiences, knowledge, and skills that the kids used in their game as they played about adult and child roles, and she noted the misunderstanding that only people get sick from pollution. She just wasn't sure whether pollution was a key element of the game or just a way to explore the themes of safety and danger, obedience and disobedience.

Ann and her coteacher decided to gather more information about the children's knowledge of pollution and their actual interest in pollution and its dangers. They added "pollution" to the drama area in the form of scraps of paper, gum wrappers, crumpled cups, and empty soda cans. They expanded their classroom library to include a few books about pollution, its sources, and its impact on people and animals. And they made plans to listen carefully to the children as they encountered these additions to the classroom.

Those initial notes sparked Ann to think more carefully about what was going on in the kitty game. They made her slow down and become cautious about leaping in with a project about pollution once she became aware of the range of themes in the kitty game.

Other ways to keep track

Tape recordings, transcriptions, videotapes, and photos can supplement teachers' notes. Each medium offers particular doorways into understanding. Tape recordings and videotapes (and written transcriptions that teachers make of these recordings) allow teachers to revisit a conversation or play experience many times—listening and seeing again, but this time with the privilege of space and time for reflection that wasn't there when the discussion or game was "live." Photos help teachers think creatively about what might be going on in children's play and notice images or background issues that they might have missed in the moment. Photos can also invite teachers to wonder about children's play in new ways: "That reminds me of . . ." or "Look at her expression," or "I wonder what he was reaching for."

Teachers have their own ways of seeing and hearing. Some may be oriented to visual images and written words, while others are drawn to audio recordings. Do your own experiments, and find the ways that work best for you to collect information about the children's inner landscapes.

Step Two: Acknowledge feelings

The second step in exploring an issue that may lead to activism is to initiate conversations with children about the feelings the issue has raised. A teacher might comment, "You've discovered something unfair. How do you feel about what you've noticed?" or "You're right, that is unfair. It looks like you're really mad—and sad, too, maybe."

Young children are quick to spill out their feelings and to notice other people's feelings. When her teacher squats down to comfort a tearful friend, for example, Reba is quick to identify her friend's feelings and to propose a plan of action: "She's crying because she's mad at those boys because they won't let her play. I know what, we'll make a sign that says 'Girls can be baseball players.'" Similarly, Casey is right on target when he announces to the class that Carl "is very, very sad because some big kids laughed at his talking, and it isn't nice, and it isn't fair, and we have to tell them that! Right?"

As teachers acknowledge children's feelings, they can also gauge their intensity and monitor their duration. Intense feelings that endure may be the clue that children are ready to embark on an activism journey. Here's a story about a time like this when Fran was teaching at Madrona.

Gregory was sad. Fran knew it, and his best friend, Toby, knew it. A child short on words but big on action, Gregory was spending much of his time in the block area, building with determination and intensity. He talked to no one, not even Toby. After a couple of days of this, goaded by Toby's concern and her own twinge of anxiety, Fran approached Gregory's mom. She explained that their family was concerned about the welfare of Gregory's brother, Victor. It seemed that the school he attended for children with special needs might not be able to provide the equipment Victor needed and depended on for his well-being. They hadn't received the funds they were counting on, funds that would cover the expense of the equipment. Victor might have to leave the school that was like a second home for him and his family.

A short time after this conversation, Gregory sought out Fran and in a quivering voice, shared his sadness and his worries. He also told Fran that he wanted to tell the other kids what was going on, which he did with Toby's support.

To Gregory's peers, this was not about equipment and "unfair" funding; it was about leaving a comforting, secure place for the unknown. The children recognized the feelings of worry and sadness from their own experiences—moving, changing schools, a new teacher, a new sibling, even leaving home to go to school each day—and they were quick to offer comfort.

For a week or so, children and teachers gave Gregory lots of space to be sad. Once or twice Fran posed a question she thought might lead them to think about the problem. The children ignored her. Clearly her job was to respect this intense and prolonged display of feelings and to protect it from unwelcome intrusion.

Only after several weeks of feeling sad did the children began stirring, readying for action. One morning, Toby's mom, a physical therapist, suggested that they all take a look at this needed piece of equipment and find out how much it cost. Later, Toby suggested a "penny drive" to buy the equipment. "My sister did one at her school," he said. "They got lots and lots of money!" The children were ready to take action.

The children were in no rush to resolve this issue with either thoughts or actions. They were, for a time, content to be with Gregory in his grief. They cared about their friend and were not put off by his unwavering display of sadness. But they were four and five year olds—curious, active learners. They grew ready to take action to help their friend, eager to explore the challenge that Toby's mom offered them.

As teachers guide children to think about their feelings and about the issues that provoke them, the children may travel back and forth between feelings and thoughts for some time, with a thought producing another feeling and a feeling another thought. "I am really, really mad because some bad people took that man's wheelchair," relates four-year-old Josh. "But someone can get him another one. What if they can't find him another one? That would be very, very sad."

Some children may need to express strong reactions before they are ready to be thoughtful and consider a plan of action. Jenny is expressing strong feelings and not an action plan when she states, "When that guy says something mean again, I'm going to kick him really hard. And then I'm going to scream too. And say a mean, mean word to him." Then, too, the children may knit their thoughts and feelings together, with the teacher helping to distinguish the two as best she can. Fran and the children in her class once went on a trip to a city park where they had encountered a homeless man sleeping under an apple tree. The conversation they had upon returning to Madrona illustrates this weaving together of feelings and thoughts.

Graham: "I think he was sleeping because he was really hungry."

Stu: "He could eat an apple. Besides, he was camping. We go camping. We got a tent."

Eula: "No! He was not camping! Don't you even know about homeless? My mom's friend does. People get wet and cold and hungry. Even kids do it."

Fran: "I feel sad about that."

Graham: "Me too."

Braden: "I'm not sad because I'm going to help him. I'm going to climb that apple tree and dump all the apples on him."

Gales of laughter follow, including Braden's.

Graham, his freckled face red with anger: "That could hurt him. Anyhow, you can't eat just apples."

Hannah: "My sister ate seven one time."

As this conversation shows, children's movement through their feelings about injustice toward thinking about action to address it is seldom straightforward. Yet with perseverance, as teachers nudge and prod, shared understandings begin to emerge from the feelings that children express.

Step Three: Support critical thinking

Hand-in-hand with acknowledging children's feelings comes encouraging critical thinking. This is the next step toward action. Teachers support children to move from "I feel angry that there's broken glass in the parking lot" to "Why is the glass there? Are there garbage cans for trash? Are they too full? Do people need reminders about using trash cans?" When teachers encourage children to think carefully about an issue before plunging into action, they invite them to move beyond a surface understanding of an issue and learn about it more deeply. Teachers ask children to consider why a problem exists, who is involved in the problem, what other people feel and think about the issue, and how the children's actions might impact other people. As the children deepen their understandings and become more articulate about an issue, teachers gather more information about children's real concerns and passions, so that the action that evolves is more likely to stay anchored in the children's interest.

To support and guide the children's thinking, teachers can ask questions like these:

- Why is this a problem?
- Why might this problem exist?
- Who is part of this problem?
- Who should know about this problem?
- What would make this more fair?
- Do you know anyone who might have ideas for us about this problem?
- What do rule-makers need to know about this problem?
- Do we have anything in our school or at home that would help with this problem?

Just as adults come together for meetings to address important issues, children's meetings provide a forum for critical thinking as they wrestle with an unfolding issue. Meetings give children an opportunity to process thoughts and feelings together, and they give teachers clues about what is going on for each of the children. Sometimes these meetings happen spontaneously, in response to the unexpected appearance of an issue. Other times, teachers may plan a meeting for children to think carefully about an issue, as Ann did in the following Hilltop story. Note the ways that Ann uses variations of the questions above to help children clarify their thinking during the discussion.

It was February, several months after a celebration of the anniversary of Rosa Parks's refusal to give up her seat on a Montgomery bus to a white man. There had been a series of bathroom disasters at school: a toilet in the girls' bathroom had repeatedly overflowed, flooding the bathroom and forcing temporary bathroom closures. During one of these floods, Ann called the kids together for a meeting to announce this most recent crisis and to remind the girls that the bathroom would be closed while the director mopped up the floor. As Ann finished her announcements, Sarah, one of the girls in the class, made her own announcement: "If Rosa Parks were here, she would not like this!"

Ann was flummoxed. What did Rosa Parks have to do with Hilltop's bathroom floods? She sat silent at the meeting, hoping someone would flesh out the connection for her. Logan spoke up: "Yeah, she'd hate it when that sign got put on the bathroom door: Stay out of the bathroom."

Sarah continued his thought: "What if the girls' bathroom was always broken, and there was a rule that said girls can't use the boys' bathroom? Then the girls would have no bathroom to use!"

Reisa added, "Girls would just have to break that rule, because that's not fair for girls to have no bathroom!"

Ann was beginning to understand the children's analysis, and she was excited. Rosa Parks had refused to acquiesce to the unjust law of her time that compelled African American bus riders to defer to white passengers. The kids were considering their situation through the lens of fair and unfair rules, drawing on Rosa Parks' civil disobedience as an example of how to respond to unfair rules. Ann was eager to encourage the children's critical thinking about bathrooms and fairness. She asked, "Why might there be a rule that says girls can't use the boys' bathroom?" *(Why might this problem exist?)*

Justin said, decisively, "My mom told me bathrooms are for privacy."

Theresa nodded. "At restaurants, my mom and me go in a different bathroom than my daddy. It's for privacy."

Ann asked, "What does *privacy* mean?" *(Why is this a problem?)*

Annie explained, "It means that people don't see you go pee or poop."

Justin added, "Like you can close the door and no one can see you be naked."

Ann repeated my first question: "Why would there be a rule that says girls can't use the boys' bathroom?" *(Why might this problem exist?)*

Sarah answered, "Because then girls don't see boys be naked."

Reisa thought about this for a moment, then challenged Sarah: "Yeah, but boys can just close the door of the toilet, you know, and then girls who are in the bathroom won't see them at all, just their feet if they look under the door." She obviously had some experience with this.

Logan had been listening to all this. Now he reintroduced Rosa Parks. "Rosa Parks might say that girls and boys should just use any bathrooms. That's what would be fair to Rosa Parks."

Annie spoke up. "Yeah, she wouldn't like rules about 'no girls' and 'no boys.' She didn't like rules about 'no black people.'"

Ann was electrified by this conversation. The children were engaged in deliberate reflection about the reasons for designated bathrooms, thinking critically together about whether those reasons justified exclusion. Ann asked, "What would be a fair rule about bathrooms that Rosa Parks would like?" *(What would make this more fair?)*

Sarah was ready with an answer. "She would like a rule that says girls can use the boys' bathroom any time they want to."

Justin took this idea a step further. "What if there wasn't a boys' bathroom and a girls' bathroom? What if kids could use any bathroom they wanted to use? That's what Rosa Parks would like."

Logan carried this forward. "We could just take down the signs on the doors that say 'Girls' and 'Boys.'"

Annie said, "Then, the next time there's a flood, kids can just use that other bathroom, the one without the flood, and it would just be regular to use that bathroom."

There was a chorus of eager assent following Annie's comment. Ann decided to push the conversation a bit further. "Do you think the other kids in our school would agree to that idea? How can we find out what they think about changing the bathrooms?" *(Who is part of this problem? Who should know about this problem? Do you know anyone who might have ideas for us about this problem?)*

Theresa suggested writing a letter to all the kids to tell them about the idea. "The teachers can read the letter to the kids, because kids can't read letters. Then the kids can tell their teachers if they agree, and the teacher can write down yes or no and send us their letter."

They decided to try this idea, and spent the rest of the meeting composing and signing a letter to the other kids in the school.

In the following story, children first articulated their feelings about dark skin, then thought together about fair and unfair ways to talk about dark skin. The teacher in the story, Fran, had only a minor role in the children's conversation; they were skilled thinkers, able to manage their meeting.

"Hey, there's no brown crayons," Jennifer called out.

"Yes, there is . . . no, there isn't! Where are the brown crayons? I need to draw a picture of my mommy!" Eula complained.

"Brown is just a poopy color anyhow," said Molly, while a few others giggled.

"No, it's not. Fran, these guys don't even know about brown. You better have a meeting and tell them."

They did have a meeting. But Fran did little of the "telling." Eula was clearly in charge of the discussion, with some help from Larry and Jennifer. She talked about how all the people in her family had brown skin and that they liked the color of their skin. She also told them about all the things that she liked that were brown, like the earth, her dog, chocolate milk, and raisins. Other children added to the list.

Larry added to the discussion with some information about his family: "I have a pink grandma and a brown grandma and they are both nice." Jennifer described the different shades of color in her family, describing her dad as "almost black." She also directed me to fetch the book *What Color Are You?* which describes "mellow stuff" (skin color and melanin production). Sean piped in with, "My mom reads me *Black Is Brown Is Tan*. You can read that, too, Fran."

Fran wanted to show support for the kids' strong feelings and clear thinking, and for their forceful response to Molly's hurtful words. Before the meeting adjourned and the children scattered, she added, "I feel really upset when I hear someone making fun of another person because of the color of their skin. There are many beautiful and different skin colors among the people in our classroom, and none of them are 'poopy.' Eula, is there anything more that you would like to say to Molly right now?" Eula, who had moved closer to her friend Molly and whose anger had dissipated while she talked, turned to look at Molly and said, "How would you like it, Molly, if I called your skin a bad name?" Molly didn't answer right away. The room was quiet until she said, "Hey, guys, let's look for brown crayons. Maybe we didn't look good enough. Anyway, Fran will have to buy some, if we need more."

Step Four: Facilitate action

A teacher's job doesn't end with embracing children's feelings and thoughts about injustice. Just as teachers move swiftly to help resolve a conflict about sharing space or a prized toy, so do they facilitate action plans that grow out of the children's understanding of inequity and injustice. When children begin to think about possible activist responses to unfairness, a teacher's job is to keep a record of the children's ideas, nudge them to think about the implications of each one, and then help the children decide on a plan that is appropriate and manageable.

Sometimes an action plan is embedded in children's critical thinking. For example, in her response to a teacher's news that some grocery stores throw away edible foods, Mia sums up her feelings, her thinking, and a plan for action: "I'm mad at them for doing that. Don't they even know that some people, even little kids, don't have any food? They are grown-ups and they should be smart. I think we have to go and tell them, and get that food from them."

Sometimes an action plan grows out of a teacher's efforts to create a framework for activist ideas to emerge. Such is the case in Ann's story that follows.

One year, Ann took her class to a highly recommended puppet theater that featured a troupe of puppeteers visiting from Uzbekistan. They performed a vaudevillian sort of play, emphasizing physical comedy over dialogue. The kids laughed and laughed during the show, enjoying the slapstick tripping and slipping and jumping around. However, the children grew very quiet and scooted closer to each other when one puppet repeatedly hit a robber puppet, making the robber fall down. Each time he stood back up, the other puppet hit him hard again, forcing him to collapse, shrieking. Like the children, Ann was taken aback by this sudden violent turn. It lasted only a few minutes, but it had a big impact. It took a while for the kids to relax again, and they appeared to be relieved when the performance ended.

In the van on the way back to school, the kids and Ann had a detailed conversation about the puppet theater, and many children reported being afraid or uneasy when the robber puppet was getting hit so many times. Once inside, Ann asked the kids to come to a meeting "to finish our talk about the puppet show."

The kids obliged, gathering in a circle on the floor while Ann found some paper and a pen. She began the meeting by reviewing the conversation from the van: "A lot of kids said they liked some of the puppet show, but that they didn't like the hitting part. Kids felt scared and sad, and they wished the puppet would stop hitting the robber. You decided that the hitting puppet liked to see the robber puppet fall down, and that's why he kept hitting him; he thought it looked funny to see the robber fall down. I wonder if you have ideas about what the puppet could do instead of hitting to make the robber fall down. I've got paper so that I can write your ideas down."

Kids began to generate ideas as quickly as Ann could jot them down. After all the children had explained their ideas, she invited them to take action. "You have many ideas about ways to make the robber fall down without hitting him. I'd like the puppeteers to hear your ideas. Could we turn your list into a letter to send to the puppeteers?"

Yes! Children were enthusiastic about sending a letter with their ideas to the puppeteer. Ann took out a fresh piece of paper and wrote a greeting, reading it out loud:

"Dear puppeteers, We saw the Uzbek Folk Theater today. We have some ideas about how to make the puppet robber fall down without hitting him."

Then she told the children that she would write their ideas in the letter. Kids dictated their thoughts to her as she wrote:

"Garrett says: The man could sneak up to the robber and tickle his feet and his legs could go up and he could fall down on the soft cushion.

"Amanda says: The man could trick him to think that he's a woman and then, when he's surprised to see a man, he could fall down and be funny.

"Katharine says: I don't like it when the puppet got whacked.

"Nicholas says: I don't want you to hit the puppet.

"Alena says: Make him fall down without pushing him down, just make him fall down and stand up.

"Sylvia says: It was funny when the man had boots on his feet and on his hands. The robber could just fall down laughing at that man."

After writing the letter, Ann invited kids to sign it. She folded it up and put it in an envelope, and they all walked to the corner mailbox to send it on its way.

Ann sensed the children's feelings during the puppet performance, and she deliberately provoked their critical thinking on the ride back to school. At the class meeting, she set the stage for action.

Sometimes children arrive at an action plan themselves, as they discuss their feelings and ideas about an issue. Other times, adults suggest ideas for activism after much careful listening and studying. Adults have a broader sense of the options available for responding to unfairness than children do. Children may need some suggestions about the options they have for responding to unfairness they recognize.

Sometimes children move quickly from feelings to critical thinking to action, and teachers barely have time to breathe. That was the case when Eula and her friends met to talk about brown crayons and brown skin. Fran's experience with Gregory was just the opposite. In that case, not only did Fran have time to breathe, she also had a lot of time to consider when to provoke thinking and action. Most typically, teachers gather up ideas that have spilled from the children's feelings and thinking, and then they take time to figure out what the children are particularly invested in and how to mold an activism project in a way that is manageable for teachers and developmentally appropriate for children. Here's a story that illustrates this process in Sam's class.

Sam had heard from kids in his class about the neighborhood association's project to beautify the local park by inviting people to plant saplings. Many of the families in his classroom had participated in this project, spending time together in the park planting trees.

Several weeks after the initial planting, Sam and the children went for a walk in the neighborhood, stopping by the park to see the newly planted trees. At the park, though, the children discovered that many of the young trees had been damaged and even uprooted. The kids were outraged; some were in tears. Sam listened and nodded as they expressed feelings of anger and sadness. On the way back to school, he asked them to think about why someone would want to harm the trees; by the time they were back in their classroom, Sam thought they were ready for his question: "What can we do about this?"

Their responses came in rapid fire: "Tell their moms!" "No, tell their teachers!" "Tell a policeman." "Set a trap!" "Go break *their* trees." Their ideas reflected the intensity of their anger and hurt. They were reactive and retaliatory.

Sam recorded them without comment. He knew his next step would be to craft some questions aimed to nudge them past retaliation and into more careful thinking. "I'll ask the kids what a teacher should do when kids tell him about hurt trees. This may help them consider other sorts of responses," Sam decided.

The next morning, as the children gathered around Sam to make plans for the day, he reminded the children about their discovery of the damaged trees. "You were so angry yesterday, and I think I know why. Some of you worked hard to plant those trees, and you were looking forward to them growing big and tall and beautiful." Children responded to Sam's comments, not with the anger and frustration of the day before, but with sadness and some murmurings about unfairness. "Yesterday," Sam continued, "you wanted to get back at the people who broke your trees—that was your idea then of how to take care of the problem. But I wouldn't let you hurt other people or their things, and I don't think you would really want to do that anyhow. But what if you were able to tell their teacher, or their mother, or a police officer? What would be your words? What would you want them to do?"

"Well," said Max, "I would tell the teacher to teach his kids about how to take care of stuff that's growing. They don't know about that yet."

"Yeah," said Becky, "then they could help other people's trees to grow."

"Anyway," chimed in Jill, "you can mess up your own toys and trees and rocket ships, but you can't mess up someone else's. My mom said that. Their mom should say that to them!"

Sam noticed that the children's responses were more thoughtful than they'd been the day before. To encourage the children to step into action, he asked, "How could we teach the people who hurt the trees?" The children decided to have a march in the park, carrying signs that said: "Don't hurt trees." "Trees are growing things." "We need trees."

Caring teachers who are invested in children's social, emotional, cognitive, and moral development cannot afford to sidestep the responsibility for facilitating activism projects. The stories in this chapter attest to children's willingness and ability to be creative and collaborative problem solvers and activists. It is teachers' responsibility to become confident risk-takers in these collaborations, without taking the project out of the hands of the children or trying to solve all the problems for them.

Stumbling blocks

Issues that spring up in a classroom and present opportunities for anti-bias activism are emotionally loaded and quite often controversial. They almost always feel heavy with the weight of social and cultural taboos or debates, and they frequently catch teachers off guard. Many teachers feel over-whelmed, nervous, or worried when they sense the beginning of an activism project; other teachers feel excited or eager. Whether you're ready to leap in or frantically grabbing for handholds, your own emotions can get in the way of exploring the issues thoughtfully with children. There are four main ways of responding that teachers need to be wary of throughout the planning of an anti-bias project.

- Teachers may want to help children feel better.
- Teachers may be tempted to moralize about an issue.
- Teachers may want to provide children with answers, or solve the problem for them.
- Teachers may want to take charge and create an activism project.

The problem with all of these instinctive responses is that they sabotage the children's opportunities to feel, think, and act when they encounter injustice. They prevent the learning that's possible through an activism project.

Of course teachers want to help children feel better when they are in the throes of strong feelings of grief, anger, or sadness about injustice. As Fran's story about Gregory shows, though, often children simply need the space and the support to experience those feelings. Trying to help children feel better when they really are feeling sad, angry, or anxious can give them the idea that they should only have happy feelings, or lead children to suppress their feelings. Supporting children's feelings can mean helping children name feelings ("Your face looks really sad to me" or "I wonder if you're feeling worried about Victor's new school") and giving them ways of expressing their feelings ("You sound angry to me. I wonder if you'd like to go pound some clay or run hard outside") as well as simply affirming that it's okay to feel them.

Similarly, flooding children with information or "right answers" to their complex questions stifles their curiosity and puts them in the position of being empty, receptive learners rather than active, engaged investigators. A huge influx of factual information can easily overwhelm children, particularly if their real wonderings are about underlying emotional issues rather than facts and figures.

It is essential to the growth and development of children that teachers allow them to work through some emotional and intellectual difficulties. It sometimes seems awkward to take a backseat. But resolving issues for kids, instead of helping them work through their own feelings and ideas, often only benefits adults by keeping things calm. Children miss the opportunity to hone their critical thinking and problem-solving skills. To help them think about when to step in, teachers can ask themselves, "Will my fixing this problem sustain and nurture the children's learning?"

That's not to say teachers should never comfort children, give answers, or provide solutions. Teachers are wise in many ways, and children expect them to have answers and information. Children can also legitimately want and expect comfort from teachers. Teachers can use their wisdom to enrich and expand children's thinking. For example, a teacher might offer her stories about an issue to help extend children's thinking ("I agree with your idea, David. I have a story about that; would you like to hear it?") or suggest a place to look for more information ("You know a lot about recycling already. We could go to the library and ask Mr. Bates, the librarian, for some more ideas").

It's a constant balancing act as teachers decide when it is important to be the adult-in-charge and when it is best to be a collaborator with the children. Teachers in Reggio Emilia, Italy, liken their relationships with children to those of a master and apprentices; there's mutual learning and constant collaboration, but also clear acknowledgment that the adults have more experience and knowledge than children.

Here's a story to illustrate this point:

Patty helped the children get into their boots, coats, hats, mittens, and scarves. She and the children were going for a walk in the swiftly falling snow. The kids had been watching it fall for the last hour, growing increasingly eager to explore their white, transformed playground. As the children bundled up for their adventure outside, one child, Tony, commented to Patty, "My mom told me that some people have to sleep outside because they don't have any houses to live in. If someone sleeps outside in the snow, they would freeze to death, right?" Several children looked up as Tony talked. They were listening carefully to hear Patty's response.

Patty paused in her work of zipping coats and adjusting mittens. She didn't want the children in her care to worry about sleeping outside or about freezing to death. She didn't want to contradict Tony's mom, but neither did she want to upset the children with a conversation about the fierceness of cold, especially as they were preparing to go outside into the beautiful snowfall that had absorbed them all morning. She decided to reassure them that they were safe and that they needn't worry: "Well, sometimes people don't have houses to sleep in, but there are warm shelters where homeless people can stay when it snows, so that they don't have to sleep out in the cold. There are people in our city who have the job of taking care of homeless people. They'll make sure that no one freezes to death. And we certainly will be warm enough outside, with our boots and coats and hats! Let's go play in the snow, and when we get cold, we'll come inside and have cocoa to warm up."

In her concern about the children, Patty sidestepped a conversation about homelessness and the dangers that homeless people face in the winter. She took care of the children's feelings by reassuring them that they ought not to worry. Patty might have chosen another route. She certainly could have assured them that they would be warm during their play time outside, and reminded them that they had warm houses to sleep in, so they would not freeze to death. But she might have agreed with Tony that people can die if they spend the night outside in the bitter cold of a snowy winter night, and then asked the kids to think with her about who might have to sleep outside, and why. She might have asked the kids if they would join her in a meeting about the problems that homeless people face in the winter and what sort of help they might need. The children might have wanted to pursue this issue, sharing their feelings, thinking about the problem, homing in on an action plan. In her efforts to protect the children from worry and unease, to guard them from the harsh truths about homelessness, Patty put up a roadblock to a potential activism project.

Fran: This has been a struggle for me, both as a parent and as a teacher. While it has been gospel for me to respect the feelings and thinking of children, I've had to work hard to quell the urge to teach the answer or eliminate the problem. Down deep, I know I believe this to be the role of the "good mother/father" and the "wise teacher."

The anti-bias curriculum challenges that response. Its very framework leads us to a different conclusion. It proposes that when children feel good about themselves, when they are becoming knowledgeable about and comfortable with differences, and when they are learning to recognize unfairness in the form of stereotypes and biases, then taking action is a natural outcome. The role of the "good mother/father" and "wise teacher" in this framework is to be a collaborator and risk-taker in the learning and the doing along with the children.

Well, yes. Of course. That makes sense. And I can think about it, and I can talk to colleagues about it, and we can agree that "kids want to be change-makers" and that "it's developmentally appropriate to support the kids in activism that they want to do." Yet, I know intimately the anxious feelings that greet the beginning moments, hours, and days of a potential activism journey: fear, doubt, excitement. I know that I have to slow down, exhale, listen, and ask myself questions. And most important for me, I have to be vigilant about not gathering up all of the threads of an issue, reweaving them into neat handi-work and handing them back to the children. That's my first impulse, and it's wrong. The children have the right to muddle around in the issues they encounter, to grow as critical thinkers and active learners.

Food Bank Rap

Robbers:
We were playing with food, I don't mean for real
But they had some play food that we had to steal
'Cause we were playing robber and they were playing store
So we swooped up their boxes with a thunder and a roar:
Food! Food! We want food!

Storekeepers:
We were playing store but they took our stuff
We were playing store, and they were playing tough,
If they'd asked nicely we'd have given them a cake.
They said, "Robbers don't ask, we just take!"
Food! Food! We want food!

Solo or everybody:
Then somebody said, "Up where I live
If you have extra food that you want to give
To people who don't have anything
There's a box at the store called the Food Bank Bin."
Food! Food! We want food!

Everybody:
So we made a box and put up a sign
That said "Food Bank Bin," and it looked so fine.
We made extra food from magazines,
We cut out pictures of pizza and beans.
Food! Food! We want food!

So we all could play, no need to fight
But somehow things still didn't seem right.
We thought about families out on the street,
Who really didn't have enough food to eat.
Food! Food! We want food!

So everybody asked their mom and dad
To give any extra food they had.
Neighbors and friends, they all chipped in,
For real food for the real Food Bank Bin.
Food! Food! We want food!

Rap lyrics copyright 1999 by Nancy Schimmel

Chapter 4

Travelers' Aid: Planning and Provisioning for an Activism Project

Planning for an activism project

E. L. Doctorow wrote that writing a novel is like driving from New York to Chicago at night. You can only see the distance illuminated by your headlights, but you can make the whole trip that way. Activism projects are similar.

When a project begins, teachers don't see its whole course laid out before them. They don't know the twists and turns that the road will take or what experiences they'll have with the children along the way. Planning for an activism project takes place day by day, rather than all at once at the beginning of a project. Teachers can't plan activism curriculum very far in advance, because the content of the curriculum depends so much on what happens with the children. The children's discoveries, questions, and passions shape the direction of the project. Teachers aren't just along for the ride, though. They plan and provision for their journey with the children.

As teachers plan for an emerging activism project, they take on the role of researchers. Researchers ask questions, form and test hypotheses, then observe and document the outcome of their testing. They continually rethink their hypotheses in light of what they see, and they are ready to change course in response to new leads. They slowly hone an idea by moving between *receptive work* (observation, documentation of what they observe, and thinking) and *active work* (testing their hypotheses).

Teachers ask questions to understand what children are feeling and thinking, form hypotheses and test them, and take notes and keep records of their observations of children and their own reflection. With their research, teachers are trying to figure out why children are interested in a particular issue, what aspects of an issue hook the children, how the children understand an issue, what possibilities the children see for action, and what help they need from adults. The information that teachers gather in their research helps them plan curriculum that meets the children's needs, interests, and developmental levels.

For example, a teacher might listen to a conversation between two children about hunger, buying food, and poor people. She takes a receptive role to gather information. Then, still in a receptive role, she might hypothesize that "Amanda and Zeke seem to be curious about how people without money get food. They've talked a lot about poor people being hungry." She might decide to take an active role and test her hypothesis: "I think I'll put some pretend money in the drama area, along with some play food, and watch what Amanda and Zeke do with those props." The teacher returns to a receptive role to observe Amanda and Zeke at play with the props she added to the drama area, gathering more information that helps her refine her hypothesis and choose another active step to take. In this way, teachers take in what the children offer and use it to create the next step in a project, moving between receptive and active roles as an activism project unfolds.

The receptive part of teachers' work is aimed at gathering information and documenting a project. Using these tools, teachers learn about what the children are feeling and thinking, and they preserve records of a project to use in their planning, to support children's thinking, and to communicate with families. Teachers take on receptive roles when they

- observe children's play
- take notes about and audiotape children's play and conversations
- take pictures
- ask questions to understand children's feelings and ideas
- represent what's happening in the classroom

On the other hand, teachers step into active roles to test their hypotheses about what children are thinking and feeling, to create discussion and debate, to stimulate children's thinking, and to facilitate action. Teachers take on active roles when they

- change the classroom environment
- make room for stories to emerge
- offer children opportunities to represent their understanding
- invite children to document their own work
- plan field trips and other excursions
- invite visitors to the classroom
- ask questions to nudge children's understanding
- use persona dolls to add voices to the classroom discussion
- hold meetings and facilitate group discussions
- enter children's play
- suggest ways of taking action

As you read the following story from Hilltop, pay attention to the receptive and active roles that Ann takes, and notice how she acts as a researcher as she and the children take on an activism project about making Hilltop accessible for people in wheelchairs.

Several years ago, the children in Ann's class decided to build a ramp at the building to make their school "more fair to people in wheelchairs." This plan, and the children's passion that birthed and sustained it, took Ann by surprise. She certainly hadn't begun the year with a plan to implement a curriculum project about accessibility! The ramp project began in early October, when Ann's focus was on nurturing a sense of community in her newly formed class. She had her own project going on when the children invited her to join them in an activism project.

Ann and the children had gone for a walk to the neighborhood library. Kids were interested in construction equipment and wanted books that would explain about backhoes, cranes, wrecking balls, and cement trucks. On the walk, they passed a blue and white sign that reserved a parking space for

people who use wheelchairs. The sign provoked a discussion about wheelchairs and stairs. The group had been talking for a few minutes when one of the children, Sophie, stopped everyone in their tracks by announcing that "my stepdad uses a wheelchair because his legs don't work. He can't even come to Hilltop because there's only stairs, and wheelchairs can't go on stairs. We have a ramp at our house for my dad's wheelchair."

Ann was stunned. She hadn't known about Sophie's stepdad. She was swamped by shame (how could she not have known that vital information?) and by an urgent desire to do something right away to make up for not having known. She wanted to say something calm and steadying about Sophie's stepdad being in a wheelchair, something that would send a clear message to the kids about respect and fairness. But the kids got there ahead of Ann. "Our school's not fair!" Sam declared. "Let's build a ramp at our school to make it fair for Sophie's dad," proposed Joel. The kids were immediately galvanized, talking together with eager voices about their emerging plans for helping Sophie's dad get into the school. Ann caught their excitement and joined their conversation about what tools and skills they would need to build a ramp at Hilltop.

They arrived back at school in time for lunch and nap. As they ate and then got ready for nap, the children continued to talk about building a ramp. Ann listened carefully, trying to learn what they understood and misunderstood about ramps, wheelchairs, and construction projects. Once the kids were asleep, she caught her breath and began to sort out the experiences of the morning.

The children were set to take on this project. They talked with clear determination about making the school more fair. They were not daunted by the prospect of a major construction project; in fact, they were eager to get started. Their conversations, though, communicated to Ann that their energy about building a ramp was as much about their fascination with construction equipment as it was about a desire to right a wrong. They talked about needing a bulldozer, a steam shovel, and "worker helmets," as well as a saw, a hammer, and a drill. They were as eager to put up a warning sign that said, "Danger: Keep out! Someone's building here" as they were to "get speed bumps for wheelchairs on the ramp." These two threads—indignation about the unfairness of the school and excitement about using real tools and writing important signs—were intertwined.

Ann wondered how they should proceed. She called Hilltop's staff trainer, Margie, eager to tell her the morning's story and to hear her thoughts about how they ought to begin their work. During the conversation, Margie helped Ann slow down. Ann was ready to leap into the construction, like the kids. She'd been ready to take on the project *for* the children, proceeding according to her initial understanding of the children's ideas and feelings. Margie, however, suggested that Ann and the children lay a foundation for their building project by investigating how ramps work, by exploring everyone's understandings of and feelings about people with disabilities, and by studying and experiencing how wheelchairs move—by provisioning the classroom for investigation and planning for the teacher's as well as the kids' learning. Ann's conversation with Margie reminded her to allow time and space for the project to unfold.

Ann decided to add some provocative props to the classroom and study how the children played with them. She stocked the block area with ramp-shaped unit blocks. She borrowed a persona doll and a doll-sized wheelchair from Margie. She contacted a hospital-supply store and convinced them to lend out a child-sized wheelchair. She searched the library for books that included people in wheelchairs. Families helped her stock the room with building supplies: hammers and nails, wood scraps, nuts and bolts, tape measures, levels, and blueprints and photos of home remodeling projects. Then, she tried to step to the side and observe the children as they navigated these new props. She took notes and photos and made tape recordings of children's conversations.

As the children played with Carmella (the persona doll in a wheelchair), practiced hammering, or matched nuts and bolts, Ann watched and listened, asking herself, "What do they already know? What are they trying to figure out? How do they feel about people whose legs don't work? What experiences have they had with people in wheelchairs?"

As she observed the children at play, Ann began to identify more clearly the two threads that came together to weave the fabric of this project: the children's fascination with construction, and their concern about the fairness or unfairness of their school. As the children played with Carmella, talked with Sophie about her dad, tried to move around the room in the loaned wheelchair, and built with ramp-shaped blocks, Ann began to understand that they were working on the concept of accessibility. In their initial conversation about wheelchairs on the walk to the library, the children's sense that the school was not fair was based on Sophie's testament about her dad's experiences. Now, the children were internalizing concepts about accessibility, learning about it from playing about it. As she observed the children's play, Ann learned that she had been too quick to assume that they knew all about disability. She'd wanted to rush ahead into building, thinking that the children understood the issue because they were talking about it so clearly. If she had pushed to start the construction right away, the children's focus might have been primarily on building, and they would have lost their opportunity to develop a deeper appreciation for the need for accessibility.

The project about building a ramp at Hilltop provided a concrete building project to ground the children's interest in construction—provided a concrete expression of their four-year-old passion for fairness (this ramp was for their friend Sophie's dad). Ann invited the children to bring together their understanding about ramps and their knowledge about blueprints. They sketched houses with ramps, then used their drawings as plans for "real" houses in the block area. Several visits were made to Sophie's house to sketch her stepdad's ramp and its relationship to the house and the ground, and to try out the ramp with the borrowed wheelchair. On one visit, Sophie's stepdad Pat gave kids rides on his electric wheelchair, up and down the ramp and along the sidewalk. The kids asked Pat all sorts of questions about his chair, about what sorts of ramps he liked best, and about what he needed to have built at Hilltop.

As a welcome by-product of this effort in social activism, the children's knowledge and skill in construction also progressed. They practiced using hammers, screwdrivers, and saws daily, and they were proud of their skills and of their ability to build real structures with real tools. They visited a family's remodeling project and met with the carpenters there, hearing about the steps involved in that construction project. An architect visited and taught about slope and its implications for safe ramp design. They took time to learn about the planning that construction workers do before they begin to build. They sorted out when a wrecking ball and bulldozer were needed and when a measuring tape and hammer were more appropriate. With this knowledge, the children were better able to talk about building a ramp. Ann didn't have to tell them, "Well, no, we won't need a wrecking ball" or "Now we have to make a plan," because they could guide the project themselves. The time they spent exploring the complexities of construction allowed the children to become knowledgeable participants rather than just cute kids talking about steam shovels. It let them maintain ownership of the project.

During the ramp project, Ann's active role consisted largely of adding materials to the classroom that invited play about wheelchairs, ramps, and construction: Carmella (the persona doll), ramp-shaped blocks, books, tools, wood, and a real wheelchair. Ann also planned trips to Sophie's house and walks through the neighborhood with the wheelchair. Simultaneously, Ann took on a receptive role, watching and listening and taking photos of children's play and tape-recording some conversations. The information she gathered in her receptive role shaped her decisions about her active role. Ann moved between active and receptive, leading and following, learning and teaching, as she planned during the accessibility project.

Teachers' receptive roles in guiding activism projects

Observe children's play

A great deal of a researcher's time is spent watching and listening, gathering information slowly over time. This is a key role for teachers throughout the development of an activism project. Observation of children's play provides information about what children are thinking and feeling, understanding and misunderstanding—information that allows teachers to keep activism projects grounded in children's experiences. This is not a passive role. When a teacher is gathering information—doing research—she is not "doing nothing" or "letting the kids play" while she is busy with other tasks. This role of careful observation takes focus and concentration. Teachers must bring all their attention to the task. (See the box on the facing page.)

Take notes about and tape-record children's play and conversations

Researchers record their observations, so that they can return to them over and over, plumbing them for information and inspiration. As teachers observe children's play and talk with children about activism issues, they, too, often take written notes or make audiotapes. Notes and tapes allow teachers to revisit children's play and conversations, to study them in depth.

Ann: Once we have the notes and photos and transcriptions, we have to figure out what to do with them. When I first began the practice of taking notes about children's play and making recordings of children's conversations, I didn't really understand how to use all the documentation I gathered. I did it

Active and Receptive Roles: An Example

The sign provoked a discussion about wheelchairs and stairs. They'd been talking for a few minutes when Sophie stopped them in their tracks, announcing that "my stepdad uses a wheelchair because his legs don't work. He can't even come to Hilltop because there's only stairs, and wheelchairs can't go on stairs. We have a ramp at our house for my dad's wheelchair."	Active: Creating opportunities for stories to emerge
Ann caught their excitement and joined their conversation about what tools and skills they would need to build a ramp at Hilltop.	Active: Facilitating a group discussion
As they ate and then got ready for nap, the children continued to talk about building a ramp, while Ann listened carefully, trying to learn what they understood and misunderstood about ramps, wheelchairs, and construction projects.	Receptive: Observing the children
Ann decided to add some provocative props to the classroom and to study how the children played with them.	Active: Changing the classroom environment
Ann observed the children as they navigated the new props, taking notes and photos, and tape-recording children's conversations.	Receptive: Observing the children's play
The class visited a family's remodeling project, met with the carpenters there, and heard about the steps involved in that construction project.	Active: Planning field trips and other excursions
An architect visited the class and talked about slope and its implications for safe ramp design.	Active: Inviting visitors to the classroom
Ann invited the children to bring together their understanding about ramps and their knowledge about blueprints by sketching houses with ramps, then using their drawings to guide their building in the block area.	Active: Offering children opportunities to represent their understanding

because I'd read about it being the right thing to do. I'd carefully transcribe a recorded conversation among children, then go on with the plans I'd already made. I mostly thought of the notes and conversations as ways to capture on paper the sweet and appealing thinking of young children. I'd share my transcriptions with parents, inviting them to "listen in" on conversations that they would otherwise miss.

As I grew into the practice of supporting emerging projects, I learned more about how to use the documentation that I collected. I noticed myself wishing to understand if my guesses about the children's interests were on target or way off base, knowing that it mattered deeply to the success of an emerging project. I began to turn to my carefully collected notes for guidance. When I studied my notes and transcriptions alone or with a coteacher, I could see underneath the children's words to the themes and issues undergirding them. I noticed when ideas were repeated or when a theme showed up over and over. I began to see through to the heart of children's play. And with an understanding of the heart of their play, I could respond in meaningful ways and take an active role in shaping an activism project. I could better supply the classroom with props that would sustain children's play. I could plan trips or invite visitors to the classroom. I could ask provocative questions of the children. I could develop strategies for the children to represent their thinking. Listening to the children is my best guide for supporting emerging projects. The documentation I collect while the children play and talk deepens my listening.

Take photos

Teachers often take photos to record key moments of an activism project. They take photos of children playing about an issue and photos of children at work on each stage of an activism project. They take photos of visitors who come to help with a project and during field trips. These photos create a visual history of an activism project, helping to tell the story of the project to the children and their families. Photos offer the children a chance to see themselves at work on a project, which often feeds their energy about a project: "I remember when we went to visit Sophie's house and went on her dad's wheelchair ramp! Let's make a ramp out of blocks for our doll to use, just like the ramp in that picture!"

Ask questions to understand children's feelings and ideas

Teachers can also ask questions to deepen their understanding about children's feelings and ideas. These questions are aimed at gathering information, not at provoking new thinking in children. A teacher may ask, "What do you know about people who are homeless?" "What's the most important thing about cleaning up the litter on the playground?" "Why is pollution a bad thing for animals?" "What makes a school fair for girls and for boys?"

Questions asked to gather information are open-ended. Teachers ask these questions with genuine curiosity, eager to hear children's authentic responses rather than to teach or move children to a right answer. Teachers respond to children's comments with acceptance and respect: "Thanks for telling me your ideas." "Your ideas make me think about new questions."

One year in Ann's class, several children (all boys) began to make and use weapons with increasing intensity. After about a week of their gun-infused good-guy/bad-guy play, a girl protested, declaring, "Those gun games scare me, and the boys shouldn't play those games. It's not fair for them to play scary games." Ann and her class decided to have a group meeting to talk about playing with weapons.

Ann was uneasy with the weapon play and had been studying the children's play for several days to try to understand what was important to them about these fierce dramas. She was glad to have a more formal opportunity to learn more about how all the children were feeling about this weapon play and to put the weapon play in the context of fairness. At the same time, she was tempted to use the group meeting to ask provocative and pointed questions, to push the children to see weapon play as bad—which was her strongly held conviction. She struggled to stay in the receptive role.

Here's an excerpt of a transcription of their first meeting about weapon play. As you read it, pay attention to how well you think she did at asking questions to understand rather than to provoke the children's thinking.

Ann: Samantha said to me, "Those gun games scare me, and the boys shouldn't play those games. It's not fair for them to play scary games." I want to learn more about what feels fair and what feels unfair about gun games in our classroom.

Kyle: It's too not safe to use weapons.

Ann: What is unsafe about using weapons?

Andrea: You hurt people.

Samantha: When sometimes a kid is around me with his finger pointing like this, making a gun, I don't feel safe. If it was a real gun, it would kill me.

Ann: So you think it's not fair for some children to scare other children with their games?

Murren: My mom has an agreement that I only make weapons at home.

Ann: Do you think that would be a fair agreement for all the children in our class?

Murren: Yes.

Samantha: I don't think that would be fair, because I can't make weapons at home.

Ryan: You can make weapons at home but not at school, because people might think you might hurt them after you make the weapons.

Ann: You think making weapons is scary to people, even if you don't use weapons?

Ryan: Yes.

Kyle: We could make weapons at school, but put them in a cubby or mailbox.

Andrea: I agree to just make them at home but not make them at school.

Samantha: But that's not fair to me because my mom doesn't let me make them at home.

Cameron: You can only make swords or guns at home, but if your mother doesn't want you to, then wreck them and throw them in the garbage.

Ann: Kids have different ideas about weapons. Some kids, like Kyle, think that it's fair for children to make weapons at school but that they should put them in cubbies and mailboxes and not play with them. Other kids, like Andrea, think that children should only make weapons at home, not at school. Samantha thinks that it's not fair to say it's okay to make weapons at home, because she's not allowed to make weapons at her home.

Andrea: My mama doesn't like weapons.

Ann: I think we ought to talk with our families about this. Let's make a plan that you'll ask your families what they think is fair and not fair about weapons at school.

Represent what's happening in the classroom

Researchers begin their work with theories or hypotheses about what may happen, but they change and refine their thinking as their work proceeds. Their notes and charts reflect what *really* happens during their work, rather than merely what they *thought* might happen. Their documents are living records of real work, rather than stale thoughts set on paper before a research project even begins. In the same way, teachers can create curriculum webs or adapt traditional planning charts to represent what actually happens during a project.

During the activism project aimed at collecting money for people who are homeless, for example, Ann made notes on a curriculum web as the project unfolded. She used the web as a way to represent the day-to-day evolution of the project, rather than as a way to plan the project from the outset. See Ann's web on the facing page.

In addition to helping teachers understand children's thinking, documents such as photos, notes, and audiotapes also support children's thinking. Teachers use them to serve as historians for children, reminding them about how and why an activism project began, describing their early thinking about an issue, and inviting them to refine it by providing them with a visual history of their work on a project. Project work often extends over several days, weeks, or even months, each step building on and extending the previous step. It is developmentally challenging for young children to carry all the steps of a project with them over time. When teachers take photos of children's play, save their drawings and other work, and provide written notes of conversations to read to the children, they weave together the experiences that create a project. They become the keepers of the collective memory.

Bulletin boards and scrapbooks can become collection centers for photos, notes, and drawings. For example, when the children were exploring the possibility of building a wheelchair ramp at Hilltop, Ann used a bulletin board in her room to post photos of children trying out the wheelchair, visiting Sophie's house, and building with ramp-shaped blocks; the curriculum web, to which she added daily notes; drawings of ramps that children made; notes from the children's meetings about ramps and construction. She also made a scrapbook containing photos that told the story of the unfolding activism project. Kids became skilled storytellers, using the scrapbook's photos to illustrate their narratives of the project. She wanted to give children as many venues as possible to understand their experiences. And she wanted to promote a collective history that nurtured children's sense of belonging to a vital community.

Dr. Wes Browning and Anitra Freeman, speakers for Real Change Homeless Speakers Bureau, visit Hilltop. They offer to be our guides as we distribute the money we collect, 2/7/97

Dr. Wes and Anitra invite us to visit the art studio for homeless folks.

Kids play with Lego with Dr. Wes, dress up with Anitra.

We buy art supplies and fruit and take them to Street Life Gallery. Our visit turns into a party with homeless artists. 4/20/97

Field trip to Real Change: The Homeless Newspaper, where we meet Misty, a homeless woman, 12/3/96

What food should we make to give to homeless people? Kids plan a menu for "picnics": PB&J, carrots, oranges, and cookies.

We shop and prepare "picnic" lunches to give away, 3/13/97

Jenny: "If we talk to homeless people, we'll learn more about them."

At the shelter kids play together. "There's not much toys to play with." We decide to buy toys.

Julia encounters a homeless boy: She tells us her story at our class meeting. "We have to help homeless people." 10/15/96

Our streetwalk: We give away food and money to three homeless people we meet, and visit a family shelter and give more food and money, 3/20/97

Conversation: What we know or believe about homeless people and their needs, 10/16/96

Ann introduces a persona doll, Francine, a homeless girl who lives in a shelter. 11-12-96

Toy collection at school

Kids write letters to their families: How can we help homeless people? 10/18/96

Trip to Magic Mouse toy store to buy toys, 4/4/97

Ideas from family discussions

Ann Ravenscroft, child advocate at a homeless shelter, visits Hilltop, helps us think about what shelter life is like and what homeless children need, 12/11/96

We visit shelter again to deliver toys, 4/4/97

Collect toys to donate

Collect clothes to donate

Collect money: "Save money in jars."

On trip to the bank, we exchange coins for cash

Francine wears the same clothes all the time; kids decide to "give clothes to homeless people," 10/25/96

Kids write a letter to families at school, 10/23/96

Kids count and roll coins

Kids' clothes collection at Hilltop

Kids meet with each class to tell Julia's story and distribute letters, 10/28/96

We collect $450 in coins

We visit Baby Boutique (a clothes resource for homeless people) to deliver clothes and help sort them onto shelves and racks.

As children reflect on their earlier play, as they revisit their carefully pre-served work, they can think in new ways about their experiences, just as we adults hone our thinking by study and reflection over time. They may have conversations with one another in which they use their earlier experiences as launching pads into new learning. They may decide to repeat an earlier expe-rience to get it clear in their minds. They may tell the story of the experience to someone who was not involved. Here are examples of the conversations Ann overheard around the bulletin boards in her classroom:

"Hey, remember when we visited Sophie's house and went on her dad's ramp?"

"Here's my drawing that I made about the ramp at her house."

"Let's build a block house with a ramp!"

"What's that a picture of?"

"It shows me taking a ride in a wheelchair. We went for a walk with a wheelchair, but it was too hard to cross the street."

"Because the wheels rolled you too fast?"

"No, that's not why. It's because of unfair sidewalks that don't have ramps."

Documentation also enriches communication with families. As an activism project begins, families appreciate detailed information and descriptive stories that assure them that the activism work grows from children's play and in turn supports children's further learning and growth. Stories, photos, and detailed notes invite families to join teachers in thinking about what's happen-ing with their children. Documentation communicates the behind-the-scenes thinking of their children and of teachers, and provides families a launching pad into understanding their children's activism.

Ann: Working in full-day child care, I don't see parents every day. Actually, there are some parents whom I rarely see because our schedules don't intersect at all. But parents come to the classroom every day, whether I see them or not, and they look around and try to get glimpses of what their children are doing.

To provide windows into children's play and learning for families, I try to create bulletin boards that reflect the evolving life of the children with photos and quotes from kids and examples of the work they are doing as a project unfolds. These windows invite families to look at children's play with curiosity and delight.

Lately, I've tried to include brief statements about my thinking in the dis-plays, so that even if I'm not there, I can "talk" with parents. I might add a question that helped guide my planning or pose a question for viewers to con-sider. I might add tips for parents to use as they study their children's work. I write things like this:

"I wasn't sure how much the children understood about using a wheelchair. So I could learn more about what they understood, I took these notes while they took turns riding in a wheelchair."

"What are your goals for your child as she or he investigates accessibility issues and ramps?"

"Notice the different ways that the children tried to draw the depth of a ramp. It's a challenge to move from three dimensions into two."

Teachers may decide to invite families to bring in photos, notes from conversations at home, and descriptions of experiences they've had that relate to a growing activism project. Many of their stories illuminate or enrich an activism project in exciting ways. As they get involved with collecting stories and photos to represent the development of an activism project, families find ways to become involved in a project. They may know a visitor to invite or a field trip to take. They may offer to go along on a trip or to come spend time in the classroom and help with a project. Documentation that represents an evolving activism project is one way to make a project accessible for families. It opens doorways for families to become involved in their children's activism.

Teachers' active roles in supporting activism projects

Change the classroom environment

As an activism project unfolds, teachers may decide to purposefully rearrange or add to the classroom environment. These physical changes encourage children to think about an issue in new ways. Here are some examples from Fran's classroom of ways that she changed her classroom to stretch children's thinking and invite them into activism:

- Fran put brooms by the doors to the playground and parking lot, commenting to the children that "I've put extra brooms near the door for those of you who want to help with the neighborhood cleanup."

- After overhearing a conversation in which children talked about "getting mad" as a response to injustice, Fran hung a picture of the Native American activist and Cherokee Chief Wilma Mankiller in the classroom. Children noticed her picture and asked about it. This began a conversation about "adults who get mad when people are hurt by unfair laws and rules."

- When the children in her class noticed the distinctions made in a toy catalog between "girls' toys" and "boys' toys," Fran decided to nudge their thinking by posting signs in the drama area announcing, "Baby dolls are only for girls to play with," and in the block area announcing, "Blocks are for boys only." These signs provoked outrage in the children and propelled them into a discussion of sexism and toys.

- Fran added a wheelchair to her classroom following a trip to a nursing home to visit one of the children's grandmother, who used a wheelchair. As the children played with it, they discovered that the chair didn't fit through the room's narrow doorways. They realized that access to their room was limited for anyone in a wheelchair.

Make room for stories to emerge

When teachers use their own stories, the children's stories, and books to nudge children's thinking, they create bridges to new understandings and to a wider repertoire of possible actions. For example, when Fran and the children encountered a man in a sleeping bag beneath an apple tree in a city park, the initial response of most of the kids was to talk about their own experiences sleeping outdoors on camping trips or in their backyards. One of the children challenged the other children to move beyond the fun of camping to the issues of hunger and homelessness. "That man was not camping," Eula exclaimed. "Don't you even know about homeless? My mom's friend does. People get wet and cold and hungry. Even kids do it." The children responded to Eula's challenge by considering the apples in the tree as solutions for the man's hunger. Fran, listening to the children's conversation, wondered how she ought to respond. She decided to tell the story of a homeless family living with her neighbor, hoping to nudge the children to think more deeply about homelessness and to recall their own experiences with homeless people. Fran's story connected homelessness to the life of a real person the children knew, and this changed the tone of the conversation. One of the children, Sean, shyly described his current circumstances as "like that family by your house, Fran." Sean's family was temporarily without a home and staying with family friends. Fran's story moved the discussion beyond camping and apples to a serious analysis of homelessness and the lives of children and teachers at Madrona.

Books stretch children's thinking and expand their understandings of an issue. As the children in her class explored accessibility issues, Ann stocked the classroom with books about people who use wheelchairs. One of the books, *Mama Zooms*, describes the adventures that a little girl has with her mother, who uses a wheelchair. This book added another child's story to Sophie's stories of living with a dad in a wheelchair. Another book, *My Teacher's in a Wheelchair*, traces a day at school for a teacher who uses a wheelchair. This book inspired investigation and conversation by the children about how their experiences at school would be different if their teacher used a wheelchair.

Teachers can invite children to create books about an activism issue or project, allowing them to stimulate one another's thinking with their own stories. When children dictate stories, they clarify their understandings for themselves and provide different perspectives about an issue for their peers and their teachers to consider. As documents that become part of the collective record and "group memory," the books that children make are a reference for further planning and action.

Offer children opportunities to demonstrate their knowledge

Children deepen and extend their thinking when they represent it using common early childhood materials such as clay, blocks, paint, markers, and writing materials. The process of building, sculpting, drawing, painting, or writing about an issue helps children think about it more fully and clearly.

Conversations between children who are engaged in this process side by side can also provide opportunities to wrestle with differences of opinion. During a project about homelessness, teachers might invite children to draw pictures of things that homeless people need or to sculpt a homeless shelter with clay. During a project about pollution, teachers might encourage children to write stories about cleaning up a neighborhood park and to draw pictures of a park that is "fun and fair for all sorts of kids."

There are many forms in which children can demonstrate their new knowledge and skills: drawing, writing, creating plays and puppet shows, building with blocks, sculpting with dough, painting, playing pretend games. It's often useful for children to use several different media to represent their thinking. Each new medium offers children a new perspective and new challenges to consider. For example, during the project about making Hilltop fair for people in wheelchairs, Ann invited children to sketch the wheelchair ramp at Sophie's house. This drawing helped kids get a sense of the slope and length of ramps. She asked children to draw pictures of houses with ramps to nudge them to think about how and where ramps attach to buildings. She encouraged children to build block houses with ramps and to try out a doll-sized wheelchair on those block ramps to focus the children's attention on the relationship between the degree of a ramp's slope and the speed a wheelchair moves down a ramp and the effort required to move it up the ramp. Each of these opportunities to represent wheelchair ramps offered the children new issues to think about. When children revisit and build on earlier work and move from one medium to another, their thinking is enriched.

Invite children to document their own work

As an activism project unfolds, teachers can invite children to record the story of their work. This practice provides children with a record of their activism when a project ends.

The practice of asking children to help document activism projects began at Madrona spontaneously, but it grew to become a key aspect of activism work. It began the day the children and Fran held a spontaneous meeting to discuss what to do about speeding vehicles on the streets near the school. As the meeting began, Fran grabbed one of the blank books that were kept at the writing table for children's dictated stories. During the meeting, she used the booklet to record children's ideas and reactions to the situation and their suggestions for resources. That meeting launched a project about how to make the neighborhood "more fair for kids who go on walks." It also initiated the practice of recording activism projects together.

After the meeting, Fran saw several children making complicated lists at the writing table. This was something new, a change from their usual practice of dictating and illustrating stories. She couldn't read these lists and reminders, but the children obviously could. It was clear to Fran that they were putting into practice something they had just learned. After that day, the children made sure that the booklet they had begun about speeding traffic was at every meeting. They named the booklet "About Cars That Speed" and showed it to family members, other teachers, and classroom visitors.

Fran and the children took the book on field trips, used it to record the comments of classroom visitors and to demonstrate their project work to them, copied the children's drawings of traffic signs into it, and used it as a place to keep brochures, signatures, and thank you notes collected during the project.

One of the families from school had been on vacation when this project began. When they arrived back at school, the kids greeted them with the book: "There are speeding drivers outside, and we are trying to teach them to slow down. Read this book. It will tell you all about it." The book provided a complete overview of the project to date and was a perfect way for the vacationing family to catch up on what the class had been doing while they were gone. It also emphasized to the children the importance of their record keeping.

As the class created this ever-expanding book about their work, the children saw that the adults took their work seriously enough to create a book about it. And the children applied their emerging literacy skills to the process of documentation, eager to add to the book and to read the story it contained. As the project about safe streets ended, the class added finishing touches to the book and invited parents to listen to the final chapter of this story. Fran made several copies of the book to keep at school, in the reading area, the dramatic play area, the block area, and the outdoor play area. The book became a cherished part of the school.

When children observe adults collecting data that tells a story, then they are eager to contribute to and even manage this process. Reviewing the record they've made gives them an understanding of where they've been and what they've accomplished. Budding activists know their story well and are eager to share it with others as the final gesture to their hard work.

Plan field trips and other excursions

Although an activism project may begin and end in the classroom, rarely is it explored entirely within those confines. Finding answers to the questions that they generate almost always takes children out into the community. Planning an excursion to collect or confirm data generally has the effect of drawing children further into an investigation and enriching their experiences with the viewpoints of other people.

For example, when some children in her class discovered that no women were depicted in a new book about firefighters, Fran suggested a walk to the neighborhood fire station to investigate the status of women there. The children were thrilled to find a woman firefighter on duty, especially when they learned that she shared their outrage about the book's omission. The firefighter invited the children to collaborate with her on a letter to the book's publisher. This spontaneous trip fed an activism project and added a new voice to that project in a way that would have not happened within the classroom.

Invite visitors to the classroom

Early in an activism project, teachers often discover that both they and the children need to consult someone who is experienced with an issue. The children may be curious about a particular aspect of an issue and have burning questions to ask. Or a teacher may want the children to encounter a person who will lead them to the next stage of thinking and acting. Sometimes a coteacher or a parent can step in as a "guest expert" on an issue. Neighbors can be experts on local issues such as safety or the environment. Community workers such as librarians, architects, bus drivers, activists, firefighters, politicians, police officers, maintenance engineers, and city planners bring professional experience and knowledge to enlarge the children's wonderings and discoveries.

Often, children can identify who they need to talk with to learn important information. As the children in Ann's class explored ways to make their school wheelchair accessible, they commented to Ann that they had better talk to "the person in charge of the building." So Ann invited the building's facility supervisor to meet with the children. Ann also decided to invite an architect to meet with her and the children, to teach them about slope and safe ramp design.

Visitors can enrich an activism project with important information and new perspectives. On the other hand, visitors may not be accustomed to talking with young children, and their messages may be uninteresting or unintelligible to the children. When this happens, teachers can jump in and manage a visit as an interview. They can invite the children to ask their questions and serve as an interpreter between the visitor and the children. This lets a teacher connect the visitor's information with the developmental level of the children.

Ask questions to nudge children's understanding

Teachers take an active role in moving a project forward when they ask children open-ended questions to help children clarify their thinking, push their thinking to another level, correct misunderstandings, or arrive at group consensus. Questions that seek more than simple answers and quick fixes invite children to think in new ways about an issue.

Teachers may ask questions to help children clarify their thinking. For example, a teacher might respond to a child's anger about a biased remark by saying, "You get really mad when kids say you can't have two dads. What would you like to say to them?"

At other times, teachers may carefully craft a question and strategically place it in order to anchor an activism project. For example, a teacher might respond to children's initial reaction to unfairness in a puppet show by commenting, "I can tell that you didn't like the way the police officer treated the old man in the puppet show. Why do you suppose he was doing that? What should the old man have done?" This sort of question focuses the children's attention on an issue of unfairness and encourages them to think about it in new ways.

In the thick of a project, teachers may ask questions about logistics: "What are some ways to get people to pay attention to the unsafe streets in our neighborhood?" "Who do you think we should talk to first about this problem?"

Towards the end of an activism journey, teachers might ask, "What are some of the things we've learned about hurtful name-calling?" "Who are some of the people that helped us to learn about that?" These questions invite children to reflect on their activism work, notice what they've done, and why.

Use persona dolls

Persona doll stories allow teachers to introduce diversity and resistance to bias to children in the form of stories about kids like them. Persona dolls have their own characteristics and life stories. A group of persona dolls used in a classroom can both reflect and expand on the experience of the children in the classroom. With persona dolls, teachers can introduce new ideas, reinforce current understandings, and challenge misunderstandings. The dolls come alive for the children. Children often respond to them by engaging them in dialogue or by making accommodations for them in the classroom. During the accessibility project, Ann used Carmella, a persona doll in a wheelchair, to spark conversations among children about the accessibility of the classroom, the needs of people in wheelchairs, the reasons that people use wheelchairs, and how people who use wheelchairs might feel in various situations.

When children are trying to make sense of an injustice they have encountered, when they are stuck and unable to look at another perspective, or when they need more information in order to choose a course of action, a persona doll story can be the catalyst that brings about a shift in feeling, thinking, and doing. Trisha Whitney's book *Kids Like Us* (St. Paul: Redleaf Press, 1999) is an excellent resource on persona dolls.

Here's a story showing how one teacher used a persona doll to head off misinformation and stereotyping in her preschool classroom.

Amy had seven persona dolls in her classroom. Each had an identity and a history, and the children knew these from their teachers' frequent use of the dolls.

One day, Amy used several of the dolls to counter misinformation that had crept into her class, which was made up entirely of white children. Four-year-old Nick had come to school full of stories about "black people being robbers." Amy overheard this on the playground and noticed his captivated audience. She assembled four of the dolls—two African American, one European American, and one Latino—and told their stories of living with their families in neighborhoods with kind friends and not-so-kind friends.

"LaKeisha lives on the same street as Miguel. They live in an apartment building where everyone shares with everyone else—like food, or batteries, or quarters for the washers. Sometimes a mommy, a grandpa, or an auntie takes care of some of the kids who live in the building. LaKeisha and Miguel really like it when this happens because they get to have more play time together. But there is a bully who lives in their building, a teenage boy, who sometimes is a friend of Miguel's big brother, Carlos. This big boy teases the younger children like LaKeisha and Miguel. Sometimes he takes their balls and jump ropes. Most of the time they are afraid of him and try to stay out of his way. But when the adults come around, he runs off, and then they feel safe."

Amy paused a moment to take in the children's expressions. Satisfied that she still had their attention, she went on. "Ruth Ann and Nathan sing in the same church choir. Sometimes after church they go to each other's houses to play. Ruth Ann is afraid of Nathan's neighbor because she yells at them if their ball accidentally goes over the fence and into her yard. Nathan likes to go to Ruth Ann's house because her mommy is a police officer and she always tells them stories about the nice things people do and the not-so-nice things too. One day, she climbed her neighbor's tree to fetch a frightened kitty. Nathan really liked that. He thought Ruth Ann's mom was very nice and very strong too."

Amy paused again, and this time Nick spoke up: "Some black people are bad. They take other people's stuff and do mean things." Amy asked the children to think about the families of the dolls and whether they were "bad" or not.

Beth said indignantly, "That's silly. I know sometimes people are good and sometimes people are mean. Sometimes people forget to say they are sorry. People are lots of different things!"

"Yes," said Paul, "and I know a lady with white skin who is very, very evil!"

"Nathan's neighbor isn't very nice," added Olivia thoughtfully. "She frightened Ruth Ann, and that isn't a nice thing to do!"

Then Amy summarized, saying, "I think we agree that there are people who are sometimes unkind and that they have different skin colors. It wouldn't be fair to LaKeisha's family or to Ruth Ann's family to call them 'robbers' or 'bad.'"

"I would never say that. I like LaKeisha the best. I would yell at that bully. I would say, 'Go away, mean old bully.'"

Maddie's shrill words were followed by the quiet, steady, and deliberate voice of Frederick: "Anyhow, those are just dolls." Looking directly at Nick, he added, "My dad has a real friend who is black. And he would never, never be bad to any person."

With the children's eyes still riveted on Frederick, Amy quickly interjected a big thought, one she hoped they would return to again and soon. "There's a word that tells about those unfair ideas about people: 'stereotyping.' That's a very long word that means saying unfair things about people just because of how they look."

The introduction of the persona dolls temporarily brought a more balanced picture of the world into the classroom. But Amy knew that these young children would need many more examples and experiences to counter the biases and stereotypes about people of color that they were already absorbing.

Amy took action when she deliberately provoked the children to think about skin color bias and stereotypes through the stories of her persona dolls. From this deliberate provocation, where feelings and thoughts were shared, activism might grow.

Hold meetings and facilitate group discussions

Regular meetings built into the daily routine, or spontaneous gatherings in response to a discovery or event, offer opportunities for children and teachers to define and summarize feelings and thoughts and to describe and anticipate next steps in a project. Teachers take the active role of gathering the children for a meeting when they want to introduce an idea, reflect on feelings and events, or make plans for a project.

> **Fran:** The four year olds at Madrona were used to meetings. Many of them attended community meetings with their families, and some had very clear ideas about what should happen. One of the kids once explained to me, "At meetings, everybody talks a lot and sometimes they argue. They drink coffee and then go home." Because the children were familiar with meetings, and because I valued opportunities to bring our group together for conversation, I decided to include two meetings in our daily routine.
>
> At the start of each day was the Check-In meeting, at which I encouraged the kids to talk about what was happening in their lives away from school. When an activism project was in process, this was an opportunity to hear what parents thought about the project and what families were doing about a project. These meetings gave me important clues about what the children might need to play about that day. They also helped me to get a clearer picture of the kind of parent support I could expect around a particular project or activity.
>
> At the end of the day was the Big Idea meeting, where the children and I pondered what had happened that day and what it meant for us as a community. When an activism project was unfolding, the Big Idea meeting offered me clues about the meaning of children's dramatic play, block play, drawing, or storytelling.
>
> Meetings were a place for children and teachers to tell stories, debate issues, and make plans. Some of the longer meetings lasted for forty-five minutes; others were short and offered a chance to re-group and re-energize for the next phase of play and discovery.
>
> Meetings were the glue of the classroom culture and the place where activism projects were molded. I always brought a blank booklet to the meetings. In these booklets I jotted down resources that the children named ("I know all about food banks because we have one at my Sunday school"), plans they proposed ("Yeah, we've got to make a sign—a big sign!"), and reactions to ideas ("Nope, I'm not picking up garbage again!"). Sometimes the children would remind me to record something they deemed important ("You should write about what Stu said, Fran"). We often read these books as reminders of what we had done, to assess what we were currently doing, and as inspiration for another round of thinking and planning.

Enter children's play

After observing the children's play and reflecting on the meanings and challenges it holds for the children, a teacher may decide to enter their play to complicate the script, make connections, redirect the energy, or shift the focus.

The following story illustrates how Fran entered children's play one day to shift their focus and direct their energy to a new understanding of a hot topic.

Dictating and illustrating stories was a daily activity for children at Madrona. Kids wrote serious stories and silly stories, stories that never ended, and some that ended so abruptly it was easy to miss the punch line. The children never tired of hearing one another's tales, especially when they were dramatized in the form of a pantomime or play.

One year, the kids were getting stuck in a particular story. Every child in the class had a version of a story about a family, candy, and the bathtub. One typical telling of the story went like this:

Once upon a time, the kids and the mom went to the candy store. And then the dragon roared at them and they ran and ran. But the mom didn't. She couldn't find any of her kids, so she asked the bus driver, and he said no. So the dad came and he found the kids in the park. Then they all got to the candy store and shut the door and bought all of the candy. When they got home, they all jumped in the bathtub and ate up all the candy. The end.

The kids thought these stories were very, very funny—especially the part about the bathtub, which was in every story. Parents working in the classroom would roll their eyes as they watched the kids dramatize this tale over and over again. Almost every adult made a stab at introducing an equally exciting topic as they took dictation at the writing table, to no avail. The adults finally agreed that they could no more dictate the content of a story than they could dictate the content of a painting or a sculpture. They were all aware that children sometimes need to practice certain themes endlessly. But the adults were bored—and they didn't approve of all that candy in the bathtub!

One day Fran had had enough. She could no longer tolerate the overwhelming presence of this sticky family drooling over candy in the bathtub. She decided to write her own story, which would relate to her ongoing report about the homeless family who lived with a friend in her neighborhood. She joined the children at the writing table and began writing her story. Adults didn't usually do this. Their job was to take dictation, not write their own stories. The kids were very curious. Fran read her story to them as she wrote.

Cory and David were instantly intrigued and had questions and suggestions for the family right away. Braden wanted to write his own story about a homeless man his dad saw one day. His story, in turn, inspired other children to tell stories about their encounters with homeless people.

With the introduction of Fran's story about the homeless family, the tide turned. Sticky-family stories: 1; homeless-family stories: 4. The children used the stories to explain their theories and explore their hypotheses about homelessness. When the children acted out these stories, they engaged in public debate and brainstorming. This storytelling enriched and complicated the dialogue that was taking place in our group about homelessness, and it eventually led to an activism project.

Fran entered the children's domain, did what they were doing, and respected the rules for being there. But the story she brought with her became a provocation, helping the children think of homelessness as a story and drama topic, and diminishing the power of the sticky family. This is a subtle way in which teachers say to children, "This is what I think is important. This is what I want you to pay attention to now."

However, teacher as "player" is a role that teachers should take on very carefully and respectfully, always mindful of the context that the children have created. Children's play is often fragile and tenuous, subject to mood shifts, changing relationships, and the ongoing challenge of negotiating and agreeing upon the direction of the play. An adult who has not taken the time to figure out the theme and supporting roles can misinterpret the intentions of the children and change the direction of the play in ways they don't anticipate or intend. In addition, an adult's presence can undermine the children's confidence in leading their own play, resulting in dependency on adults. In both cases, there is a lost opportunity for the children to represent their feelings and concepts through play.

There are times when it is appropriate for a teacher to enter children's play. Kids may play out a theme over and over until they've got it down, but their play doesn't necessarily move them into deeper thinking or new perspectives. When children's play reflects their struggles to understand bias and inequity, they may need adult help to consider new ideas and concepts. Teachers can notice what children are playing about and engage them in dialogue about those issues. They can give children props to extend their play or ask questions to nudge them to think more deeply about particular issues, or bring in books that are related to their play. After studying the script and the roles of the players, a teacher may choose a character and enter the play on the children's terms, as Fran did, careful to match her rhythms and stride with those of the children.

Suggest ways of taking action

It is sometimes appropriate for teachers to put on the hat of "expert" and provide children with a direction for their musings. This can happen when, after expressing feelings of concern, anger, or disbelief about an unfairness issue, and having mulled over the causes and consequences, the children either strike out to take action that is inappropriate or are unable to come up with any action plan at all. For example, at Madrona, children expressed outrage that a neighbor's car had been vandalized. They initially wanted to "set a trap for the mean guys" and "hide in the bushes with swords and clubs." Fran acknowledged those ideas and suggested one of her own: Call or write the police and ask them to step up surveillance in the neighborhood.

Stepping into the role of expert is something that children expect adults to do. They look to adults to be wise and to set limits on what they can and cannot do. Adults who have answers for big problems are reassuring to children. However, taking on the expert role must be balanced with encouraging the children to be reflective and creative problem solvers, as well.

Whenever possible, teachers should set up opportunities for children to make discoveries and form conclusions, demonstrate their knowledge, and dig deeper into the meaning and origins of unfairness. The role of expert should be reserved for those times when the children have wandered off the mark with their thinking and planning, leaving them vulnerable to misunderstandings and perhaps even biases: for example, believing that one person, the mayor, can fix the problem of homelessness, or that providing skin color crayons to every preschool will eliminate skin color bias. Even then, a few well-considered and well-placed questions can often help children come up with new ideas to explore. Taking the role of expert is really a last resort.

Activism projects and the everyday life of the classroom

While children are moving into a focused project, the regular life of the classroom continues. Kids play in usual ways, engaged in dramatic play in the dress-up area, building with blocks, assembling puzzles, experimenting with sand and water. There are periods during the day or week when no obvious project is under way. These times give teachers and children a break from the often intense and focused nature of activism—a chance to be together in easy companionship. In this way, the project, like other activities, is folded into predictable daily routines.

It may be tempting to put an activism project front and center in a classroom, pushing all other pursuits and play to the side while a project is going on. When children first encounter and name an unfairness issue, for example, a teacher may want to set all else aside and spotlight the emerging project. She may want to postpone changing the toys in the sand table or rearranging the drama area, or she may consider rescheduling a cooking or science project. A teacher may feel swept up in the children's reaction to unfairness and interpret their energetic response as a cue that the kids want only to attend to that unfairness. However, young children need many outlets for their passion and enthusiasm, many opportunities to make choices and change their minds. And everyone, adult or child, needs time away from an issue to reflect and recharge.

An activism project should never smother the life of the program. Indeed, coercing children to maintain daily interest in a topic is a surefire way to turn them off. Nothing could be more deadly to a project than the prospect of no escape. Projects develop their own rhythm as they take shape. Every activism project has its own timetable, with periods of outpouring and periods of quiet, days that are filled by the project and days during which no overt work is done.

Some projects are brief and intense, ending in several days with no lingering questions, no driving curiosity. Others unfold evenly and may be sustained over a period of months. Still others may peak several times before finally fizzling out. The rhythms are organic to each process and can rarely be predicted. Fran recalls that at Madrona one year, the children first encountered homelessness in the fall but didn't pursue any action about it until spring. In the interim, there were encounters with other interests and a range of topics to explore. She also experienced a project about speeding cars that was urgent, intense, and quickly finished. Another project about cleaning up the neighborhood began with a rush, crept along for a while, then dried up several months later.

Children make different investments at different times in an activism journey. Not all the kids in a class will necessarily be involved in a project as it unfolds. Some children may be uninterested at the beginning but become interested later, while others who are there at the beginning may take a back seat as the project continues. Some are hooked at a deep level, while others have a more casual relationship with a project. Just as with everything else that happens in the life of a classroom, children make choices that determine when and how long they will be invested in an activism project. Their choices reflect individual developmental needs and patterns.

> **Fran:** When I think of the group of kids at Madrona that included Eula and her friends, I can identify the "specialists." Cory and David liked to keep records and send out messages. Braden loved to put together protest marches, harnessing other kids to make big posters and signs. Eula loved to plan outings; she knew a lot about what went on in the community. Graham and Larry regularly broadcast the unfairness they observed both in and outside of school, and joined with others—like Hannah, Jennifer, and Zoe Alice—to create hypotheses for the group to test. Erik and Sean checked in every once in awhile; their passion was building with blocks, and not much could distract them from that.

Managing an activism project when you teach alone

Teachers and children share full, busy days together. They play indoors and outdoors, eat and nap and eat some more. They paint, work with wood, play in the sand, and build with blocks. There may be formal group activities like music and storytelling circles. Teachers may plan science or cooking activities. Children may create elaborate games that carry over from one day to another. Teachers may feel that their days with children are full enough—and then along comes an activism project, which adds to the complexity of daily life in the classroom for children and for teachers.

When teachers work in a team or with teaching assistants, one teacher can focus most of her time on an activism project. She can, in effect, become the full-time project manager. When teachers divide up classroom responsibilities, it's important to consult with each other often, exchanging news about the work they are doing with the children. This helps teachers receive and give support to each other, have a more complete picture of the life of the classroom, and stay informed about each child's developmental challenges and successes inside and outside of the activism project.

When a teacher works alone in a classroom, the challenges inherent in an activism project are amplified. In the face of these challenges, teachers working alone might try

- simplifying schedules and routines
- setting aside a time each day for activism work
- finding ways to involve all the children at once in the activism project
- recruiting parents or other volunteers to help in the classroom

One strategy is to simplify schedules and routines, setting aside theme work and complicated art projects, for example, while the children are investigating an injustice issue. There is a measure of spontaneity and flexibility required by an unfolding activism project, as teachers allow the rhythms of the project and the children's interest to shape each day, rather than holding tightly to a preestablished schedule of activities.

Another possibility is to set aside a time each day to work on the project with interested children. For example, during free play time, a teacher might set up a writing table for children to dictate letters, or she might invite children to join her in the block area to build a model of a school that's fair for people in wheelchairs.

Some days, a teacher may decide to involve all of the children in an activity, for her own convenience and to keep all the children connected to an activism project. She may use a class meeting to pose provocative questions or to summarize the work that children have been doing on an activism project. She might take all the children on a field trip related to the project. There will probably be some children in a group who are not at all interested in a project. Forcing them to participate in a group activity that they don't care about is disrespectful and often derails the activity for the other kids, so it's wise to use this approach thoughtfully and sparingly. However, it can build community within the classroom. It is a way to keep people informed about the feelings and ideas about unfairness that some children are engaged with, the work that they are doing, and ways that other people can join them.

Teachers can invite parents and other volunteers to help out in a classroom and on field trips. This gives a solitary teacher the additional hands she needs when not all of the children are taking part in an activism project. Some programs require parents to spend time in the classroom each month. In these programs, parents could supervise children's play while the teacher and interested children work together on an activism project.

Letting the children set the pace

Children have ways of letting teachers know whether or not they are comfortable with the pace of an unfolding project. When a project is moving too fast or when teachers complicate things too much, children are likely to say, "I wanna play!" When children are overwhelmed, they take refuge in their familiar play scripts. On the other hand, children may convey, through words or body language, that they are bored, that nothing much is happening that interests them. The children are the barometer. Teachers pace themselves according to feedback from the kids.

> **Fran:** When I first began to be more intentional about responding to the children's observations of unfairness, I felt like I had to respond to every idea that the children had, every suggestion they made. I thought that if I didn't, I would miss important discoveries or derail their enthusiasm. One time, in one week, we went on two investigative field trips and hosted a guest speaker—this along with my probing questions and the new, provocative props I'd added to the room. On the Monday following this hectic week, when I once again returned to the topic, two children put their hands over their ears, and one who was bolder, said, "I don't want to talk about this any more." I was crushed, but also relieved. This wasn't a pace I could keep up either.

The chart below summarizes the growth of a project on hunger at Madrona one fall. The observations were made by Fran in the classroom as the topic unfolded. The reflections show her looking back at each day's notes and trying to decipher the children's passions and concerns. As you read it, think about all the issues discussed in this chapter: the active and receptive roles Fran takes on as the teacher; the days when nothing connected with the project is recorded; the revisiting of the issues involved over and over again by the children and their deepening understanding as they worked through the issue of hunger in their play.

The Life of an Activism Project: Thinking about Hunger at Madrona Cooperative Preschool

September **15**

There was a crisis in the dramatic play area today, with robbers stealing the banquet food of the royal family and its entourage. The conflict was negotiated by the children. Anya said, "Everybody has to have food!"

The children all comply with Anya's moral edict. Do they all feel this way—that everyone is entitled to food?

September **18**

Toshio came to school today with his hiking boots on. He also had a coil of rope. Together he and Frank built a huge mountain with the hollow blocks. Later they added a tent—a blanket over two chairs. Sean came by to visit them. He didn't join in but asked a bunch of questions about camping.

I bet that Sean has never experienced camping. His questions are aimed at accommodating the ideas he is picking up from Frank and Toshio. I could read him the book we have about camping in our library, or maybe he and I could ask to join the play as fellow campers and learn more about it that way.

September **19**

Today, robbers swept up all the food from the children camping in the block area and from the children serving the royal banquet. This time, Jessie and Stacy called for a meeting. Their issue was manners: the robbers should ask first before taking the food. While one of the robbers rolled on the floor in laughter, the other, Jake, said, "Robbers don't ask for nothing. They just take it!" "It's not fair," roared Anya. "We didn't have enough food for all our guests. We're tired of robbers!" I intervened to ask, "What if you invite the robbers to the banquet? Then they won't have to steal your food, and they won't be hungry." No takers for that idea. The robbers were reprimanded and slunk off to their cave. The campers brought their food to the banquet, and all was well at the palace.

We sidestep what I'd pose as a key question: If, as Anya says, everyone needs food, is it okay to steal some when you don't have any? Time for me to ask questions to get at the heart of what the kids know and think about when it comes to the need for food and the etiquette around obtaining it.

September **20**

The robbers have been distracted by the new puzzle in our room. The campers spent most of play time making a grocery list for their next outing. They really got excited about copying words from a grocery flyer I put on the writing table. At the Big Idea meeting, I asked two questions: "Why do we need food?" "What happens to people when they don't have any?" There was consensus on the first: "We need food so we'll grow!" To the second, Emmett said, "You die, of course!" It got quiet. Finally Frank said, "Everybody should get food."

I think that kids often hear that they need to eat in order to be healthy and grow strong. But dying if you don't have food is another matter, one I think a lot of the kids haven't considered before. They may have a moral dilemma to resolve now: Everyone should have food, because if you don't you will die. But you can't steal it.

September **21**

Two interesting food-related developments: some of the children who play palace banquet brought empty food containers from home to add to our supplies, and the campers began making their own food by cutting out pictures from ads and gluing them to cardboard.

I am interested to see the children's response to the food ads that I put out on the writing table. I expect the children to practice writing food-related words or make food signs, copying words from the ads. I've seen them do this before when they were playing clothing store and buried treasures. But instead, the campers cut up the pictures, glued them onto cardboard, and created their own food supply! I think the kids are figuring out ways to reduce some of their anxiety around the need for food and food shortages.

September **24**

Kenji discovered "gold" today in rocks on the playground. To qualify as gold, a pebble had to have sparkles in it. He and Toshio were experts by the time the other children took notice. They had sorted through the gravel around the sandbox and made piles of "gold" and "not real gold." Jessie, Stacy, Margaret, and Anya were the first to join them. As the piles started to mount, I brought out paper cups with their names on them, anticipating that there would be children who would want to keep some gold to bring inside. Margaret, Anya, and Kenji did, carefully washing their gold in a pan of water when we came indoors at the end of the day.

Reminder: I want to ask the librarian to find us a book on panning for gold. And Toshio's dad knows a lot about rocks and minerals. Maybe he has a story or two that would interest the kids. I'll give him a call this evening.

September 25

The robbers were back! A quick-thinking Sean gathered a bunch of food containers and put them outside the palace gates. "Here's your food! Now don't take ours!" It worked for a while. Later, at a meeting, I praised Sean for feeding the robbers. "We was the food bank," he replied. Some of the children didn't know what a food bank was, so Sean explained: "You go there when you don't have any food and when you don't have any money to buy some food. I go there sometimes with my mom. But sometimes we have food stamps and sometimes we have real money. Then we get our own food. Then I can get my favorite cereal!" "I know about food banks," Toshio added. "We take food from our garden to the food bank. So does other people that we know. You shouldn't waste food!" A chorus of "I don't do that" followed.

Drawing from his experience with food shortages and food banks, Sean set up a food bank for the needy robbers. He certainly didn't give all his food away. He made sure the castle was stocked too! It seems like the children have agreed that somehow everyone has to eat, even robbers. Another thought: Having money to buy food is a big deal in Sean's life. Money means the difference between choosing what you want to eat and taking what you get. I wonder what might happen if I introduced money into the play. How would the dynamics of robbing and of hoarding change?

September 30

The children in the palace decided to give all the play money to the robbers in exchange for the gold (pebbles from the playground) that the robbers were flaunting. After hoarding it for a while, the robbers came to me asking for help to build a grocery store. They chose blocks for the building material and soon added a cash register and paper bags. Wresting the food from the folks at the palace was the next challenge. Jake, a reformed robber, called for a meeting. They pleaded their case and the royals bought it except for the matter of money—they would only use gold. The robbers-turned-proprietors agreed that palace royalty could use gold, and they could give some of their money to the campers to use in the store.

By adding money as a prop to the drama area, I hope to introduce another element into the "food and fairness" issue the kids are exploring—the link between food and money. Sean had already pointed the way to that when he defined the difference between buying food and going to the food bank. I didn't expect the money to fall into the hands of the robbers so easily, and I certainly would never have predicted building a grocery store as their next move! But with money in hand they have also taken over food distribution. Clever! Powerful!

October 3

Today was the first day of disharmony among the grocery store proprietors, the palace residents, and the campers, who had become ocean-going explorers. The proprietors began hoarding the money! As the availability of money and gold shrank, the campers, forever resilient, returned to making their own food at the writing table. But the palace was in an uproar and Margaret, the reigning queen, called for a meeting. "They are not fair! They have lots of money and we don't have any. We have to buy some food for our banquet! Give us some money!" I suspected the converted robbers were feeling even more powerful in their new role. I inserted a couple of questions that I hoped would provoke some shift in this deadlock between the haves and the have-nots: "We agree that people have to have food to live, right? And we've been sharing our food, sometimes by giving it to people and sometimes by selling it to people. Some people buy food at the grocery store and some people go to the food bank. But where does that food come from?" I made a list of their responses: the store • the farm • people grow it • sometimes hunters • fishermen • sometimes you just find it in the bushes, like berries • you make it at your house, or your grandma's • the food bank • McDonald's

No one mentioned growing food in our greenhouse, which we can do year-round. I think I'll "plant" this idea tomorrow.

October 4

Lots of takers for planting in the greenhouse. We made a plan at the Big Idea meeting. The kids wanted to grow things they like to eat. I prodded them to plant things that will grow well and quickly in the greenhouse during the fall and winter. I read a book about settlers planting, harvesting, and storing food. The kids thought about good places to store our food from the greenhouse and decided to ask Father Tim, the parish priest (and the "boss" of the school) if they can use the basement to store their food.

We are at a very concrete place in our thinking and actions. This plan is manageable and involves everyone in equitable ways, unlike the scarcity and power struggles we've had around food and money.

October 5

I brought in seed packets today. The kids wanted to dig into the ground of the big planting boxes in the greenhouse right away. But I also brought some peat moss and fertilizer to put in first. We created teams of diggers to work at different times in the greenhouse. Fifteen minutes was about the limit for most of the kids, but Anthony, Toshio, and Frank worked for more than an hour, talking to one another about how hard they were working, interspersed with questions for me about making the soil rich.

It really doesn't surprise me that Frank, Toshio, and Anthony spend so much time preparing the soil. Their families all have gardens and spend time working in them together. I'm going to borrow a dehydrator to preserve the apples the children have been bringing into school lately (does everyone in this class have an apple tree in their back yard?). We might try some other fruit too. Margaret's mom wants to make pickles with the kids. She'll bring in the supplies the day after tomorrow. With parents helping, we can offer children the choice of working in the greenhouse, pickling, or dehydrating fruit.

October 7

Today we made pickles, after dehydrating fruit yesterday and the day before. The kids were really into this, with some still preparing the soil in the greenhouse and others preparing fruits and vegetables for dehydrating and pickling. Several kids took flashlights and brooms to the dingy, cold basement to prepare a storage area for our preserved food. Actually, Kenji and I did most of the work, as the others scattered to hide and scare one another. Emmett's mom brought in a book that describes how some coastal Native Americans continue to preserve food as they did in the past.

I continue to be amazed by the intensity and focus the children are maintaining around these projects. Although adults generate the activities, they seem to fit with the kids' notions of a self-sustaining food supply. And there is so much harmony! We talk about this at a parent meeting, and several parents tell stories about growing up on farms or in families with large gardens, which they depended on for their food. Although culturally based (a Filipino American grandmother, a Japanese American mother, a European American mother, and an African American father), the stories have common threads that each person can relate to. I encourage them to come to school and tell these stories to the children to enrich the curriculum they are pursuing.

October **8**

Stacy was upset when Jessie tossed her leftover snack into the garbage can. "You should only take what you can eat! Then you don't waste!" Frank agreed, adding, "Then there will be enough food for everyone, and some left over for kids that are really, really hungry." Toshio announced that he was "really, really hungry" because he didn't eat his breakfast. Anya commented, "What if there wasn't even any breakfast to eat? That could happen, you know." There was silence after Anya added this idea to the conversation. Margaret looked like she was ready to cry when she said, "It's not fair. Kids shouldn't be hungry. Their mom has to find them some food, just like Sean's mom did at the food bank." "Or grow it," added Jake. Silence. I added, "So it sounds like a good rule that Stacy is proposing: that we only take what we can eat. That way we save food for our hungry friends at school, and perhaps we can save food for hungry children everywhere." End of discussion. Nothing to add now.

Wow! This conversation seems to hit close to home. They have all experienced hunger, I'm sure, but mostly it has been quickly relieved. What if it weren't? Unsettling thoughts and feelings. Having a rule about not squandering food seems to lessen anxiety and restore faith in the notion that ultimately no one will go hungry.

October **11**

Other than routine checks of the plants growing in the greenhouse ("Boring," says Jake. "The stuff isn't even growing!") and the larder (to make sure mice aren't into the stores, but mostly to play chase in the dark with flashlights), not much was happening by way of play and conversation about food. The kids continued to monitor one another at snack time, though, making sure no one was wasting.

The kids are getting impatient. It takes a long time to grow food. To help the kids wait and to give them a sense of progress and action, I'll create a chart to keep track of time and the growth of our plants. It'll give the kids some tangible thing to do every day other than waiting. I've borrowed some plastic food models that I'll add to the drama area. Perhaps different props will generate renewed interest.

October **12**

The kids made a restaurant, and the food was free! You could have as much as you wanted, but no waste! Sean remarked: "You need some money to buy some more food to cook for the people!" Margaret retorted with, "We have the biggest garden you ever saw. And a greenhouse too!"

The children have rolled several issues together here—an ongoing source of food with free food for everyone. Utopia! I don't have the heart to ask where the eggs, bread, and syrup at the restaurant came from.

October 13

Emmett's dad and the kids were building a sukkah beneath the climber to celebrate the Jewish holiday of Sukkoth. They lashed boughs to the metal bars, and when it was done, they played inside. Some will bring food from their gardens, some from the store. They'll put it around the sukkah. Later, a family will take the food to a food bank.

I'm wondering about the whole class taking the food to the food bank. What would they get from this? Would it fill holes in their understanding of food distribution, availability, and hunger? How comfortable would Sean be? Many questions. I'll try to get some answers from some of the parents and from a couple of my colleagues.

October 15

Jake arrived at school upset. "Emmett gets to go to the food bank and we don't. That's not fair!" I was caught off guard. At the Check-In meeting, I encouraged Jake to explain what he was thinking. Everyone—even Emmett—agreed that it would be unfair if only Emmett's family was involved in delivering the food to the food bank. I explained that my plan was for all of us to go, and we made plans for our trip. Sean said, "I'm the one who tells you how to get there." We plan to go three days from now, by bus, with Emmett's mom bringing the food in her car. I asked if anyone had questions about what it would be like to visit the food bank, but they didn't. Some were anxious to get back to playing restaurant. Frank had a new twist. He wandered about the classroom asking for money donations for the restaurant so that they could buy more food when they ran out of garden supplies.

It seems that the children in their thinking and play are working out ways to make sure that people don't experience hunger: The restaurant offers free food, with Frank insuring supplies with his donations, and all of the children want to witness the food by going to the food bank. Perhaps to think about it in any other way would be intolerable.

October 18

Anthony's grandfather stopped by with some carrots, turnips, and potatoes he'd just dug up from his fall garden. He was getting ready to turn the soil, and he invited us all to come in a few days to help him. The kids were buzzing with excitement and anticipation. They added his crop to the boxes they were loading for the food bank, and Anthony and Toshio took him outside to show him the greenhouse garden.

Are the children getting ready to be finished, feeling satisfied that they have worked through the problem and know the solutions? What can four and five year olds do about world hunger, anyhow? Perhaps their response to the food bank field trip will give me clues.

October 20

The children did not enter the cold, cavernous food bank boldly. They were quietly taking it all in, almost with a sense of reverence. A young man greeted us and showed us where to put fresh produce and where to put canned goods. The children sorted the food. When they had finished and been abundantly thanked by all of the workers, the kids relaxed a little and asked many questions as they explored the unloading, sorting, and storage areas. They saw where people pick up the food and asked where the people who needed food were. On the way out, a few folks were lining up, and Jake told them we had brought some food. Mostly the children stared and I felt relieved when we were finally walking toward the bus stop.

I struggle at sorting out my feelings from what the children might be feeling. I am overcome with class issues—issues about people with privilege taking care of people who have less privilege. No one is free of the threat of hunger. We will walk in one another's shoes from time to time. But it isn't simple, and I wrestle with my privilege.
I think it's simpler for the kids. They just don't want people to be hungry, ever!

October 21

We debriefed at Check-In. Anya worried that we didn't bring enough food to the food bank. Toshio said, "Well, we can go back again. I know where it is." Several children voiced their desire to return. Sean said he liked it better when the crowds weren't there: "Sometimes you have to wait one whole day to get your food!" The children seemed impressed by this news. "I don't hardly have to wait when I go to the store with my mom," said Jessie. "Well, it's not the store—it's the food bank," countered Stacy. She said, "People don't have money to buy things when they go to the food bank." Some of the kids began naming food items that they observed were missing there: ice cream, candy, and their favorite breakfast cereals. Frank said, "They had good food there for the people. They had lots of rice, and beans, and bread, and stuff like that."

I sensed that the kids were more grounded now in their feeling and thinking about food and hunger. Today, for the first time in several weeks, their imaginative play did not reflect food issues. Even the restaurant was gone, as was Frank's fundraising. Their drama play and stories, with their intense feelings, and the real work they've done in the greenhouse and with food preservation provided a foundation for a concrete and satisfying act—collecting and delivering food to the food bank.

October 25

We all had great fun in Anthony's grandparents' garden. Anthony's dad, who is Deaf, was there too. He taught us some ASL signs for vegetables. Anthony had already taught us a few. Anthony's uncle speaks Tagalog, and he volunteered to teach them the words for corn, beans, and carrots. We trudged back to school with the last of the crop and settled in on the blue rug to rest and reflect. "Now we have more food to take to the food bank," said Frank. "That's not enough," Kenji responded. "Well, we can collect more. I can bring some soup from my house," offered Margaret. "I know," said Sean. "We can get a big, big, big ol' bag and put food in it from our houses and our gardens. After we fill it, we can take it to the food bank." "And then we can start another one," said Jake, getting excited. "I got it! I can get a huge box from someplace. That would make a lot of food!"

The kids seem really satisfied with this plan to continue collecting and delivering food to the food bank—their solution, I think, to the problem that everyone needs food but not everyone has the money to buy it. They have been working on this problem from different angles for several weeks now, and I think they are satisfied that they are addressing it. At least for the time being, there are no more food issues to be worked out through play. In fact, for five days in a row their dramatic play has featured fires, rescue, and a runaway baby. Perhaps it's time to pull together the photos, the dictated stories, and my notes, and provide the children with a map of where they have been and what they have accomplished.

October **29**

At the end of the day, at the Big Idea meeting, I shared the two picture collages I had made. One showed the children preparing and taking care of their garden in the greenhouse and preserving food. The other began with Sukkoth and ended with the trip to the food bank. They beamed with delight. Then I read several stories that children had dictated to me along the way. They laughed uproariously at Jessie's tale of the mean ol' robbers and nodded their heads in agreement with Anya's description of the restaurant. I read my story, too, which is a summary of our project. The children made a few corrections, adding their perspectives, and I announced that the books would be in the reading corner. As parents arrived to pick up kids, they joined our informal celebration of our work. Even those children who were only minimally involved wanted their parents to see the photos and hear the stories. Parents looked pleased. I told them to look for the photo collages and stories in the entry hallway and in the reading corner. I also planned to make a copy of my diary of this project for each family.

This really felt like the ending. The children were celebrating their hard work and their accomplishments. In their play, they had worked through their feelings of anxiety about food and hunger, and they invented solutions like making food from food ads, serving free food at restaurants, and learning how to produce and preserve food. The activism project held a big solution, though: the trip to the food bank to deliver food.

Epilogue:

A few more books were added to the collection and food continued to pour in for the food bank. Only Toshio, Anthony, and Frank stuck with the garden. It was a long haul and yielded a small crop of lettuce, radishes, and green onions for a winter salad. Everyone enjoyed the dried fruits and pickles during the winter months. We got them before the mice did! After Halloween, the play scripts focused on some imaginary characters like pirates, magicians, and extraterrestrial beings. When Kenji began building a train at the carpentry bench, there was a lot of interest in tools and the strength of materials. Emmett and Jake learned how to make pinch pots with clay and mass-produced them for birthday, Hanukkah, and Christmas gifts. For the rest of that school year, no one ever wasted any snack food.

What Do I Do?

**Words and Music
by Ruth Pelham**
©1982 Ruth Pelham ASCAP

2. What do I do when my brother is crying?
   What do I do? I don't know what to say.
   You take your brother in your arms
   And you hug him.
   You take your brother in your arms and you love him.

3. What do I do when my friend is crying?
   What do I do? I don't know what to say.
   You take your friend in your arms
   And you hug her (him).
   You take your friend in your arms and you love her (him).

4. What do I do when the whole world is crying?
   What do I do? I don't know what to say.
   You take the world into your heart
   And you love us.
   You take the world into your heart and you love us.

5. What do I do when I am crying?
   What do I do? I don't know what to say.
   You go deep into your heart
   Love will find you.
   You go deep into your heart, love will find you.

6. What do I do when I am crying?
   What do I do? I don't know what to say.
   Well, you can climb into my arms and I'll hug you.
   Yes, you can climb into my arms and I'll hold you.
   Yes, you can climb into my arms because I love you.

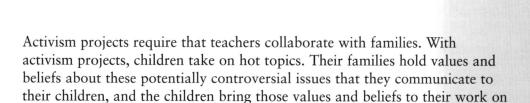

Chapter 5

Traveling Companions: Involving Families in Activism Projects

Activism projects require that teachers collaborate with families. With activism projects, children take on hot topics. Their families hold values and beliefs about these potentially controversial issues that they communicate to their children, and the children bring those values and beliefs to their work on activism projects. Parents' values play a role in the growth of activism projects, whether that role is acknowledged or ignored.

When parents' values are acknowledged, there is true collaboration between parents and teachers, and teachers can do their best work. When teachers intentionally include parents, seek out their perspectives, and aim for mutual understanding and collaboration, differences can be acknowledged openly (rather than allowed to fester) and support can be frankly offered and received. Children get to draw on their parents' ideas and feelings to deepen their learning about an issue. Teachers, too, have opportunities to extend their own thinking and broaden their perspectives about an issue. They build relationships with parents, discover new resources that parents offer, and receive help and support from parents. In this way, teachers build bridges for children between their experiences at home and at school, open doors for family involvement, and deepen their understanding of the beliefs and values of children's families.

Ann learned about the importance of including families during an activism project early in her teaching.

During the summer in Seattle, there is a month-long festival called Seafair, with neighborhood fairs and street dances and parades, that culminates in a weekend extravaganza of hydroplane races, a torchlight parade, and an air show. During Ann's first year at Hilltop, the Blue Angels—six Navy pilots flying F-18 Hornets, fighter/attack aircraft—were the featured performers in the air show. They arrived in Seattle about a week before the air show, so they would have time to adapt their stunts to the geography of the area before the actual show. The pilots practiced several times during the week leading up to the show.

The first day of the Blue Angels practice, Ann was at a neighborhood park with the kids in her class. The kids were immersed in an elaborate pretend game about princesses and dragons and guards. They ran and climbed and chased each other, laughing and yelling. Suddenly, the planes were overhead, the blasting roar of their engines obliterating the children's game. As quickly as they had appeared, the planes disappeared, zooming away with frightening speed. The kids had frozen during the few seconds that the planes were overhead, staring up at them. As they disappeared, the children rushed to where

Ann was standing. They gathered around her in a tight cluster, looking terrified and shaken.

One of the kids asked, "What are those airplanes doing?" Ann's answer was bigger than his question: "Those are Navy airplanes. They're built for war, but right now, there is no war, so the pilots learn how to do fancy tricks in their planes. They're here to do a show about fancy flying."

Ann's response sparked more questions: "How are they built for war?" "Do they drop bombs?" "How do they do fancy tricks?" "Will they fly over us again?" "Why are they so loud?" "Do people go on trips in those airplanes?" "Are the pilots Army guys?" "Will we see the show about the tricks?"

They talked and talked. Eventually, the tension dissipated and one of the kids exclaimed, "Let's play!" The kids raced back to the climbing structure, reclaiming their game from the Blue Angels.

The next day, the Blue Angels zoomed over again, and the conversation continued. The kids were skilled in articulating their feelings and ideas, so Ann suggested that they take action, that they write and draw about their feelings and send their messages to the pilots. Ann thought that would give the children their voices back, voices that were silenced by the roar of the planes' engines. It also would humanize the pilots for the kids, reminding the children that the pilots were people who would listen to children's messages.

We went back to school, and the children leaped into the project of communicating their feelings about the Blue Angels. They drew pictures of planes with Xs through them: "This is a crossed-off bombing plane." They drew bomb factories labeled "No." Ann wrote down their messages: "Blue Angels, stop." "Respect our words, Blue Angels. Respect kids' words. Don't kill people." "This is a book to tell you, 'Stop, Blue Angels. Don't kill anyone.'" "If you blow up our city, we won't be happy about it. And our whole city will be destroyed. And if you blow up my favorite library, I won't be happy because there are some good books there that I haven't read yet." The children drew and dictated their messages for about 45 minutes, then their focus gradually shifted to more typical drawings about their families, rocket ships, and pirates. They had poured out their strong feelings about the Blue Angels in their messages and seemed relieved and relaxed.

During nap that day, Ann made copies of the children's drawings and letters and wrote a note to families explaining what they had done. She felt clear that the activism work of writing to the pilots was an appropriate response to the children's experience of the flyovers. The children's ready leap into the drawing confirmed that they were eager to communicate their feelings and ideas. Ann didn't ask for parents' input about their letter-writing—she didn't genuinely want it. She felt passionately that they had done the right thing, and she wasn't interested in hearing otherwise.

She did worry, though, about parents' responses. She was afraid that parents would think that she told the kids what to write, that she had promoted her political agenda with the kids. She worried that parents who were more supportive of the military would be offended or angry. She felt that she ought to have talked first with parents before launching the activism project, not so much to get their permission, but to learn how they felt about the presence of the Blue

Angels in Seattle, what sorts of conversations their family had about the flyovers, as well as to talk more openly about her own feelings about and experiences with the Blue Angels and her thinking behind the activism project.

Despite her worries, some families were right there with the kids and their teacher, ready to add their voices to the protest. They talked with Ann about how they valued their children's experiences of speaking out for what they believed was right and about their hopes that their children would have many more experiences like this. Ann soaked up their comments with relief and gratitude.

Several families, though, were not so supportive. One mom said that she had explained to her child, "You can't always believe what you hear," referring to the discussions about the Blue Angels being war planes. Her comment stung. It touched Ann's awareness that she could and should have proceeded differently with this project.

Parents and teachers can support children's activism even if they do not entirely agree on all the issues. They can talk together about their perspectives on an issue and find ways to accommodate or acknowledge a range of perspectives during an activism project.

For example, if, during the Blue Angels project, Ann had talked right away with families about what the children had experienced during the Blue Angels flyovers, about what parents thought of the Blue Angels, and about her feelings about the military, the project might have unfolded differently. She might have learned that a family valued the Blue Angels as symbols of military protection. She could have shared her sadness and anger at the thought of the many military and civilian deaths during wars. Together, they could have listened to the children's comments about the overwhelming noise and the physical intimidation of the planes. They might have agreed that the planes were frightening for children and shared a hope that the planes would never have to be used for anything but aerial stunts. They might have decided together that the children could write letters to release some of their fear and to find some power in the face of the frightening flyovers. They might never have agreed on the role or value of the military, but they probably would have found their way together to an activism project that responded to the children's feelings and ideas and that respected family beliefs.

When teachers create links between children's home and school experiences, they open opportunities for children to learn about the values of their parents, peers, and teachers. Children learn about differences, how they can be respected and acknowledged, and how people with different perspectives can work together with respect and appreciation for each other. When there is an open and honest relationship between parents and teachers, children can relax, play, learn and explore, confident in the relationships that surround them. When children can carry a conversation from their family dinner table into the classroom, when they can bring an encounter from a field trip home to discuss with a parent during bath time, when they can trust that their families and their parents are in close communication, they can delve deeply into an activism project instead of worry about how to reconcile the differences and distances between home and school. They can call on all the resources available to help them understand their world. Parents feel invested in shaping and supporting the activism project as an extension of their teaching about values. And teachers gain invaluable perspectives and new understandings of the children and their families.

Partnership-building strategies

Every group of parents is different. Some readily become involved with activism projects. Others loudly protest anything that looks like social activism. Strategies that have successfully bridged barriers with one group may miss the mark with another. Teachers need to bring an open mind and an open heart to their work with parents. Here are the strategies we've used to build partnerships with parents in our programs:

- Create a program that is relevant to family cultures.
- Ask parents directly about their values and goals.
- Be honest, clear, and forthcoming about your own values and goals.
- Encourage dialogue among the parents.
- Maintain communication with parents.
- Nurture adult dispositions for activism.

Create a program that is relevant to family cultures
Teachers have the responsibility to learn about the cultures of children's families and to reflect those in the classroom. The values and goals of children's families and the communities in which they live significantly shape their approaches to activism projects. For example, they affect what children have experienced and understand about social injustice and social change.

Teachers can learn about families' cultures, values, and goals in many ways. Here are some strategies:

- Some teachers include questions about family cultural history, heroes, holidays, and rituals in their enrollment process.

- Teachers often meet with families at school or during home visits and ask about their goals for their children.

- Often, teachers learn about a family's values and goals by listening carefully to their questions that they ask about what happens at school ("Will the kids get to learn about reading?"). Or they listen to the requests that families have for their children ("I want her to stay clean during the day—I want her to be respectable, not grubby").

- Teachers can tell stories about the play they see in the classroom and ask families to think with them about the children's pursuits and questions reflected in their play. Teachers can invite families to help them understand their children.

- Teachers can bring their observations about children to parents (for example, telling a parent about his child's tendency to speak out when she encounters unfairness) and invite parents to describe how they have nurtured a particular disposition at home, how they convey their values and their community's values to their children, and how they encourage their children to respond to unfairness.

- Teachers can create a bridge between home and school by making space for children's activism dispositions in the classroom. For example, providing poster board and wood pickets for sign making for a child whose family often organizes protest demonstrations.

When teachers use strategies like these to truly collaborate with parents, rather than seeing themselves as experts who relay information, families participate actively in the classroom rather than passively receiving teachers' services. And when families are actively involved in their children's classrooms, then activism projects can't help but be grounded in the children's cultures and community.

Teachers may find that they share many values with children's families and that it is easy for them to build their classroom around those values. Sometimes, though, teachers discover that the dispositions that families want their children to develop are quite different than the dispositions that they seek to foster. Conflicts of values and goals, whether small or large, are bound to come up when a teacher begins to work with children to identify and address issues of unfairness. At times like these, it's the teacher's job to understand the reasons behind these different wishes and to find or create common ground with parents.

Fran: In my classroom, I valued long stretches of play, interspersed with meetings to debrief and plan more play. However, many of the families at Madrona valued direct teaching as a way to pass on cultural values and strategies: they viewed preschool as a preparation for life. And they liked the idea of sharing what they were teaching their children at home with others in the preschool. This was a way to bring their culture into the classroom and to provide enrichment for other children and adults. They took great pride in assembling materials and setting up a learning station for a lesson in origami, for example, or preparing latkes, working on a quilt, or learning the basics of carpentry.

I respected families' goals for their children and wanted to be responsive to their requests, so I worked with parents to build a daily flow that allowed for both play and direct teaching. This balance was negotiated at parent meetings, where the importance of play was a regular topic of conversation, as was cultural relevancy. In the course of processing these values and priorities, the parents and I decided to set aside space in the art room in which parents could instruct children. We agreed that participation in these activities would be a choice for children, never a requirement. I coached parents about ways to make the activities feasible for young children. As structured activities led by parents became part of every day, children began to stop by, first to observe and then to participate. I noticed that these supervised and structured activities were more attractive to children who had particularly low energy than to children whose play energy was abundant and focused. I learned to welcome these activities not only as a source of cultural enrichment, but also as a haven for wandering, scattered energy.

Because parents were learning to value and respect the children's play, and because Fran was learning the value of cultural sharing and enrichment, everyone was open to negotiating a way for both to happen in the classroom.

Ask parents directly about their values and goals

- Enrollment forms
- Home visits
- Cultural stories
- Parent meetings

When teachers set the tone for open, honest discussion about values and beliefs, they create an atmosphere in which a range of ideas and feelings are honored. Begin seeking out parents' values, beliefs, and ideas when a family first enrolls in a program. On the enrollment form itself, parents can be asked to share their goals and hopes for their children, as well as to describe their cultural heroes and important family days. Home visits by the teacher continue this sort of sharing. Some teachers devise ways for families to tell their cultural stories, knowing that their values are often embedded in them. For example, once some level of trust has developed amongst families, and between families and teachers, an entire parent meeting can be built around sharing cultural stories. Teachers can ask families to think about questions like, "What are some important beliefs and traditions that your family life is built around?" and "What are the ways in which you pass those traditions from one generation to the next?" Or teachers can ask families to describe their family sense of humor, or primary celebrations, or the origins of a name. Teachers can ask family members to bring a photo or memento to share during the meeting; this can spark rich conversations among parents and teachers, sometimes revealing the interplay of past and present and hopes for the future.

Or, in a less public way, parents can be invited to respond to a questionnaire that will give teachers a cultural profile of the children and their families.

Questions may range from "Who lives in your home? Include family pets!" to asking for specific ways a family's home culture (including beliefs and values) can be supported and reflected in the classroom.

> **Fran:** At Madrona, there were monthly anti-bias meetings where big issues like cultural values and the impact of bias on family cultures were discussed. These were important meetings, but not everyone could attend. So I developed the Family Story as a strategy to include a greater number of voices in our discussions and planning. Knowing that families have different strengths and skills when it comes to communicating, I suggested several ways in which they could offer up their cultural stories: They could write their stories, they could record their stories on audiotape, or they could share their stories with me during our home visit. Or they could even share them with me as we chatted before or after school. Regardless of the mode, I invited each of them to "describe your family's history, what you like to celebrate, your values and priorities, and your cultural identity." Once done, these stories informed much of what happened in the co-op throughout the year. And although I was the custodian of the stories, and the spokesperson on behalf of each family, I brought this rich data to board meetings, to curriculum planning meetings (both parents and teachers), and to event planning meetings to assure that the multiple perspectives of the co-op members were represented. And I often asked for clarification of the values and beliefs embedded in these cultural stories as we navigated the often bumpy terrain of a social activism project. What I learned helped me understand what sorts of activism projects they would be likely to support, as well helping me make bridges between home and school in other ways.

Be honest, clear, and forthcoming about your own values and goals

- Informal conversations
- Phone calls
- Parent conferences
- Open houses
- Bulletin boards, newsletters, and notes home

Conversations about values and beliefs call on teachers to open their hearts, to share personal experiences, to be known by families in a more intimate way, and to acknowledge the possibility that they may hold values different from those held by the families in their programs. Even teachers who easily discuss such difficult developmental topics as biting or toilet learning generally steer away from these more vulnerable and risky conversations about values and beliefs. However, teachers' work grows from their values and beliefs; this is particularly true of activism projects.

It is disingenuous for teachers to pretend that their values and beliefs do not play a significant part in their work with young children, particularly when it comes to activism issues. Activism projects are not simply about supporting the children's social, emotional, and cognitive development; they are not simply about children's awareness of unfairness, but also—and significantly—about teachers' deeply held beliefs about injustice and inequity in the classroom, in the community, and in the larger world.

When teachers are honest and straightforward with parents about what they value as social activists and about their intentions to support activism with the children, they can build deep and authentic relationships with parents—not necessarily always based on complete agreement, but definitely based on trust. Parents know that the teacher has no hidden agenda that they must ferret out or guard against; they can talk openly about the values and beliefs that undergird the life of the classroom.

Whenever teachers meet with families, whether informally in hallways, classrooms, or playgrounds or more formally during home visits, open houses, parent meetings, or conferences, they can make clear what they value about children's growth and learning and the ways that activism feeds that growth and learning.

Here are some specific ways that teachers can share their values with parents:

- Some teachers hold an open house or parent orientation in the fall. During these meetings, make sure to describe your understanding of anti-bias work with young children, reflecting on how you've come to value this work and how it influences your teaching.

- Some teachers give parents written information when they begin in the program. You may decide to include a note to families about your values and goals, and how those values and goals shape your work in the classroom.

- In the written materials you give to parents when they join your group, you might include the pamphlet written by Louise Derman-Sparks, María Gutiérrez, and Carol Brunson Phillips titled, "Teaching Young Children to Resist Bias: What Parents Can Do." (This inexpensive pamphlet is available from the National Association for the Education of Young Children.) Attach a brief note to this pamphlet, describing to parents that you'll be addressing issues of bias and fairness with the children in your class, and offering the pamphlet as a way to understand the thinking behind this work and to support children's efforts at home.

- In your regular newsletter to parents, you might include a space in which you and other teachers can share your passions, beliefs, and values about teaching. You might tell the story of how you came to be a teacher or describe what sustains you as you do this work. You might reflect on a core belief that you hold and how that belief shows up in your teaching.

Ann: I seek to build a foundation of honesty and openness with families, beginning with easy topics like what I really appreciate about their children, why I do this work, why I stay at Hilltop. I try to focus our early conversations on what my goals are for children—not just the "academic" learning that I hope they experience (and on which parents place high value) but also the social and emotional learning that I prize. These sorts of conversations build relationships that can carry the weight of the heavy stuff, the feelings and experiences that give rise to activism projects. I continue to feel shy with families, especially talking about myself, yet every year I am rewarded by the response. Parents seem to deeply appreciate knowing who I am—which really isn't surprising, since I'm with their children for many hours each week. And they typically respond by sharing their hopes and values with me, often relaying their struggles, hopes, concerns, and dreams for their children.

During these conversations, teachers can begin educating parents about the ways in which activism grows from children's developmental tasks even when children are very young. For example, two-year-old children respond to unfairness in unmistakable ways. Claudia fiercely takes back the teddy bear that Lucy snatched out of her stroller. Ian screams to let everyone know that he is outraged that Deirdre knocked him to the ground. LaVonna growls as she yanks on Willie's hair after he pushes her aside at the water table. Snatching, screaming, growling, and pulling hair are a few of the many ways that very young children let one another and adults know that they object to unfairness.

Teachers can point this out to parents, communicating ways that they support young children's response to unfairness: "When LaVonna pulled Willie's hair, I saw that she was mad that he forced her out of the way at the water table. I told her, 'That really made you mad when Willie took your place at the water table. You pulled his hair to let him know. But pulling hair really hurts people, so next time say "No" in your biggest voice. I'll come help you and Willie solve your problem.' I wanted to help LaVonna learn a new way to stand up for herself when something unfair happens. I gave her a name for her feelings, validated her thinking, and then offered a better solution—an action plan—for her. This is how even very young children learn to work together to address unfairness."

Four year olds seem to be on "unfairness watch" full time. The refrain, "It's not fair!" echoes through preschool classrooms as children notice inequity, bias, and injustice. This is a critical time for families and teachers to acknowledge children's feelings, extend their thinking, and help shape thoughtful actions instead of impulsive reactions. Teachers can help parents understand that four and five year olds are developmentally eager to take on issues of unfairness. Teachers can point out that adults nurture children to care about other people and the environment when they encourage them to be active rather than passive or indifferent in the face of unfairness. They can remind parents that four- and five-year-old children are stepping into a solid sense of their power, competence, and goodness, and that adults can support that developmental work by supporting children's observations of and responses to injustice.

Encourage dialogue among parents

- Parent articles in the newsletter
- Parent meetings and other events
- Phone trees and buddy systems

Some parents may come to an understanding of and involvement in activism projects through their conversations with other parents rather than with teachers. It may be the insights of other parents that bring credibility to the idea of young children's being activists. Or it may be that as parents talk together, they come to a shared understanding of the role that activism plays

in their children's growth and learning. Here's a conversation Fran overheard at Madrona one day:

Hazel: "I am really amazed at what the children are talking about at school, especially during the daily meetings. And at home too. Graham is challenging all of us to talk about difficult problems. Some of his solutions are pretty impractical, but we're just delighted that he's so aware. When we talked about anti-bias goals in that parent meeting at the beginning of the year, I thought to myself, 'Activism—that's ridiculous. That's for adults, not children.' But then I began to notice that the kids really care when something is unfair. It must be annoying to have adults say, 'It's fine, don't worry about it' or 'Life's not fair,' or, maybe worse, not even respond. How disrespectful! If we want kids to grow up thinking they can make a difference, then we shouldn't turn them off at age four!"

Bev: "Right on! I only wish every kid had these opportunities. I want my kids to know they can speak up on behalf of themselves and others in the face of discrimination and injustice. Because my kids already go to rallies and protests and organizing meetings, this is right up their alley. They know what to do, and they want to do it. I'm all for it."

Karen: "Well, to tell you the truth, I didn't think Braden would even notice the sorts of issues Fran talked about at that first meeting—he's too busy with dinosaurs and blocks, especially at school. But there he was the other day talking about relieving world hunger! And just last night he assured his older sister that she could be a pilot if she wanted to!"

James: "I don't like the word 'activist.' It makes me think of loud, pushy people who are always minding other people's business. And I sure don't want that for my girls. But to survive in this world they need to be strong and they need to speak up for themselves and for others who aren't getting a fair deal. What I like about these projects is that the kids are thinking about a lot of things that kids at this age don't usually trouble themselves with. And we're really involved in what they're doing. Some days I get to feel like an expert instead of just a dad."

During parent meetings, parents can share feelings and insights about emerging activism projects with one another; this can happen both spontaneously, as families and teachers talk together about children's experiences in the classroom, and intentionally, as teachers plan for parent discussion. If a family misses a parent meeting, teachers can ask another family to fill them in on the discussion and decisions; this provides an opportunity for parents to exchange ideas and to stretch one another's thinking.

Teachers can encourage dialogue among parents in other ways. They can create a regular space in the school's newsletter for parents' views. They can plan activities for parents at school open houses and other gatherings in which parents talk in small groups about specific issues.

Fran: During the Persian Gulf War, I became acutely aware of how difficult it is to honor families' values when those values are different from mine. In the classroom I emphasized peaceful resolutions to conflicts and talked often with the children about elements of peace. Most families felt comfortable with these classroom conversations and with our language about "peaceful solutions to problems." But when our conversations about peace expanded to include discussion of the Persian Gulf War, some families became uneasy.

Many of the children came to school wanting to talk about weapons and destruction and their own feelings of vulnerability. They wanted to figure out how the war could be ended so that "people wouldn't get hurt." Yet there were others for whom war seemed exciting: their families talked about the necessity of war to overthrow oppressors and to protect and free people. War-related issues showed up frequently at outdoor time, in dramatic play, and in the block area.

This was a really uncomfortable time for me and for many of the parents. Passions flowed strongly in both directions. The fierce differences among families grew from their experiences and feelings about war and freedom and oppression. Because our school was built around diversity, we could not sidestep differences of beliefs. Parents were talking about the war and their beliefs about it all the time—in the hallways, in the front yard, in the classrooms. There seemed no way for us adults to come together on how to approach conversations about the war with the children, other than emphasizing that we all hoped it would end soon. Despite the tension, I was glad we were having conversations about our conflicting values rather than avoiding one another.

Maintain communication with parents throughout an activism project

- Updates
- Notepads for feedback
- Parent folders or mailboxes
- Journals
- Display boards
- Project books
- Audio- or videotapes
- Phone trees

When an activism project begins to grow, it is important that teachers maintain close communication with families about the children's thinking.

Certainly, some children keep their families posted about what happens at school, and some parents are able to hang out in the classroom regularly enough that they are aware of the ways in which projects are unfolding. However, teachers need to be intentional about keeping parents informed about the course of activism projects, so that parents are aware of what their children are exploring and how they can be involved.

Some ways that teachers can do this include the following:

Post regular updates about an activism project near the place where parents sign their children in each day. These updates might be simple statements like "Today we had a group meeting about the ways that our school is unfair for people in wheelchairs." Include comments from children: "Sophie said, 'It's not fair because there are so many stairs to get to the classroom.' Sam said, 'A person in a wheelchair can't reach the blocks on the bottom shelf.'" Also include questions that families can ask their children about the project: "Ask your child about how our school can be more fair for people in wheelchairs." "Ask your child about the drawings we made today of wheelchair ramps." Finally, ask for feedback: "Let me know a good time to call you to check in about this project."

Keep a notepad near the place where parents sign their children in for parents to write notes to teachers about their questions, comments, and conversations with children. Remind families about the notepad in your daily project updates: "Please jot me a note about what your child said about the drawings we made of ramps." "Please let me know what you're thinking and feeling about our project; you can leave me a note on the pad by the sign-in."

Create a place for personal written communication to each family. Some schools use standing files, with a folder for each family. Other schools have parent mailboxes.

Provide a journal for each child that teachers and parents add to throughout the year. These journals can be a place for photos, stories about children's play and learning at home and at school, and documentation and reflection about activism projects.

Create display boards in the classroom that tell the story of an activism project. Add to the display as a project is happening, rather than waiting until a project is over. The evolving display reflects the current life of a classroom and keeps families up to date. Include children's drawings, quotes from children, teacher reflections about a project, photos of the children at work on a project, documents collected during a project (like maps and brochures), and space for families to add their thoughts.

Create books with the children that tell the story of an activism project. Children, teachers, and parents can add to these books regularly as a project unfolds. At the end of a project, make these books available for families to take home to read together.

Make available audio- or videotapes of the children's work on a project for families to borrow. Encourage them to make written comments about the project after listening to or watching the tapes; add their comments to journals, display boards, or project books.

Organize telephone trees to quickly relay messages to families and to keep them connected to one another as an activism project ebbs and flows.

Nurture adult dispositions for activism

- Respect parents' knowledge.
- Make observations.
- Invite parents' observations.
- Ask questions.
- Be open to changing your mind.

Some parents already see themselves as seasoned activists, while others do not identify themselves as activists at all. Teachers can nurture parents' dispositions to act in the face of unfairness at the same time that they nurture those dispositions in the children. When parents come to see themselves as activists, they are often eager to build partnerships with teachers in support of children's activism.

An important aspect of teachers' work involves educating parents about child development and children's learning and about issues in the community that impact families. Teachers have important information to share, and they are often eager to educate parents.

But parents also have knowledge in some of the same areas. They, too, are preparing their children to be successful in the world beyond home and preschool. Just as teachers are eager to share their expertise, so are parents eager to advocate on behalf of their children.

It certainly is not teachers' intent to silence parents. However, teachers may unwittingly promote one-way communication and education by talking at parents or taking every opportunity to fill parents with ideas and advice. Parents soon learn to show up and listen rather than show up and contribute. To genuinely include parents in classroom projects and activities, teachers need to create a more equitable balance between talking and listening.

Some simple strategies for including parents' voices include:

- Ask parents to share their knowledge, experiences, and ideas (rather than just their questions) during parent conferences and meetings.
- Schedule time to talk with parents about suggestions for curriculum that strengthens the connection between home and school and provides cultural continuity for children.
- Post agendas for parent meetings, making it clear that parents will have time to bring up important issues and concerns.
- Make space in school newsletters for articles by parents.
- Showcase ideas and insights from parents on project bulletin boards.

When teachers deliberately shift from the role of educating parents to the role of collaborating with parents, opportunities for teachers and families to work together will naturally grow.

As soon as an activism project begins to bubble up—when children first notice and express strong feelings about unfairness—teachers can begin to comment to parents about what they observe in the children's behavior. They can invite parents to pay attention to children's feelings and to think about how their children understand unfairness. Teachers can ask parents what they observe about their children at home and at school in connection with the burgeoning issue.

> **Fran:** At a parent cooperative preschool, parents expect to be "in the know." That's a great thing, because it keeps parents attuned to what's happening in the classroom, but it also has its drawbacks.
>
> I experienced some of those drawbacks when I tried to build curriculum around children's play, experimenting with the ideas of emergent curriculum. This was hard for parents: They wanted to know, from the beginning of the year, what was in store not only for the children but also for themselves. They had contributed to the monthly curriculum planning, they were there as assistants in the classroom, and they were invested in seeing their curriculum plans come to life.
>
> I began to coach parents to notice what the children were doing, asking them to think about why the children were doing it. I invited them to document the children's play. I put a notebook in every room of our school and asked parents to record what they saw the children doing and saying.
>
> As parents stepped into the practice of recording what they saw and heard, they began to pay more attention to what the children were really doing. They began to understand the ideas I had been trying to communicate about emergent curriculum and could identify the ways in which children worked on issues of unfairness on their own, outside the activities we planned. At parent meetings and during classroom time, parents began to share with one another

their hypotheses and conjectures about the meaning of children's play. They took on the challenge of noticing and communicating what seemed to be important to the children.

At the co-op, asking parents to document children's play was a way to educate parents and to enrich the dialogue we had with one another. Parents became more active members of the teaching team, more willing to identify issues and offer their skills and resources.

As they become aware of children's feelings, parents may become more aware of their own feelings and ideas about injustice. Recognizing that parents, like their children, need opportunities to reflect on their feelings and ideas and to collaborate with others, teachers can ask parents about their experiences with activism. Some parents may have forgotten passions and commitments from an earlier time; other parents may not see their work with churches, schools, and community organizations as activism. When parents reconnect with their histories of activism, they more deeply understand their children's work for fairness.

As an unfairness issue gives rise to an activism project, teachers can ask parents questions like, "How does your family talk about this issue?" and "Do you think that this is an important problem to solve?" These sorts of questions can encourage parents to think about unfairness issues in new ways. Once parents begin identifying themselves as active participants in a project rather than passive observers of it, they become increasingly eager to support their children's work as change-makers.

When teachers authentically involve families in activism projects, there is a good chance that projects will grow in ways that teachers don't expect. For example, during a project about homelessness in Ann's class one year, one family offered to organize a toy and clothing collection for children at a homeless shelter. This was not part of Ann's original thinking about the project, but grew out of that family's deep support for the children's passionate efforts to help people who were homeless. Ann initially resisted the idea of a toy and clothing collection, mostly because it wasn't in her plans. After realizing that her resistance was based on her reluctance to share her position at the hub of the project, Ann was (sheepishly) able to welcome the family's offer to coordinate a toy and clothing collection, appreciating the family's involvement.

When teachers are willing to change their minds in response to parents' ideas and misgivings, they enhance the trust that families feel in their partnerships. Parents experience teachers' taking their ideas seriously and teachers' willingness to learn about and accommodate values and ideas different from their own. This willingness is at the heart of cultivating authentic partnerships with parents.

Barriers to partnerships

Although many teachers say that they value working closely with families and complain when it doesn't happen, many factors discourage parents from becoming involved. What keeps teachers from being able to achieve full partnership with parents? What prevents this open sharing and discussion of different perspectives that can support flourishing activism projects in early childhood programs? The barriers to authentic partnership with parents can be circumstantial or attitudinal. Here are some of the ones we've observed:

■ **Teachers' time and energy is limited.** It's a challenge for teachers to find time and energy to communicate with coworkers about all that's happening in their classrooms, or to collaborate about curriculum projects, children's developmental journeys, and the logistics of classroom life. Adding more adults into the mix can feel overwhelming. It takes time to write to or call parents, to make displays that tell the story of an activism project, to fill parents in on the daily details.

■ **Teachers develop habits and routines.** Teachers set up their classrooms in certain ways, plan particular sorts of activities, and have habitual ways of relating to families. These routines often work better for some parents than for others. It helps to think carefully about evolving routines that invite parents' participation in many different ways.

■ **Teachers may have set expectations about parent involvement.** Traditional forms of parent involvement include helping maintain buildings or equipment; coming to meetings, potlucks, and conferences; and helping to supervise field trips. However, some parents can't or don't want to lend their expertise, skills, or time. If there aren't other ways for parents to be involved, then some parents will be left out, and so will their cultural stories and skills. The expectation that parent involvement ought to take only certain forms gets in the way of true collaboration by applying a one-size-fits-all mentality to an issue that cries out for inclusive, flexible, and creative thinking.

Eligio's grandfather, Manolo, delivered his grandson to school each morning. Always friendly, he greeted every adult and child with a smile as he hurriedly came and went. He seemed to ignore all of the paperwork that was pressed into his hands; he was seldom aware of events involving families at the center. The teachers noticed and were frustrated by this, but they also noticed that at least once a week, he stopped to ask about his grandson, to hear evidence that he was "a good boy and working hard." He appeared eager to build connections between Eligio's home life and what happened at school. The teachers reciprocated with anecdotes, photos, and sometimes something that Eligio had created for Manolo to take home.

One morning Manolo arrived at school with a very excited Eligio in tow, bearing a large platter of still-warm *lumpia* for the teachers. Another day he invited the class to visit his stall at the market, giving them fresh vegetables and flowers to take back to school. During this visit, Eligio's friends and teachers got to meet his mother, aunts, uncles, and some other members of his Filipino community. The children learned about growing vegetables and decided to plant their own garden back at school.

Eligio's grandfather, Manolo, was actively involved with his grandson's school. His involvement took the form of warm and genuine interactions with teachers and children rather than careful reading of written letters or attendance at meetings. When Eligio's teachers recognized this and were willing to change their expectations about how family members ought to be involved in

their program, they were able to begin really listening to Manolo. They were able to hear Manolo's wishes and dreams for his grandson, his expectations for Eligio while at school, and his trust that Eligio's teachers were preparing him to thrive in the world beyond home and preschool.

■ **Partnerships require that teachers share their authority.** Many teachers are accustomed to having the final say in their classrooms, shaping the life of their classroom in the way that they think is best—from how the space is arranged to how time is allotted to what curriculum is in place. Sharing decision making, inviting other people to offer ideas and feedback, and asking for information opens the door to possible conflicts. Parents' suggestions may be really different from teachers' plans. Parents may have feedback about a project that is critical or challenging. Parents may share insights into their children that contradict teachers' perceptions. However, if parents are to participate actively in the life of the classroom, teachers must let go of their comfortable position as the final authority in the classroom. Teachers need to make room for parents; include them in decision making; share their thoughts with parents; listen openly to parents' ideas; and invite parents to contribute ideas, resources, and honest feedback. Here's a story from Ann's experience with this process at Hilltop.

Ann: I'd been working for about a month with a group of five children on a project when the mother of one of the children approached me. "Can I talk with you about the project?" she asked me. "Ben is not engaged by this project. He's not invested in it—in fact, he asked to stay home today so he wouldn't have to do this work." I was shaken by her words. I'd invited Ben to work on the project because he'd seemed really interested; in fact, his initial interest had drawn other children to the project. I had a lot invested in having this project be fulfilling for the children involved, an example to families of the sort of really good teaching that facilitates deep and enjoyable learning.

I felt embarrassed and defensive. I wanted to be right about Ben's interest in the project. I wanted to be perceived as a wise, insightful teacher, one who tenderly nurtures each child's development. I wanted Ben's mom to defer to me in my wisdom.

I had to breathe deeply and force myself to listen to Ben's mom without leaping to my own defense. She said, "I think Ben was interested at the beginning of this project, but he's moved on to a new passion. Here's what I think would be really satisfying for Ben right now. . . ." She described Ben's interest in superhero play and suggested ways I might respond to that. As she talked, my defensiveness began to soften. She spoke with respect for my teaching and with trust in my responsiveness both to her and to her son. In fact, she wasn't offering suggestions because she thought I was doing a poor job, but because she believed that I cared about her insights. I realized that she initiated this conversation because she felt a partnership with me, and that I could easily have blown it by refusing give up my final authority on her child and on curriculum.

- ■ **Teachers and parents may experience language, culture, and class differences.** Teachers often come from cultures different from those of the children and parents in their programs. Some teachers work in programs with families who literally speak a different language than they do. Many times teachers and families occupy different social and economic classes. It seems easier to ignore these differences than to tackle them head-on; however, whether they are acknowledged or go unnamed, they provide a constant undercurrent to adult interactions, and they pose barriers to including parents in early childhood programs. Teachers have the responsibility to investigate these differences and understand how they affect their relationships with parents.

Fran: I really thought a lot about cultural differences when I thought about how to involve families in the classroom. Teachers are gatekeepers of sorts, deciding what will and what will not happen in the classroom. As a white woman of European descent, I was concerned about occupying the gatekeeper role, especially in a classroom with children from a range of cultures. Some of the questions I found it useful to ask myself were, How might my membership in the dominant culture impede the flow of other people's cultural agendas into the classroom? What behaviors and expectations of mine might get in the way of building trust, stifling the urge in parents to share with me their dreams and visions for their children? What could I do to be an ally for parents of color?

What about me would invite them to share the hard issues and how they would impact their children's futures?

- **Working parents are typically not available during the school day.** It's a challenge to maintain daily communication with working parents, who often have limited time to spend at school when they bring their children in the morning and when they pick them up in the evening. Parents may see one teacher in the morning and a different teacher in the evening; there may be some teachers whom they never encounter. In addition, many parents' jobs need their full attention all day; they can't leave work to join in classroom projects or to accompany children on field trips. Teachers sometimes perceive these parents as distant from the daily life of the classroom, uninvolved, and unaware of what's happening. Without deliberate attention to the particular challenges of involving working parents, chasms can open that separate parents from their children's daily life.

- **Some parents may be consumed by day-to-day survival issues.** Some parents are legitimately focused on survival—feeding their children, maintaining or finding a place to sleep each night, getting medical care when someone in the family is sick. These parents may not have energy or time available to be involved in their children's classrooms. They may want to be fully connected to the school but unable to surmount such barriers. Fran worked one year with a family who lived in interim housing; while they waited for federal assistance so they could rent an apartment, they lived in a motel. The family took two buses to get to school and two buses home. The children wrestled with poverty and homelessness through their play; one of the children developed an eating disorder. For this family, involvement in classroom projects was not an urgent concern; their immediate efforts were concentrated on making it through each day.

- **Parents and teachers fear being judged.** As adults who are involved intimately in different ways with the welfare of the same children, parents and teachers worry about being judged by each other. For instance, a parent may worry that his child's teacher thinks he lets his child watch too much television or eat too much junk food or that he fails to provide regular bedtimes. A teacher might worry that a child's parent thinks that she doesn't have a strong enough relationship with his child, or maybe that she has too strong a relationship with his child, or that she doesn't know enough about his child's particular developmental issues to be his teacher. These worries cause an undercurrent of tension that promotes distance rather than partnership between teachers and parents. Parents want teachers to understand the challenges of working and being a parent, the juggling that they do, the vast amounts of time and energy it takes to raise a child. Teachers want parents to understand the hard work that they do, the many complexities involved with supporting many children's growth and learning, and the low pay and low social status of their work.

- **Parents pay teachers in child care programs.** It's challenging to build a partnership when one partner pays the other. Teachers sometimes wonder how parents perceive them: As their hired help? As vastly underpaid but irreplaceable professionals? As teachers, baby sitters, child development experts, or parenting consultants? This conflict can be exacerbated when parents, struggling themselves, nonetheless are substantially better compensated than teachers.

Parents and teachers both want what's best for children, and for the most part these dreams are much the same. This is revealed when parents and teachers figure out ways to come together to share beliefs and hopes, values and goals. When authentic partnerships are forged as an outcome of this sharing, very little can stand in the way of parents and teachers collaborating to support flourishing activism projects.

Speaking Up

Words and music
© 1999 by Nancy Schimmel

Chapter 6

The Journey Ends: Concluding an Activism Project

Many activism projects have specific goals: children will collect food and deliver it to the food bank, families will meet on Saturday for a neighborhood trash cleanup, a teacher will buy paint for the art area in a range of skin colors, kids will rearrange the classroom furniture to make their room more accessible for people in wheelchairs.

It seems as if figuring out when a project is over ought to be simple—once the goal is accomplished, the project is finished. Unfortunately, it's not nearly so straightforward! Whether or not a goal has been accomplished doesn't necessarily reflect whether or not the children have finished with an activism project.

Children may be long done with an issue before the formal goal of a project is realized. For example, children outraged by the garbage on their playground may give voice to their feelings by making signs to post that firmly request people to "Put your garbage in the garbage cans." They may plan a cleanup day and write an impassioned letter to their families informing them about the need to pick up trash on the playground. However, by the time a cleanup day arrives, the children may not be much interested in cleaning up the playground. Perhaps the urgency and outrage that they felt earlier has abated, and they are now eager just to play at the playground with their friends and families rather than cleaning up garbage. Maybe it is enough to make signs and write a letter—they may not need to take more action. The children's involvement in the project may be over sooner than their teachers and families expected it to end.

Ann: Several times in the past years, I've worked with children to write letters protesting unfairness. We've written to an oil company following an oil spill, to a puppet theater after we'd seen a particularly violent show, and to the Navy after frighteningly loud fighter planes descended on our city to practice for an air show. Each time, I wondered what might grow from the children's clear sense of unfairness and the careful thinking articulated in their protest letters. Would the letter writing be a first step in a bigger activism project? What would happen after the children received a reply to their letter? And each time I was surprised by how quickly children were done with the issue. I'd be ready with provocative questions, books, and props to stimulate further thinking about the unfairness issue while we waited for a reply—and the children were unresponsive. They had moved on to other concerns. When replies to their letters did come, the children were uninterested. The responses inspired brief retellings of the events that had sparked their letters, but nothing more. Their letter writing was their activism, and once their letters were in the mail, they were done with the issue.

On the other hand, children may stay deeply engaged with an issue long after the formal goals of a project have been accomplished. Ann was also involved in a project in which the children in her class set out to give money to people who were homeless. The children collected several hundred dollars and made three trips downtown to distribute it. The last trip did not mark the end of the children's involvement in the issues of poverty and homelessness, though. Even with the money they'd collected long gone, the children continued to share stories about homeless people they encountered, to build homeless shelters out of blocks, to write letters to their families about ways they ought to continue to help homeless people, and to save money from allowances and birthdays to give to homeless people. Although the formal action plan was accomplished and Ann was no longer actively facilitating a project, the children were not ready to let go of the project's focus. The project was not yet over for them.

The world of children is rarely orderly and sequential. Children have not yet learned to compartmentalize, and they are just learning how to prioritize. Yesterday's passion may be replaced by today's discovery. Today's experiences may shape many days to come. Endings are not always clear and straightforward—they do not necessarily come when adults expect them. Children do not politely feign interest in a project that no longer engages them, and at the same time they may surprise adults by their capacity for sustained and focused work.

Signs that children's interest is waning

When teachers pay attention, they hear clear messages about where children stand with a project. Children may communicate that their focus is shifting away from an activism project in any of the following ways.

They say they've had enough

Children may boldly and directly declare that they have had enough of working on an unfairness issue. "I don't want to do this anymore." "I'm not picking up another piece of trash ever!" "That's enough food for the food bank. I'm not bringing any more food there."

They squirm during meetings

Children may resist coming to meetings about an activism project or come only under duress and wiggle and squirm and ask when they can go play. Children may exclaim, "Oh, no, not another meeting about that!" They might protest, "I can't stand to talk about this anymore!" or "When will this meeting be over so we can do what we want to do?" During a meeting, they might poke at each other, giggle, or make whispered plans about a game they want to play outside. They might respond with silence to a teacher's questions about a project: "Eula pointed out that we're running out of brown crayons. Who would like to sort through the crayons today to find all the brown ones? No one?"

Children's play shifts focus

Children's play may shift to a new focus that has arrived on the scene that absorbs their attention. For example, a teacher might observe that children whose drama play had been full of pretend name-calling and powerful confrontations are now playing about the newest Disney film. Or a teacher might notice that it's been several weeks since a child last dictated a story about elderly people and their experiences. Instead, she observes that the children's stories have been full of monsters under the bed.

Is it really over?

When children's interest in an issue seems to wane, teachers can feel befuddled. Are the children really finished with this issue? What happened to their passionate feelings and careful thinking? Is it time to end the project?

These behavioral changes may mean that children are simply done with one aspect of an issue. They may be ready for more complex work on that issue. Or it could mean that children are done with it completely. Here are some strategies that teachers can use to determine if a project is really over or if children just need a nudge from a teacher to continue their work.

Offer children provocative props to use in their play

Sometimes a new prop related to a familiar idea can spark new thinking. For example, a Filipino child in Mira's predominantly European American group declared, "It's not fair that there's no doll who can be my baby—they all have white skin and I have dark skin." Her statement sparked a passionate conversation about the unfairness of having only light-skinned dolls, led to a trip to a toy store to buy a new dark-skinned doll for the classroom, and inspired several weeks of exploration about skin color with paints and crayons. When Mira noticed the children's interest beginning to wane, she decided to add bandages to the doll area, calling the children's attention to the label on the package that said the bandages were "flesh toned." She watched to see if the incongruity between light-colored bandages and the dark skin of the doll reignited the children's interest in fairness issues related to skin color. She hoped that this new prop would move children's thinking to a new level of complexity and feed their energy for activism. At least it would tell her if the children were really done with the project about skin color fairness or if they were simply hungry for new ideas to consider.

Call children's attention to stories and photos of the project

Sometimes hearing the story and seeing photos of their work reinvigorates children. The story and photos may start the children talking about what they want to do next in a project. Other times, the story and photos simply remind children of where they've been. They respond to the story as an interesting event that happened in the past. Children's responses can help determine whether they have had enough or are eager to do more.

Tell a story connected to the project

When children hear a new perspective or approach to an issue, they may feel reenergized about their activism work. Or they may feel bored. Ann used this strategy after children in her group wrote a letter to an oil company after an oil spill. The children seemed to be quickly losing their passion for the issue of pollution and harm to sea animals, so Ann told them a story about a group of school children in coastal Alaska who were working to take care of animals rescued from the oil spill. Ann hoped that the story would inspire the kids in her group to continue their activism. Instead, children responded to the story with comments like, "I'm glad those kids are taking care of the animals." "Those kids are doing good work, just like we did good work when we told that oil company to be more careful." The children were not interested in taking more action. They had written a protest letter and were done with the issue.

Invite children to a meeting "to decide what comes next in this project"

At this meeting, teachers check the pulse of a project by asking the children: "Is there more work that we need to do?" "Do you have new ideas?" "What is our next step in this work?" Children's responses to these questions are typically honest and insightful: "Well, there's more work that we haven't even talked about yet." "I think we're done." "My mom told me an idea that no one even thought of before." "We already did that work." "We still have to do more, but first we have to go to the park because it's really sunny out today." Teachers often get a clear sense of whether the children are finished working on an issue by their comments about what ought to come next in a project.

Invite a visitor to the classroom or plan a field trip

During the project at Hilltop in which children collected money for homeless people, there was a lot of inaction as the children waited for families at the school to bring their donations of coins. Ann worried that the children were losing interest in the project because of this inaction, so she planned several field trips and invited homeless people to visit. These events infused energy into the project, nudging the children to think in new ways about homelessness, rather than abandoning their work in the face of a lot of waiting.

Teachers may use several of these strategies to gauge children's involvement in a project and finally determine that kids are finished with an issue only to be surprised by the reemergence of the project with a new slant or a different goal. This happened at Hilltop during the project about building a ramp to make the school accessible for people in wheelchairs. The children, working with an architect, had reluctantly acknowledged that they couldn't build a ramp without a major renovation of the building. They were beginning to move away from their project and get involved with other ideas and new games when they received a reply to a letter they'd written to a city traffic safety engineer about the need for sidewalk ramps. The engineer invited the children to join her in a few weeks' time at an intersection near the school to break apart the old sidewalk and pour a new one with a ramp. The children responded to her invitation with enthusiasm. They spent the intervening weeks studying the intersection and nearby sidewalks, assessing them for wheelchair accessibility, and talking with people in wheelchairs about how they navigated city sidewalks. The accessibility project resurfaced with a different focus.

This refueling of an activism project may also happen when a child encounters the activism issue in a new way and recounts her experience to the other children. Endings are seldom neat and orderly. Some children may finish with a project in short order; their interests lie elsewhere. Others may want to pursue a topic at length. Other children move in and out of a project all the way along. When there is group consensus about a project being done, life is simple. When some children are interested and others not, teachers do some juggling.

Teachers can continue to work with individual children even when the group momentum for a project has dissipated. It's important to support a child's interest in an activism issue by providing materials, space, and time for her work. When a child has more work to do on an activism project, her teacher may need to create more letter-writing opportunities for her, make room for continuing discussions at meetings, provide resource books to help her continue and extend her thinking, or offer her puppets to act out issues.

Ending a project for adult reasons

There are times when teachers decide to end a project because it no longer serves the best interests of the children, the school, or the community. This story from Fran's days at Madrona exemplifies several of the reasons a teacher might make that call.

> One year, most of Fran's riding vehicles were stolen from the outdoor storage shed. This was especially upsetting to the children because the stolen items included a couple of brand-new, long-awaited shiny red wagons. The children were outraged that someone took trikes and wagons that didn't belong to her. The moral and ethical implications of ownership (when is something really yours and not just something you use and give back?), sharing (when to share, with whom, and for how long), and the difference between stealing and borrowing eventually led the class to the topic of punishment. Although everyone agreed that the thief should be punished, the proposed sentences ranged from vengeful ("We'll go and get all of her stuff that she really likes") to harsh ("She has to go to jail forever") to rehabilitating ("She could say that she is sorry and clean our wagons and bring them back. And we could say, 'Don't ever do that again or you'll get a whipping'").
>
> When the detective who was working on the case came to school to investigate, he got an earful. The children had plenty of ideas on how to catch the thief and what to do with her when they did. The detective, a pleasant and soft-spoken man, listened respectfully to the children. Then he put on his "detective as educator" hat and invited the children to visit the courthouse and a detention center to learn more about the criminal justice system.
>
> It was after he left that Fran put her foot down—gently. Yes, it was unfair that someone had taken the riding vehicles, especially the new red wagons. And

yes, people shouldn't take things without asking first. But this is where the children's involvement would end, Fran decided. They had shared their feelings and recommendations with the adult in charge of the problem. That was enough. Fran wasn't comfortable having the children explore the punitive side of this injustice.

Teachers may end a project when it crosses the boundary from childhood to the world of adults

Teachers have a moral obligation to safeguard childhood by pulling back from activities and experiences that are clearly developmentally inappropriate for young children. Fran recognized that children do not have the cognitive structures or the social and emotional maturity to weigh all the factors and conditions that bring people to take what is not theirs, particularly in a world that unfairly divides its goods and resources, or to understand the emotional and political complexities of the American criminal justice system. This was the terrain of adults, not children. By choosing not to bring the children to the courthouse and detention center—places where adults negotiate issues of crime and punishment—Fran protected the children from an experience she thought they would find frightening and which they did not have the developmental maturity to understand.

Teachers may end a project when it threatens community support for the program

Sometimes teachers' ideas about what is developmentally appropriate activism for young children are different from the understanding held by people in the community. In itself, this need not derail an activism project. Indeed, it may give rise to education of the larger community about the work of young children as change-makers. However, when public scrutiny threatens community confidence in and endorsement of a school, teachers ought to weigh the merits of moving ahead at the risk of losing community support.

In her consideration of the detective's invitation to visit the courthouse and detention center, Fran thought carefully about community values and priorities.

She understood that for the parents, grandparents, and friends of her students of color, as well as for neighbors and community members of color, the judicial system was often considered a tool of oppression, a system that had harmed rather than protected individuals and communities of color. A field trip to the detention center would have put Fran in the position of condoning a system perceived as faulty by the children's families.

Community approval has its roots in cultural values, experiences, and priorities. Teachers whose cultural yardsticks are similar to those of the families and the community will have less difficulty predicting community responses to activism projects. Teachers with different cultural experiences have the ongoing task of learning about the cultures of the children and families they work with and responding to events in culturally sensitive ways.

Teachers may end a project when it lacks parent support

It is unlikely that many parents would list activism as an activity they prioritize for their children in preschool—at least, not until they witness an activism project firsthand. However, when a significant number of parents raise concerns about or objections to an activism project, teachers need to consider whether or not the objections are well founded or strong enough to change course and end the project.

When parents are involved with children's activism projects, they are typically impressed by the ability of the children to think critically and act creatively in response to issues of unfairness. They become excited by the rich array of experiences that activism offers their children. When individual parents express discomfort or disapproval, teachers can best respond by listening openly to their worries, fears, and understandings, and by explaining the ways in which teachers keep activism projects appropriately grounded in the lives of young children.

When a number of parents raise concerns or objections about an activism project, teachers need to take stock. Have teachers misjudged the appropriateness of the activity? Have parents been adequately prepared and informed along the way? Have there been clear invitations to families to be involved? Is the activism issue culturally relevant?

It is difficult to carry out an activism project without the involvement of parents. It is nearly impossible to carry it out without their approval. Even when teachers feel clear that an issue is worth pursuing with children, it can be exhausting to butt heads with parents every step of the way. More importantly, teachers may offend the cultural values of the families with whom they work.

More than likely, if Fran had chosen to accept the invitations of the detective, the parents would have voiced their disapproval. For many, the courthouse and detention center were places where injustice was perpetuated—there was nothing to be gained from a field trip there.

Teachers may end a project when there are concerns for the children's health and safety

Like many places teachers visit with young children, the courthouse and detention center in the story above were not designed with young children in mind. Nor are other places frequented mostly by adults: construction sites, manufacturing plants, office buildings, soup kitchens, fire stations. Investigating unfairness and remedying injustice may take adults and children to places where the safety of the kids is at risk. Adequate planning and preparation, like learning before a trip about possible environmental risks (sharp things, hot things, easy-to-reach and out-of-reach things, for example), can help to compensate for this, as can ample adult supervision. However, the time may come when the risks to the children's safety are too great to offset the learning the field trip might bring.

In addition to concern for the children's physical safety, health concerns may also provide reasons to end or redirect an activism project. Generally, health issues aren't a problem when activism projects take place in a classroom. But when activism carries children out of the classroom, a wide range of concerns enters the picture, ranging from basic cleanliness to toxic fumes. Even fluctuating room temperatures and inappropriate dress can put children at risk for catching colds and other illnesses. (Fran once found herself with a group of children in the cold storage unit of a warehouse!) It may be possible to adjust the project to take account of these concerns. For example, a neighborhood cleanup project could focus on paper litter in order to reduce health risks—and even then, people may decide to wear gloves.

Teachers and parents may be reluctant to end an activism project because of health and safety issues. They may reason that "children do this all the time," that "we'll miss a priceless learning opportunity," or that "risk is a part of learning." All this may be true, but nonetheless there are times when it's not possible to make a particular project safe enough for young children.

Teachers may end a project when there are cost or time constraints or other logistical problems

As teachers work with children to flesh out ideas and understandings about unfairness, they often hear children recommending investigations and solutions that are unrealistic, especially in terms of cost and time. Children's brainstorming and problem solving is imaginative and creative, and their idea of what's possible often differs substantially from that of adults. Children don't consider feasibility when they think about taking a stand against unfairness.

Sometimes instead of ending a project because of logistical constraints, a teacher can help the children reformulate it. For example, children won't be able to build a house for the homeless family they heard about on TV, but they might be able to collect money to help a neighbor replace his stolen wheelchair. They may not be able to buy a new collection of Japanese story tapes for Shiho and Keiko and Spanish story tapes for Miguel and Carlos, but they can begin a collection by asking parents to tape stories in Japanese and Spanish for the classroom. Most likely they won't be able to travel to the next town to see a playground especially designed for children with special needs, but they can write to the children at the school to ask them to send some photos. And it will be hard to get to the karate *dojo* (school) to see strong girls who excel at aikido, but the children can ask the librarian to set aside books for them about strong girls and women without having to negotiate for either time or money.

Logistical challenges such as transportation (Can we walk or will we need to arrange for drivers or take a bus?), scheduling (What hours is that agency open? Can we get back in time for lunch?), adequate supervision (We need at least three parent volunteers), and availability of materials (Where can we find sturdy materials to make signs?) can quickly bog down a project. Teachers can help children reformulate a project, or draw it to a close, when time, logistical, or cost issues present barriers.

Planning the end of a project

When teachers determine that a project is coming to a close—either because children are done with their work on an issue or because teachers have decided to end a project—they must consider these questions: How can the end of a project be acknowledged? What is the best way to talk with children about the outcome of their activism? How can teachers help children locate their activism work in the context of ongoing struggles for justice?

When teachers plan endings to activism projects, they create opportunities to celebrate the children's work. Usually, this involves telling the story, beginning with the initial provocation for the project and noting the children's thought and action along the way. Children are anchored in their immediate experiences. It's challenging for them to mentally carry the first steps of an activism project with them through to the final days. When teachers revisit the story of a project as it comes to an end, the children can hold the project in their minds all at once, as a story in which they were the protagonists. It allows them to see all the pieces and fit them together as a single, successful journey.

Intentional endings highlight the sense of community that grows during activism work. They honor the journey that children, teachers, and families have taken together. The story of an activism project includes many people's feelings, ideas, and actions. When teachers, children, and families revisit the story of a project, they acknowledge the many people involved and notice the range of roles that people played in moving the project forward. This emphasizes the relationships among people, their collaborative work, and the community that grows from relationships and collaboration.

Intentional endings to activism projects give teachers the opportunity to call children's attention to the feelings and critical thinking that led to activism, to underscore the dispositions that lead to activism, and to highlight children's power to stand up for fairness. In this way, teachers can reinforce these dispositions: "This work started when Sam noticed that there were no books in our library that people who are blind can read. He told us that wasn't fair. Other kids agreed. You notice when something's not fair and you want to work to make it fair." "You pay such close attention to ways that people are the same and ways that people are different. You noticed right away that we were missing some colors of paint to match children's skin colors." "As soon as you learned about the problem of people with no homes, you started thinking about why that's not fair and how you could help with that problem. You want to work together to solve problems."

Intentional endings can be as simple as telling the story of an activism project from start to finish and as elaborate as a party for children and their families. There are many ways to intentionally bring a project to a close. Whatever form they take, intentional endings allow children to reflect on their work.

Use the children's and teachers' documentation to make a visible record of a project

Teachers can serve as keepers of memories and history for children, reminding them about how and why a project began and the course it followed. During the project, they take notes and photos, transcribe taped conversations, and encourage children to document their work. At the end of an activism project, teachers can gather all this documentation into a notebook or display to create a record of the project and a testament to the children's shared history. When presented to the children and their families, this notebook communicates to the children that their activism work is valuable. Creating a visual history of an activism journey allows the children to reconstruct the journey, remember their feelings, ideas, and effort, as well as reflect on the meaning a project holds for them. With a written record always available in the classroom, children can work out their own conclusions about an activism issue.

Acknowledge the end of a project by celebrating with family and friends

"We should have a party!" a child, teacher, parent, or member of the community might declare at the end of an activism project. After recounting their frustrations and achievements and taking a deep breath and looking around, children, families, and teachers can gather to celebrate and conclude a successful project.

> The children at Madrona had spent months thinking and planning about building a shelter for homeless people in the vacant lot down the street from the school. However, their plans were dashed when construction began at the site for a bank. The children were sad and discouraged. Fran suggested other ways that they might help people who were homeless, but the children were not interested. They had wanted to build a shelter, and that was not going to happen.
>
> After a week of quiet play, during which the children seemed to be adjusting to the idea that they would not build a shelter, one of the children arrived at school with an idea. The children could put on a concert to raise money to buy toys for children at a homeless shelter near the school. Her plan was quickly accepted by the children. There would be dancing and singing, jokes and food, and admission tickets sold to family members, friends, and neighbors.
>
> The families supported their efforts. Together the adults addressed the many details that four- and five-year-old children overlook. Parents cleaned the school, printed the invitations, rounded up props, and made sure that the children would show up with the food they had promised to bring.
>
> Fran helped the children rehearse. They wanted their performances to surprise their families. There was some tension. A few of the children wanted to "get it right," but mostly they laughed and enjoyed one another's antics. Several children rarely came to practice. They were not committed to performing. Everyone sold tickets, though, and finally the day of the concert arrived.
>
> Moms, dads, aunts, uncles, grandmas, grandpas, siblings, and friends showed up. Father Tim, the parish priest, warmly welcomed everyone and explained to the audience how the children had arrived at their decision to perform. Then Father Tim announced the beginning of the concert, and, as family

members cheered, applauded, and videotaped, the children sang, danced, counted in a number of different languages, told jokes, and pantomimed. The concert ended quickly and the children began serving food: hot dogs, macaroni and cheese, ice cream, and cherry pie. After dinner, beaming with pride and filled with satisfaction, the children followed Fran to their meeting rug while the parents cleaned up. Fran spread out the photos, stories, drawings, and copies of letters that told the story of the children's work to help people who were homeless.

This was their story and their ending. As parents gathered quietly at the edges of the rug, they listened respectfully to what the children were remembering: the sad things and the happy things, the people they met whom they liked and the people whom they didn't like much at all, the exciting times and the disappointing times. "I guess I liked most of it," said Graham of the long journey these young activists were just completing. A few tears rolled down the faces of some admiring adults, and Fran felt moved herself by the power of the children's feeling and thinking.

Focusing on children as change-makers

Sometimes activism projects end with their goal accomplished—food is delivered to the food bank, money is collected for toys for a homeless shelter, brown crayons in a range of shades are added to the art area. Other times, projects end because their goal cannot be accomplished. Building a wheelchair ramp at Hilltop, for example, proved to be too big a project for the children and their families to undertake. Teachers may worry about how to talk with children about the outcome of their activism, especially when a project ends in seeming failure. In this case, it's useful to focus on children's willingness to work for fairness, rather than on the success or failure of an activism project. Teachers can convey messages like these to the children: "We couldn't do everything we planned, but we did do the important work of learning about this problem and trying to solve it. You're people who care about fairness, and I know you'll keep noticing when there are problems about fairness to solve." "You've thought hard about how to make this more fair, and you helped other people pay attention to this problem too. As more and more people learn about this problem, it will become easier to solve. You're teaching people to pay attention to this problem, so that we have more help solving it."

Ann and her class weren't able to build a wheelchair ramp at Hilltop. The undertaking was not nearly as simple as she'd hoped it would be. She thought they could replace stairs with a ramp, but the architecture of the building required major renovations to incorporate a ramp. This was a discouraging end to a long project. The children did not easily reconcile themselves to this conclusion. Ann worried about them. Would their disappointment overwhelm them? What feelings about activism would this experience inspire? Would they be discouraged from future activism?

Ann and the children talked together about the importance of the work that they did—the value of noticing unfairness, explaining it to other people, and working to make it more fair. Ann emphasized how deeply she appreciated that they were people who were willing to take a stand for fairness. She wasn't sure how much that message mattered to the children, until several weeks had passed and she began to notice the way that the children approached issues of unfairness.

Ann and the children took a trip to a beach a couple weeks after the final decision was made not to build a ramp at school. On that trip, Ann briefly parked the school van in a parking space designated for wheelchair users while she adjusted the van's mirrors and driver's seat. The children were outraged: "Ann, you are parking in a place for people in wheelchairs. That's not fair!" "You should not take up this space from people who really need it, like Sophie's dad!" "You have to move the van right now." Delighted by their passion and conviction, she quickly moved the van.

After this experience, Ann observed the children emphatically pointing out unfairness and acting on what they noticed. "It's not really fair that your block house doesn't have any ramp for people in wheelchairs. You better build one on your house." "It's not fair that boys use up all the blocks. Girls should get a turn, too, you know." "It's not fair that I only get three crackers for snack, because I'm really hungry. I didn't eat any lunch, and now I need more crackers than the sign says I'm supposed to have."

Truly, the children had become change-makers.

At the same time, as children come to the end of an activism project, teachers sometimes are concerned that children will feel that a problem is solved forever, or that their responsibility to help others is fulfilled. With their adult awareness, teachers recognize that injustice continues, and they may be tempted to emphasize that to the children. Children, though, are rooted in the immediacy of life. Often, the activism that they undertake is about helping specific people in specific ways, rather than engaging in long-term social and political campaigns. They see clearly when their work is done—and they leave a project with a strengthened sense of themselves as change-makers.

This sense of themselves is the doorway through which children enter the community of people committed to fairness. Rather than communicate in serious and weighty tones that there is still much unfairness in the world to address, teachers can tell children stories about other people who work for justice. As children hear stories of other people's activism work, they develop an understanding that activism is an ongoing, community effort. Teachers can point out to children that they are part of that community, that they are change-makers doing important work alongside other people.

Safe, Strong and Free

Words and music
©1984 Judi Fjell (BMI)

Safe strong and free! That's how we all should be! Safe strong and free in our lives!

Safe strong and free! That's how we all should be! Safe strong and free in our lives! 1. Rich or

poor, young or old, on a cit - y street or a coun - try road, ——

Man or wom - an, boy or girl, we should all feel safe in this old world! ——

2. At home or school, work or play
In the middle of the night, in the middle of the day
With strangers, friends and family
We should all feel safe as safe can be!

3. No more secrets that shouldn't be
When we are safe and strong and free
So let's work until we understand
How to stop all those hurting hearts and hands!

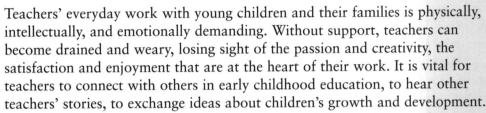

Chapter 7

Rest Stops and Other Oases: Finding Support

Teachers' everyday work with young children and their families is physically, intellectually, and emotionally demanding. Without support, teachers can become drained and weary, losing sight of the passion and creativity, the satisfaction and enjoyment that are at the heart of their work. It is vital for teachers to connect with others in early childhood education, to hear other teachers' stories, to exchange ideas about children's growth and development.

Teachers who expand their work to include activism projects need support more than ever. You are stepping into a nontraditional arena, breaking new ground, working on the cutting edge of anti-bias education. Your role as trailblazers may leave you feeling proud, uncertain, self-conscious, excited, overwhelmed, isolated, inspired. It is crucial to be in contact with like-minded people who understand and support activism work to exchange reassurances, encouragement, and reflections on your ideas for moving a project forward.

Teachers need support as activism draws community attention

Activism projects are different from typical early childhood programming. A typical early childhood curriculum project might cover dinosaurs, with field trips to a museum to study skeletons. Most people expect early childhood programs to focus on similarly innocuous curriculum. When teachers and children go instead to the mayor's office carrying a request for more homeless shelters, or when children put up signs in the neighborhood asking people to join them in a clean-up campaign, or when children send drawings and messages to a television station asking for more cartoons about girls, people notice. Activism with young children can draw the attention of people who usually ignore what is going on in child care settings.

Similarly, teachers encouraging activism need to become aware of the relationships connecting their programs to the larger community—relationships that they might otherwise take for granted. They have probably never worried about how an agency administrator will respond to a project on dinosaurs. They need not consider the effect of a trip to the zoo on the church pastor's work. But teachers need to consider what neighbors will think about an activism project aimed at improving traffic safety. They may well worry about how the elementary teachers with whom they share a building will perceive a project about wheelchair ramps. It is important for teachers to acknowledge that their activism can cause reverberations in the community, and that it can engender conflict or at least a little extra work in educating others about what is going on.

Teachers who engage in activism with young children are not necessarily seasoned activists themselves. In fact, many may just be awakening to the possibility of taking action in the face of injustice, even as they recognize this potential in children. Regardless of whether this aspect of their identity is emerging or solid, all teachers who engage in activism work with young children are continuously growing and learning, developing new skills and deepening established skills.

There are no particular answers or formulas for how teachers ought to respond to their new roles and to other people's curiosity and interest. Mostly, it is important for teachers to notice their feelings, to be thoughtful about how their feelings affect their work, to be aware of how they communicate with people in the community, to listen for and be open to feedback from people in the community, and to find support for themselves as they step into activism with young children.

Publicity in the local news media can cause a flood of new emotions, as well. Teachers may feel proud that their efforts have been publicized—and simultaneously angry that the reporter has not shared the same vision or interpretation of the project. Nearly everyone feels this way about the news media, but teachers bear the extra responsibility of helping children, their families, and the programs they work for respond to the sometimes unwelcome attention. It is natural to feel mixed emotions about coverage in the local news.

Ann: One year, the children in my class decided to collect money for people who were homeless and to distribute the money through a series of walks downtown where many homeless people in Seattle spend their days. As our first "giving walk" approached, one of the parents called the newspaper, proud of the children and eager to call attention to their work. A columnist, intrigued, came to meet with the children and me. He spent most of a morning

That's Not Fair! A Teacher's Guide to Activism with Young Children

with the children, talking and listening to them, even helping them count some of the coins they'd collected. He highlighted the children's project in a column that appeared on Christmas Eve, emphasizing the children's good-hearted, straightforward, and simple approach to helping people who are homeless: "They're not going to solve any broad problems this way," he wrote. "But they are going to chip away at some pretty hard hearts out there on the downtown sidewalks. Little chips, but still. Happy Holidays."

When the column appeared, I was proud of the children's work and of my work, glad for the homelessness project to be publicly recognized. But I also felt protective, wanting the project to be acknowledged not as innocent and charming, an appealing holiday story, but as a powerful and determined effort to address injustice. I was aware of the public scrutiny of my work. Would people read the column and be aghast, thinking that it was not appropriate for young children to walk around downtown handing out money to homeless people? I felt vulnerable and self-protective, wondering about people's assessment of my judgment as a teacher. I also felt pressure to do a really good job with the project in light of the public recognition—to show people that activism with young children is appropriate and empowering and quite manageable, that I was a wise and competent teacher and the children were capable and strong.

Teachers need support for their own continued growth

Through activism, teachers hone documentation skills, learn new ways of planning, and build communication skills with families. They learn how to nurture genuine partnerships with parents. Teachers who engage in activism with young children are always growing and learning, developing new skills and deepening established skills.

Teachers need support for this continuing education. They need opportunities to discuss the disequilibrium that often comes with learning. They may want coaching from coteachers and teacher educators. They may just want time to read about a particular topic related to activism work. Support for teacher learning might take many forms. The key principle is that teachers don't undertake this work alone, that they don't have to learn in isolation, that they can find support and resources for learning.

Support for activism with young children

You can find support from a range of people and places. We've generated a list of places to begin building support. You can probably add to the list we've begun.

- Friends and partners
- Coteachers and administrators
- Teacher educators and parent educators
- Parents in your programs
- Workshops and conferences
- Support groups and teacher networks
- The Internet

Friends and partners

With friends and partners, teachers can share their deepest fears, doubts, excitement, and hopes—feelings that you might not be comfortable sharing with the teachers and families with whom you work. Your friends and partners know your personal histories, your ongoing struggles, and your fiercest passions. They can help you reflect on how these influence your activism work with young children. When a project flourishes, they celebrate with you, and when a project hits a snag or falls apart, they offer comfort and tenderness. Set up a regular weekly time with a friend or with your partner to talk about your anti-bias work with children. Explain that you want their support for this important and challenging work. You might arrange a phone call after your kids are in bed one night a week or an afternoon meeting at a coffee shop. You might plan to spend half an hour or an hour focusing on your anti-bias work. Make a plan with your friend or partner that you'll really keep to that topic, and ask them to help you stick to that plan. You may feel self-conscious focusing your conversation on your work, or you might worry that your friend is not really interested. You might be tempted to set aside a conversation about anti-bias work to talk instead about other things happening in your life. Remember, though, that you've asked your friend or your partner to support you and that she or he has agreed because they care about your and the work you do. Your work with children is challenging and provocative and often stirs up big emotions. You deserve to spend time exploring your feelings and reflections with people who love you.

- When you're not involved with an activism project, use your weekly conversations with a friend or partner to explore what's important to you about anti-bias activism. Why do you want to do this work? What scares you about it? What excites you? What strengths do you bring to this work? What are your biggest challenges?

- When an activism project is under way, use your weekly conversations to reflect on feelings that come up for you. What's going well? What feels overwhelming? How are your interactions with families going? Where do you feel stuck? What's energizing about the project for you? Is there something that you feel uneasy about? Is there something you're eager to celebrate?

- During your conversations with a friend or your partner, practice talking about anti-bias activism as though you're talking with parents, explaining, for example, why you believe this work is important for young children, or describing how you keep anti-bias projects grounded in the children's understandings and feelings. Ask your friend or partner for feedback about how you communicate about anti-bias activism.

- You may find that regular meetings with a friend become difficult to schedule, with the challenges of balancing family, work, and community commitments. You may decide to have regular conversations in cyberspace, taking advantage of e-mail to "talk" with a friend.

Coteachers and program administrators

Coteachers and program administrators know the context in which you work. They understand the complexities of your program in ways that people outside the program don't, and they understand the intricacies of teaching. Coteachers and administrators also know the specific children and families with whom you work. With this shared knowledge, coteachers and administrators can be part of your support network. They can offer insights about children and families, and they can suggest ways to overcome challenges that grow in your programs. They may be able to help you free up some time for activism project work and for documentation. They may join their voices with yours in talking with parents about the value of anti-bias activism.

Here are some ways you can begin to draw on your coteachers and program administrators for support:

- Ask that time be set aside at every staff meeting to talk about anti-bias issues that the children are encountering, burgeoning activism projects, aspects of anti-bias work like the anti-bias goals, or ways to acknowledge children and teachers' cultural identities in the classroom.

- Identify other staff members at your school who might be interested in forming an anti-bias work group. You might agree to read a book about anti-bias teaching and talk about it together at a monthly potluck. You might decide to meet after school on a regular basis to help each other think about what you each can do to support children's anti-bias learning. You might spend time in each other's classrooms, helping each other arrange your classrooms to encourage anti-bias activism projects.

- Ask another teacher to work with you to write an article for your program's newsletter about anti-bias work. This opens the door to continuing conversations about anti-bias work with this fellow staff member and also lets the families who read the newsletter know that there are several people on the staff who think about anti-bias work.

- Suggest that your program schedule an in-service training workshop about anti-bias work with young children.

Teacher and parent educators

Some early childhood programs have teacher or parent educators, or trainers, available to help support teachers' work with children and families. They come to programs ready to help teachers develop new teaching practices, extend relationships with families, and grow professionally in other ways. They understand children's growth and can help teachers anchor their activism work in children's development. They are skillful in talking with parents about children's learning and about important teaching practices, as well as in helping teachers learn about parents' values and beliefs. If your program does not have access to a teacher or parent educator or to a trainer, you may be able to get some of the same kinds of support from a director or a mentor teacher from another program.

In her work at Madrona, Fran relied on Barbara, the parent educator, for support as she learned how to talk about anti-bias activism with parents. Barbara helped Fran think about how to ground her work in inclusive, developmentally appropriate practice and coached her about ways to respond to parents' issues. Ann relies on Margie, the teacher educator at Hilltop, to help her think about children's developmental understanding of activism issues. Margie also offers Ann logistical help when a project is under way. She gathers resources for Ann and helps with documentation, taking notes, photos, or videotape; arranging a bulletin board to keep families posted on what's happening; and putting photos in notebooks for the children to see.

Teacher and parent educators come to you ready to support your work. Here are some of specific ways you can enlist their help:

- If your center has access to a teacher educator or trainer, ask that person to help you strengthen the skills that support anti-bias activism. (If you work in a center where regular supervision meetings with a director are part of the system, that might be another place to do this work.) You might want to deepen your ability to observe children's play and identify the issues that children are thinking about. Or you might want to develop new ways to talk with children to understand their ideas. Or you might want to learn how to create an informative and attractive display to tell the story of a project. Your teacher educator can help you with your professional development if you describe skills you would like to acquire.

- When an activism project is unfolding, ask your teacher or parent educator for ideas about how you might proceed. You can describe some of your feelings and questions to her or him, and ask for input about challenges and puzzles. Your teacher or parent educator may have access to resources that you can use in the classroom; keep her or him posted about activism projects in your classroom.

- Ask your teacher or parent educator to review your written messages to families, to make sure that your ideas are clear. Ask her or him for suggestions about how to learn about families' ideas and values when a project is under way.

- Invite your teacher or parent educator to a parent meeting to help you talk about anti-bias activism with families.

- Ask your teacher or parent educator to help you in the classroom with observations of the children: she or he may be able to spend time videotaping the children, taking notes while you facilitate group meetings, or jotting down observations of children during their play. She or he may also be able to help you think about your observations of the children as you try to understand the children's understandings and questions.

- Ask your teacher or parent educator to help mediate any conflicts or misunderstandings with families that arise during an activism project.

- Invite your teacher or parent educator to advocate for anti-bias activism and your work with young children with other members of the community, for example, with the administrators of other programs housed in your building, at a community center gathering, or at local elementary school Parent–Teacher Association meeting.

Parents in our programs

You may not immediately think of parents as part of your support systems, but nonetheless they can help you in your work. Parents offer new perspectives growing from their cultural values, beliefs, and life experiences about activism issues and about their children. These new perspectives help you widen your understanding, and may suggest new ideas. Parents can talk with other parents about the value of anti-bias work, lending their voice to your voices—a great source of support. And parents may have culturally specific resources and life experiences to offer that make activism work much richer than it otherwise would be.

Here are some ways to include parents in your support systems:

- Ask a parent who shares your understanding of the value of anti-bias activism with young children to help you lead a parent meeting. This builds a solid partnership with that parent, and, too, gives you concrete support in talking with other parents about activism.

- Ask a parent who supports anti-bias activism to write an article for your program's newsletter or a letter to families in your classroom, describing why she or he thinks anti-bias activism is a good thing for children.

- Alert parents to emerging activism projects from the very beginning, asking them to share ideas and resources with you.

- Ask parents for help in understanding the cultural aspects and implications of working on a particular social justice issue.

Workshops and conferences

Workshops and conferences can help to connect you with other teachers who share your commitment to anti-bias work with young children. They help you stay aware of the most current thinking in early childhood education, and offer you opportunities to extend our learning. Workshops and conferences support your growth as teachers.

- To learn about conferences and workshops in your area, join your local affiliate of the National Association for the Education of Young Children (NAEYC). To learn about membership, contact: NAEYC, 1509 16th St. NW, Washington, DC 20036-1426. The phone number for NAEYC is 800-424-2460. Their e-mail address is membership@naeyc.org.

- Other organizations hold conferences that address anti-bias and diversity issues. Like NAEYC, they hold conferences at national and local levels. Some of these groups are:
    Council for Exceptional Children, Division for Early Childhood: 1920 Association Drive, Reston, VA 20191; 888-232-7733.
    National Black Child Development Institute (NBCDI): 1023 15th Street NW, Suite 600, Washington, DC 20005; 800-556-2234.
    National School-Age Care Alliance (NSACA): 1137 Washington Street, Boston, MA 02124; 617-298-4012.

REACH: Helping People Understand and Value Diversity: REACH Center, 4464 Fremont Avenue North, Suite 300, Seattle, WA 98103; 206-545-4977.

YMCA: 101 North Wacker Drive, Chicago, IL 60606; 800-872-9622.

For help locating conferences or workshops in your area, call the Educational Resources Information Center (ERIC) Calendar of Education Conferences at 800-538-3742 or find the calendar on the Internet at www.accesseric.org.

■ When you attend a conference, think of your time as an opportunity for in-depth study. Read the conference program ahead of time and choose a series of workshops related to one topic, rather than dividing your time—and your attention—among several different areas. This lets you explore several aspects of one topic, deepening your understanding.

■ Encourage your local early childhood organizations to hold workshops about anti-bias teaching, and ask other teachers and parents to do the same.

■ Several regions of the country have been the site for training about culturally relevant, anti-bias work as part of a national project; teachers in Seattle, St. Paul/Minneapolis, and New Orleans have been working with the Culturally Relevant Anti-Bias Leadership Project, and are available to speak and lead groups. Teachers in other cities, such as Chicago, Boston, and San Francisco, have also received special training about leading workshops about anti-bias education. To learn more about this training and people available to lead workshops in your area, contact Louise Derman-Sparks at Pacific Oaks College in Pasadena at 626-397-1306.

■ In many communities, child care resource agencies sponsor classes and workshops. Contact your local resource and referral agency to learn about teacher training that they sponsor.

■ As you become comfortable with anti-bias curriculum and anti-bias activism projects, offer to lead workshops or host discussions for teachers in your community. This is a surefire way to meet other teachers who are interested in anti-bias work.

Support groups and teacher networks

Fran helped create a support group in Seattle for teachers doing anti-bias work. The group met monthly for teachers to share stories about anti-bias work, to offer each other suggestions about resources and teaching strategies, and to listen to each other's feelings and reflections about doing this challenging work. Fran describes these meetings as "little booster shots of courage."

To form a support group, consider these suggestions:

■ Whenever possible, work with people from different cultural groups to establish a teacher support group. This helps assure that a range of perspectives is represented.

- Choose a meeting place that is centrally located, convenient for people who ride the bus, and feels safe and welcoming. This may be a person's home, a church hall, a community center, the classroom of a community college, or the teacher lounge of a child care center.

- Decide on how frequently you will meet. You might choose to meet weekly, monthly, every six weeks, or once a quarter.

- Send an announcement about the group's meetings to child care centers and preschools, community college early childhood education programs, organizations and agencies that work with teachers of young children, and teacher and parent educators. Useful information to list in your announcement includes the focus of the group's meetings, the meeting place and time, and the name and phone number of a person to call to get more information.

- Design the group's meetings to include plenty of time for informal discussion and sharing stories, as well as time to explore an area or topic in depth. Sometimes an emerging issue will swell to fill the whole meeting time. Other times, it may be most useful to the teachers in the group to share resources.

- Expect a slow start. You may decide to make follow-up phone calls after sending your announcement, to send a more personal invitation. Persist even when the going gets rough, or when only two or three folks show up. It is important for the community to know that a group exists that takes anti-bias activism seriously. Send out another batch of announcements every six months reminding people about the group's meetings.

- The book *Future Vision, Present Work* (Cronin et al.: St. Paul, Redleaf Press, 1998) offers detailed descriptions, based in real experience, of support groups for teachers doing anti-bias and cultural relevancy work.

On the Internet

Many teachers feel isolated from other early childhood teachers who are committed to anti-bias work. The Internet can help you dissolve that sense of isolation by connecting you with teachers all over the United States (and all over the world) who are trying to do this work. Teachers share stories, suggest resources, think about challenges, and offer one another support using Internet connections. Here are some ways that the Internet can provide support for your work.

- When you meet a like-minded teacher at a conference or workshop, be sure to exchange e-mail addresses. This way, you can offer each other support for your anti-bias teaching. If you don't have e-mail at work or at home, most public libraries have free public access to the Internet, and there are free Internet-based e-mail services available (two of the most widely used are Hotmail and Yahoo!).

■ ERIC is an education resource on the Internet sponsored by the National Library of Education. You can access this database of documents and journal articles at http://ericir.syr.edu. In addition, ERIC hosts more than 20 "listservs" focused on various topics in education, with links from their site. Listservs are a way to have ongoing conversations with other teachers over the Internet.

As you step into the challenges and gifts that anti-bias activism holds, you can draw strength and inspiration from many sources. Your deep-rooted commitment is key to this work. Anti-bias activism grows out of

■ your concern that every child will grow up in a world that is fair and equitable for all people
■ your commitment to children's whole growth and development
■ your respect for children's ability to recognize and challenge unjust acts and deeds
■ your passion for and your practices of taking action to address social and environmental injustice
■ your deepened understanding of the anti-bias goals and principles and how they work to liberate the lives of all children and families you work with, and yourselves

In supporting young children's eagerness to remedy injustice, you honor their moral passion. You teach children to be aware and responsible, committed to relationships with other people and with nature. You affirm that their hearts, minds, and bodies are all vital to learning. And you set children on course to be change-makers, decrying injustice and actively working to create a world of equity, freedom, and peace for all people. What a gift you offer children, what a difference you make in their lives, when you invite them to join you on a journey into anti-bias activism.

Resources

Books for teachers

Anti-bias and diversity education

Judith Bernhard, Marie Louise Lefebvre, Gyda Chud, and Rike Lange (1995) *Paths to Equity: Cultural, Linguistic, and Racial Diversity in Canadian Early Childhood Education*. North York, ON: York Lanes Press.

Julie Bisson (1997) *Celebrate! An Anti-Bias Guide to Enjoying Holidays in Early Childhood Programs*. St. Paul: Redleaf Press.

Hedy Nai-lin Chang, Amy Muckelroy, and Dora Pulido-Tobiassen (1996) *Looking In, Looking Out: Redefining Child Care and Early Education in a Diverse Society*. San Francisco: California Tomorrow.

Gyda Chud and Ruth Fahlman (1985) *Early Childhood Education for a Multicultural Society*. Vancouver, BC: Pacific Educational Press.

Sharon Cronin, Louise Derman-Sparks, Sharon Henry, Cirecie Olatunji, and Stacey York (1998) *Future Vision, Present Work: Learning from the Culturally Relevant Anti-Bias Leadership Project*. St. Paul: Redleaf Press.

Lisa Delpit (1995) *Other People's Children: Cultural Conflict in the Classroom*. New York: The New Press.

Louise Derman-Sparks and the ABC Task Force (1989) *Anti-Bias Curriculum: Tools for Empowering Young Children*. Washington, DC: National Association for the Education of Young Children.

Janet Gonzalez-Mena (1997) *Multicultural Issues in Child Care*. Second Edition. Mountain View, CA: Mayfield Publishing.

Janice Hale (1986) *Black Children: Their Roots, Culture, and Learning Styles*. Baltimore: Johns Hopkins University Press.

Nadia Saderman Hall and Valerie Rhomberg (1995) *The Affective Curriculum: Teaching the Anti-Bias Approach to Young Children*. Scarborough, ON: Nelson Canada.

Susan Hopkins and Jeff Winters (1990) *Discover the World: Empowering Children to Value Themselves, Others, and the Earth*. Gabriola Island, BC: New Society Publishers.

Frances E. Kendall (1996) *Diversity in the Classroom: New Approaches to the Education of Young Children*. New York: Teachers College Press.

Gloria Ladson-Billings (1994) *The Dreamkeepers: Successful Teachers of African American Children*. San Francisco: Jossey-Bass.

Enid Lee, Deborah Menkart, and Margo Okazawa-Rey (1998) *Beyond Heroes and Holidays: A Practical Guide to K-12 Anti-Racist, Multicultural Education and Staff Development*. Washington, DC: Network of Educators on the Americas.

Bonnie Neugebauer, Ed. (1992) *Alike and Different: Exploring Our Humanity with Young Children*. Washington, DC: National Association for the Education of Young Children.

Patricia G. Ramsey (1998) *Teaching and Learning in a Diverse World: Multicultural Education for Young Children*. Second Edition. New York: Teachers College Press.

B. D. Tatum (1997) *Why Are All the Black Kids Sitting Together in the Cafeteria? And Other Conversations About Race*. New York: Basic Books.

The Teaching Tolerance Project (1997) *Starting Small: Teaching Tolerance in Preschool and the Early Grades*. Montgomery: Southern Poverty Law Center.

Trisha Whitney (1999) *Kids Like Us: Using Persona Dolls in the Classroom*. St. Paul: Redleaf Press.

Leslie Williams and Yvonne De Gaetano (1995) *Alerta: A Multicultural, Bilingual Approach to Teaching Young Children*. Menlo Park, CA: Addison-Wesley.

Stacey York (1999) *Big as Life: The Everyday Inclusive Curriculum*. St. Paul: Redleaf Press.

Conflict negotiation and peacemaking

Diane E. Levin (1994) *Teaching Young Children in Violent Times: Building a Peaceable Classroom*. Cambridge, MA: Educators for Social Responsibility.

Kathleen McGinnis and Barbara Oehlberg (1988) *Starting Out Right: Nurturing Young Children as Peacemakers*. Oak Park, IL: Meyer Stone Books.

Vivian Gussin Paley (1992) *You Can't Say You Can't Play: The Habit of Rejection*. Cambridge, MA: Harvard University Press.

Ronal Slaby, Wendy Roedell, Wendy Arezzo, and Kate Hendrix (1995) *Early Violence Prevention*. Washington, DC: National Association for the Education of Young Children.

Susanne Wichert (1989) *Keeping the Peace: Practicing Cooperation and Conflict Resolution with Preschoolers*. Philadelphia: New Society Publishers.

Supporting children's dispositions for activism

Elizabeth Crary (1982) *I Want to Play*. Seattle: Parenting Press.

Elizabeth Crary (1996, 2d edition) *My Name Is Not Dummy*. Seattle: Parenting Press.

Nancy E. Curry and Carl N. Johnson (1990) *Beyond Self-Esteem: Developing a Genuine Sense of Human Value*. Washington, DC: National Association for the Education of Young Children.

Carolyn Pope Edwards (1986) *Promoting Social and Moral Development in Young Children: Creative Approaches for the Classroom*. New York: Teachers College Press.

Marion C. Hyson (1994) *The Emotional Development of Young Children: Building an Emotion-Centered Curriculum*. New York: Teachers College Press.

Lilian G. Katz and Diane E. McClellan (1997) *Fostering Children's Social Competence: The Teacher's Role*. Washington, DC: National Association for the Education of Young Children.

Patricia G. Ramsey (1991) *Making Friends in School: Promoting Peer Relationships in Early Childhood*. New York: Teachers College Press.

Judith Spayth Riley (1984) *How to Generate Values in Young Children*. Washington DC: National Association for the Education of Young Children.

Child-centered curriculum practices

David Armington (1997) *The Living Classroom: Writing, Reading, and Beyond*. Washington, DC: National Association for the Education of Young Children.

Louise Boyd Cadwell (1997) *Bringing Reggio Emilia Home: An Innovative Approach to Early Childhood Education*. New York: Teachers College Press.

Margie Carter and Deb Curtis (1994) *Training Teachers: A Harvest of Theory and Practice*. St. Paul: Redleaf Press.

Sydney Gurewitz Clemens (1983) *The Sun's Not Broken, A Cloud's Just in the Way: On Child-Centered Teaching*. Mount Rainier, MD: Gryphon House.

Deb Curtis and Margie Carter (1996) *Reflecting Children's Lives: A Handbook for Planning Child-Centered Curriculum*. St. Paul: Redleaf Press.

Carolyn Edwards, Lella Gandini, and George Forman, Eds. (1998) *The Hundred Languages of Children: The Reggio Emilia Approach to Early Childhood Education*. Second Edition. Norwood, NJ: Ablex Publishing.

Elizabeth Jones and John Nimmo (1994) *Emergent Curriculum*. Washington, DC: National Association for the Education of Young Children.

Elizabeth Jones and Gretchen Reynolds (1992) *The Play's the Thing: Teachers' Roles in Children's Play*. New York: Teachers College Press.

Gretchen Reynolds and Elizabeth Jones (1997) *Master Players: Learning from Children at Play*. New York: Teachers College Press.

Documentation

Margie Carter and Deb Curtis (1996) *Spreading the News: Sharing the Stories of Early Childhood Education*. St. Paul: Redleaf Press.

Judy Harris Helm, Sallee Beneke, and Kathy Steinheimer (1998) *Windows on Learning: Documenting Young Children's Work*. New York: Teachers College Press.

For teachers growing as activists

Maurianne Adams, Lee Anne Bell, and Pat Griffin, Eds. (1997) *Teaching for Diversity and Social Justice: A Sourcebook*. New York: Routledge.

Cecelia Alvarado, LaVita Burnley, Louise Derman-Sparks, Eric Hoffman, Linda Irene Jiménez, June Labyzon, Patricia Ramsey, Annette Unten, Beth Wallace, and Barbara Yasui (1999) *In Our Own Way: How Anti-Bias Work Shapes Our Lives*. St. Paul: Redleaf Press.

Margaret L. Anderson and Patricia Hill Collins (1992) *Race, Class, and Gender: An Anthology.* Belmont, CA: Wadsworth Publishing.

Lillian Bridewell-Bowles (1998) *Identity Matters: Rhetorics of Difference.* Upper Saddle River, NJ: Prentice Hall.

Antonia Darder (1991) *Culture and Power in the Classroom: A Critical Foundation for Bicultural Education.* New York: Bergen and Garvey.

Angela Davis (1983) *Women, Race, and Class.* New York: Vintage Books.

Louise Derman-Sparks and Carol Brunson Phillips (1997) *Teaching/Learning Anti-Racism.* New York: Teachers College Press.

Janice Hale (1994) *Unbank the Fire.* Baltimore: Johns Hopkins University Press.

bell hooks (1992) *Ain't I a Woman: Black Women and Feminism.* Boston: South End Press.

bell hooks (1994) *Teaching to Transgress: Education as the Practice of Freedom.* New York: Routledge.

Gary Howard (1999) *We Can't Teach What We Don't Know.* New York: Teachers College Press.

Paul Kivel (1996) *Uprooting Racism: How White People Can Work for Racial Justice.* Gabriola Island, BC: New Society Publishers.

Alice McIntyre (1997) *Making Meaning of Whiteness: Exploring Racial Identity with White Teachers.* Albany, NY: SUNY Press.

Vivian Gussin Paley (1979) *White Teacher.* Cambridge, MA: Harvard University Press.

Vivian Gussin Paley (1995) *Kwanza and Me.* Cambridge, MA: Harvard University Press.

Vivian Gussin Paley (1997) *The Girl with the Brown Crayon.* Cambridge, MA: Harvard University Press.

Vivian Gussin Paley (1998) *The Kindness of Children.* Cambridge, MA: Harvard University Press.

Suzanne Pharr (1988) *Homophobia: A Weapon of Sexism.* Inverness, CA: Chardon Press.

Elizabeth Tertell, Susan M. Klein, and Janet L. Jewett, Eds. (1998) *When Teachers Reflect: Journeys Toward Effective, Inclusive Practice.* Washington, DC: National Association for the Education of Young Children.

For parents

Sara Bullard (1996) *Teaching Tolerance: Raising Open-Minded, Empathetic Children.* New York: Doubleday.

Elizabeth Crary (1996) *My Name's Not Dummy: A Children's Problem-Solving Book.* Second Edition. Seattle, WA: Parenting Press. (Other books in this series of children's problem-solving books are *I Want It, I Want to Play,* and *I Can't Wait.*)

Marian Wright Edelman (1992) *The Measure of Our Success.* Boston: Beacon Press.

Darlene Hopson and Derek Hopson (1993) *Raising the Rainbow Generation*. New York: Simon and Schuster.

Derek Hopson and Darlene Hopson (1992) *Different and Wonderful: Raising Black Children in a Race-Conscious Society*. New York: Simon and Schuster.

Barbara Mathias and Mary Ann French (1996) *40 Ways to Raise a Nonracist Child*. New York: HarperCollins.

Maureen Reddy (1994) *Crossing the Color Line*. New Brunswick, NJ: Rutgers University Press.

Maureen Reddy (1996) *Everyday Acts against Racism*. Seattle: Seal Press.

Journals and magazines

For teachers

Rethinking Schools is a journal advocating for reform of elementary and secondary public schools that focuses on "urban schools and issues of equity and social justice." Although it doesn't specifically focus on early childhood issues, this important journal keeps teachers abreast of issues affecting children as they enter kindergarten and describes the ways that teachers are actively working to make schools more just for all children. To subscribe:

> Rethinking Schools
> 1001 E. Keefe Avenue
> Milwaukee, WI 53212
> 414-964-9646

Teaching Tolerance is a national forum in which teachers share their experiences and learn about new strategies for promoting tolerance and diversity. This free magazine has been recognized as a leader in the movement to teach fairness, justice, and equality to students of all ages. It is published semiannually by the Southern Poverty Law Center. To subscribe:

> Southern Poverty Law Center
> 400 Washington Avenue
> Montgomery, AL 36104

For children

Skipping Stones: A Multicultural Children's Magazine is a children's magazine that encourages cooperation, creativity, and celebration of cultural and linguistic diversity. In their own words, they "explore and learn stewardship of the ecological and social webs that nurture us." It is published bimonthly, except July/August. To subscribe:

> Skipping Stones
> P.O. Box 3939
> Eugene, OR 97493
> 541-342-4956

Books for children

Books about taking a stand against unfairness

This collection of children's books covers a wide range of topics dealing with social and environmental injustice. Some events occur in the past, as far back as slavery. Others are about more recent events and highlight such issues as homelessness, hunger, and homophobia. In some books, an individual stands up to bias and unfairness. In others, people (and fish!) work together for justice. All underscore the importance of taking action in the face of individual and institutional bias.

Some of the books listed here use language more appropriate for older children. Teachers can edit, paraphrase, or modify the stories to suit their audience. We encourage teachers to modify old favorites to reflect different social relationships and to spotlight environmental concerns. We also encourage teachers to write and tell stories to kids, stories that come from experiences they have shared with the children and their families and communities, as well as stories arising from their own personal experiences with unfairness, bias, and activism.

Gloria Anzaldua (1993) *Friends from the Other Side/Amigos del Otro Lado*. San Francisco: Children's Book Press. Having crossed the Rio Grande into Texas with his mother, Joaquin is confronted with prejudice by his peers but receives help and friendship from his friend Prietita.

Joyce Durham Barrett (1989) *Willie's Not the Hugging Kind*. New York: Harper Trophy. Willie really does like to be hugged and finally challenges his friend who says hugging is silly.

Eve Bunting (1993) *Someday a Tree*. New York: Clarion. Alice's favorite tree is dying. If she can't save it, maybe there is something else she can do to honor her cherished tree.

Evelyn Coleman (1996) *White Socks Only*. Morton Grove, IL: Albert Whitman and Company. A grandmother tells the story about her first trip alone into town during the days when segregation still existed in Mississippi.

Robert Coles (1995) *The Story of Ruby Bridges*. New York: Scholastic. This is the extraordinary story of Ruby Bridges, the first black child to attend an all-white elementary school. Amidst a storm of hatred and prejudice, she prevails with courage and dignity and becomes an important part of history and an example to all Americans.

Tomie dePaola (1989) *Oliver Button is a Sissy*. New York: Harcourt Brace Jovanovich, 1979. Oliver is teased for liking to do things that "girls like," but that doesn't stop him from doing what he likes best—dancing!

DyAnne DiSalvo-Ryan (1991) *Uncle Willie and the Soup Kitchen*. New York: Morrow Junior Books. A young boy spends the day in a soup kitchen with his Uncle Willie, who works preparing and serving food for the hungry and tries to make a difference in the lives of his neighbors.

Alice Faye Duncan (1995) *The National Civil Rights Museum Celebrates Everyday People*. Mahwah, NJ: BridgeWater Books. This book pays homage to the men, women, and children whose courage and determination helped advance the cause of freedom for all.

V. S. Epstein (1984) *History of Women for Children*. Milwaukee: Quality Press. The difficulties and successes of women's search for equality are highlighted in this book.

Virginia Fleming (1993) *Be Good to Eddie Lee*. New York: Philomel Books. Christy's friend calls Eddie Lee, a child with Down's syndrome, a "dummy" and tells him to go away. But Christy decides to venture out and make friends with Eddie Lee.

Peter Golenbock (1990) *Teammates*. New York: Harcourt Brace. When Jackie Robinson became the first black player in major league baseball, he experienced intense prejudice. This book depicts the acceptance and support he received from Pee Wee Reese, one of his teammates.

Eloise Greenfield (1973) *Rosa Parks*. New York: Harper. This story for young children is about Rosa Parks and the Montgomery Bus Boycott.

Nikki Grimes (1994) *Meet Danitra Brown*. New York: Lathrop, Lee & Shepard. This is a collection of 13 poems about a special friendship between two girls who stand by each other in good times and in hard times.

Donna Guthrie (1988) *A Rose for Abby*. Nashville: Abingdon Press. Abby, whose father preaches in a large urban church, sees a homeless woman searching the trash cans nearby and is inspired to do something for the neighborhood's many street people.

Betsy Hearne (1997) *Seven Brave Women*. New York: Greenwillow Books. A young girl tells the story of seven women in her family. Each woman lived during a war and did many brave things but did not fight in or support the war.

Eric Hoffman (1999) *No Fair to Tigers/No Es Justo Para los Tigres*. St. Paul: Redleaf Press. Mandy asks her family members to help her put her old stuffed tiger back together, but their suggestions don't seem fair. This story about a girl with a disability and her stuffed tiger shows how they ask for fair treatment and solutions to the problems they encounter.

Mary Hoffman (1991) *Amazing Grace*. New York: Dial Books. Although classmates say that she can't play Peter Pan in the school play because she is black and a girl, Grace perseveres with the love and support of her family.

James Howe (1999) *Horace and Morris but Mostly Dolores*. New York: Atheneum Books for Young Readers. Three young mice friends overcome gender stereotyping by learning to do what they like rather than what others say they should like.

Bud Howlett (1993) *I'm New Here*. Boston: Houghton Mifflin Company. Jazmin has just moved to the United States from El Salvador. Her first day in the fourth grade is a disaster: everyone mispronounces her name, she can't understand what anyone says, and she's taunted for having dark skin. But she perseveres, finding acceptance on the soccer field and with a new friend who defends her from racial taunts.

Norma Klein (1973) *Girls Can Be Anything*. New York: Dutton. A young girl challenges her friend Adam's ideas about gender roles.

Margy Burns Knight (1993) *Who Belongs Here?* Gardiner, ME: Tilbury House Publishers. This book describes Nary's life in America. Nary, a refugee from Cambodia, must deal with many incidents of prejudice in this new country.

Kurusa (1995) *The Streets Are Free*. Buffalo, NY: Annick Press. A group of children in San Jose, Venezuela, campaign for a city park. Their efforts take them to the mayor's office and involve their parents and neighbors.

Arthur Levine (1993) *Pearl Moscowitz's Last Stand*. New York: Tambourine Books. When the city government tries to chop down the last gingko tree on her street, which was planted many years ago by her family, Pearl, with the support of her friends, takes a stand.

Leo Lionni (1963) *Swimmy*. New York: Alfred A. Knopf. One small fish, the sole survivor of a school of fish swallowed by a huge tuna fish, organizes another school of fish to stand up to the big, powerful fish that are a constant threat to their survival.

Marybeth Lorbiecki (1998) *Sister Anne's Hands*. New York: Dial Books. Seven-year-old Anna first learns about racism when an African American nun comes to teach at her parochial school.

B. Mack (1979) *Jessie's Dream Skirt*. Carrboro, NC: Lollipop Power. At preschool, a young boy dresses up in a skirt and is teased by his classmates. He finds support in his male teacher.

Margaret Merrifield (1998) *Come Sit By Me*. Toronto: Women's Press. Some of the children at school aren't allowed to play with Nicholas because he has AIDS, but Karen still plays with him.

William Miller (1998) *The Bus Ride*. New York: Lee and Low Books. An African American child protests an unjust law in this story loosely based on Rosa Parks's historic decision not to give up her seat to a white passenger on a bus in Montgomery, Alabama, in 1955.

Ken Mochizuki (1993) *Baseball Saved Us*. New York: Lee and Low Books. Surrounded by guards, fences, and desert, Japanese Americans in an internment camp create a baseball field. A young boy tells how baseball gave him a purpose while enduring injustice and humiliation both in the internment camp and when he returned home.

F. N. Monjo (1970) *The Drinking Gourd*. New York: Harper & Row. A young white child works to help free slaves in the underground railroad.

Holly Near (1993) *The Great Peace March*. New York: Henry Holt. "We will have peace, we will because we must. We must because we cherish life." A story adapted from a song that describes people's coming together to march for peace.

Min Paek (1978) *Aekyung's Dream*. San Francisco: Children's Book Press. Aekyung, an immigrant from Korea, is unhappy in her new country. She is teased about her looks and her language. But she is inspired by her family, her dreams, and the words of the 15th century King Sejong: "You must be strong like a tree with deep roots."

Rascal (1994) *Oregon's Journey*. Mahwah, NJ: BridgeWater Books. A dwarf in a circus helps the circus bear escape and takes him back to the mountains of Oregon. In the process, the dwarf also becomes free.

Christopher Raschka (1990) *R and Я: A Story About Two Alphabets*. Elgin, IL: Brethren Press. Members of the English and the Russian alphabets are at war. One day, several letters from the two alphabets meet accidentally and discover their similarities. They begin a movement toward peace.

Faith Ringgold (1992) *Aunt Harriet's Underground Railroad in the Sky*. New York: Crown Publishers. With Harriet Tubman as her guide, Cassie retraces the steps escaping slaves took on the Underground Railroad in order to reunite with her younger brother.

Faith Ringgold (1995) *My Dream of Martin Luther King*. New York: Crown Publishers. The author/illustrator brings her own voice and artistic vision to the life of Martin Luther King Jr. and the history of the civil rights movement.

Anne Shelby (1993) *What to Do About Pollution*. New York: Orchard Books. A look at what individuals can do about such problems as pollution, hunger, and loneliness.

Judith Vigna (1992) *Black Like Kyra, White Like Me*. Morton Grove, IL: Albert Whitman & Co. When Christy's friend Kyra, who is African American, and her family move into Christy's all-white neighborhood, prejudice and cruelty appear. But Christy and Kyra's families confront the prejudice and remain close friends.

Judith Vigna (1995) *My Two Uncles*. Morton Grove, IL: Albert Whitman & Co. Elly's grandfather has trouble accepting the fact that his son is gay. Elly learns about homophobia when his son, Elly's uncle, refuses to attend a family gathering when his partner is not welcome.

Sharon Dennis Wyeth (1998) *Something Beautiful*. New York: Bantam Doubleday Dell. When a young girl goes looking for "something beautiful" in her city neighborhood, she find beauty in many different forms. Then she takes action to create beauty in her own backyard.

Charlotte Zolotow (1972) *William's Doll*. New York: Harper & Row. William is called a sissy for wanting a doll, but his grandmother understands the importance of a boy's having a doll and buys one for him.

Books about similarities and differences

This collection of books is useful in helping children understand and become comfortable with differences.

Arnold Adoff (1973) *Black Is Brown Is Tan*. New York: HarperCollins. A biracial family uses playful language to describe their different skin colors.

Charles E. Avery (1992) *Everybody Has Feelings*. Seattle: Open Hand Publishing. Using candid photographs and minimal text, children will recognize their feelings in the faces of this diverse collection of children.

Rochelle Bunnett (1995) *Friends at School*. New York: Scholastic. This book conveys the importance and warmth of children with many differences who share, support, love, and learn from one another.

Eve Bunting (1991) *Fly Away Home*. New York: Clarion Books. A homeless family moves between airport terminals trying not to be noticed.

Shelley Cairo (1985) *Our Brother Has Down's Syndrome*. Toronto: Women's Press. A child describes the things that are the same and different about herself and her brother with Down's syndrome.

Margery Schwartz Chalofsky, Glen Finland, and Judy Wallis (1992) *Changing Places: A Kids' View of Shelter Living*. Mount Rainier, MD: Gryphon House. Eight homeless children describe their experiences living in homeless shelters.

Cheltenham Elementary School Kindergarten (1991) *We Are All Alike, We Are All Different*. New York: Scholastic. This delightful book was written and illustrated by children. They notice differences first among snowflakes and then among themselves.

Norah Dooley (1991) *Everybody Cooks Rice*. Minneapolis: Carolrhoda Books. As Carrie travels from house to house in her multiethnic neighborhood looking for her brother at dinnertime, she discovers everybody cooking and eating rice.

Laura Dwight (1992) *We Can Do It*. New York: Checkerboard Books. Gina, David, Jewel, Emiliano, and Sarah are five children with special needs. In this book, we see all the different things they can do.

Rosamund Elwin and Michele Paulse (1990) *Asha's Mums*. Toronto: Women's Press. A child faces having to put two moms' names on a field trip permission slip.

Mem Fox (1997) *Whoever You Are*. San Diego: Harcourt Brace. "Every day, all over the world, children are laughing and crying, playing and learning, eating and sleeping. They may not look the same. They may not speak the same language. And their lives may be quite different. But inside, they are just like you."

Ina Friedman (1984) *How My Parents Learned to Eat*. Boston: Houghton Mifflin. An American sailor courts a Japanese woman. Each tries to secretly learn the other's way of eating.

Carmen Garza (1990) *Family Pictures/Cuadros De Familia*. San Francisco: Children's Book Press. A bilingual story of an Hispanic family and their community experiences.

Roberta Grobel Intrater (1995) *Two Eyes, a Nose, and a Mouth*. New York: Scholastic. This book celebrates people's similarities and differences through brilliant, colorful photographs of many multicultural faces.

Aylette Jenness (1990) *Families: A Celebration of Diversity, Commitment, and Love*. Boston: Houghton Mifflin. This book features seventeen children who tell the stories of their different families.

Barbara Joose (1996) *I Love You the Purplest*. San Francisco: Chronicle Books. Two boys discover that their mother loves them equally but in different ways. This book celebrates the unique qualities that make every child an individual.

Katie Kissinger (1997) *All the Colors We Are: The Story of How We Get Our Skin Color*. St. Paul: Redleaf. This book helps children understand the truths about skin color and that it is one way we are special and different.

Susan Kuklen (1992) *How My Family Lives in America*. New York: Aladdin Paperbacks. Sanu, Eric, and April are three American children, each of whom has a parent that didn't grow up in the United States. This book, filled with photographs, describes the mingling of cultures in each family.

Patricia Lakin (1994) *Dad and Me in the Morning*. Morton Grove, IL: Albert Whitman. As a Deaf boy and his father begin a day together at the beach, they talk with each other about the beauty of the sunrise and their plans for the day.

Ada Litchfield (1980) *Words in Our Hands*. Chicago: Albert Whitman. A hearing child describes his experiences living with Deaf parents.

George Littlechild (1993) *This Land Is My Land*. Emeryville, CA: Children's Book Press. Artist George Littlechild describes his experiences growing up, relating them to the struggles of Native Americans.

Pili Mandelbaum (1990) *You Be Me and I'll Be You*. Brooklyn: Kane/Miller. A European American dad explores his biracial daughter's feelings about wanting to be white.

Bill Martin and John Archambault (1987) *Knots on a Counting Rope*. New York: Henry Holt. A blind child asks his grandfather to tell the story of his birth and childhood in a traditional Native American community.

Leslea Newman (1989) *Heather Has Two Mommies*. Boston: Alyson Wonderland. At playgroup, Heather discovers that there are many different kinds of families, and she proudly draws a picture of herself with her two mommies.

Naomi Shihab Nye (1994) *Sitti's Secrets*. New York: Simon & Schuster Books for Young Children. An Arab American girl travels to the Middle East to meet her Palestinian grandmother.

Jeanne Whitehouse Peterson (1977) *I Have a Sister—My Sister Is Deaf*. New York: Harper & Row. A girl describes the things her sister can do and the things her sister can't do because she's Deaf.

Daniel Manus Pinkwater (1977) *The Big Orange Splot*. New York: Scholastic. A man lives on a street where all the houses are the same. When a seagull drops a can of orange paint on his house, he is inspired to change his house so it reflects him. He convinces his neighbors to do the same.

Mary Beth Quinsey (1986) *Why Does That Man Have Such a Big Nose?* Seattle: Parenting Press. This books shows a positive attitude toward differences in people and how they look.

Maxine B. Rosenberg (1983) *My Friend Leslie*. New York: Lothrup, Lee, and Shephard Books. Karin's descriptions of her friend Leslie address many of the questions and feelings that children may have when they first meet a child with special needs.

Ellen B. Senisi (1998) *For My Family, Love, Allie*. Morton Grove, IL: Albert Whitman. Allie struggles to find a way to give a gift to her large, extended, biracial family.

Muriel Stanek (1989) *I Speak English for My Mom*. Niles, IL: Albert Whitman. A Mexican American child translates for her mother until her mother learns English.

Michael Valentine (1991) *The Duke Who Outlawed Jellybeans*. Boston: Alyson Wonderland. This book is filled with fairy tales about kids who have lesbian and gay parents. The emphasis is not on lesbian and gay identity issues. It simply weaves lesbian and gay characters into the fairy tales.

Darwin Walton (1985) *What Color Are You?* Third Edition. Chicago: Johnson Publishing. Filled with color photos, this book explores similarities and differences, with an in-depth focus on the reasons for skin color differences.

Michael Willhoite (1990) *Daddy's Roommate*. Boston: Alyson Wonderland. A boy describes his life with his gay father and his father's partner.

Songs for children in songbooks and on tape/compact disc

Peter Blood and Annie Patterson, Eds. *Rise Up Singing: The Group Singing Songbook*. Available from Sing Out! P.O. Box 5253, Bethlehem, PA 18015.

Woody Guthrie. *Woody's 20 Grow Big Songs*. Rising Son Records.

Ruth Pelham. *Under One Sky*. Available from Music Mobile, P.O. Box 6024, Albany, NY 12206.

Sarah Pirtle. *Linking Up: Using Music, Movement and Language Arts for Caring, Cooperation, and Communication*. Available from The Discovery Center, 63 Main Street, Shelburne Falls, MA 01310, or from Redleaf Press (800-423-8309).

Malvina Reynolds. *Artichokes, Griddle Cakes, and Other Good Things; Funny Bugs, Giggle Worms, and Other Good Friends; Tweedles and Foodles for Young Noodles*. Available from Sisters Choice, 704 Gilman Street, Berkeley, CA 94710, or at www.sisterschoice.com.

Sing for Freedom: The Story of the Civil Rights Movement Through Its Songs. Available from Sing Out! P.O. Box 5253, Bethlehem, PA 18015.

Sweet Honey in the Rock. *All for Freedom*. Available at most music stores.

Red Grammer. *Teaching Peace*. Available at most music stores.

Various artists. *Peace Is the World Smiling*. Available at most music stores.

The Children's Music Network is an excellent resource for teachers. Their mission statement declares that "quality children's music strengthens an understanding of cooperation, of cultural diversity, and of self-esteem . . . and that it enhances children's thinking skills and feelings of empowerment." They can be reached at P.O. Box 1341, Evanston, IL 60204-1341; (847) 733-8003; www.cowboy.net/~mharper/CMN.htm.

Smithsonian Folkways Recordings carry the music of Ella Jenkins, Suni Paz, Pete Seeger, and others who have collected and created music for children that reflects and validates American cultures outside the dominant mainstream. Available from Center for Folklife Programs and Cultural Studies, 955 L'Enfant Plaza, Suite 7300, Smithsonian Institute, Washington, DC 20560.

Index

academic learning, 8. *See also specific activities*
accessibility, 83. *See also* wheelchair ramp project
active work, 71. *See also* teacher roles; teaching strategies
activist dispositions, 21–42
    comfort with differences, 23, 29–33
    defined, 21
    empathy, 22, 23, 35–37
    examples, 21–23
    and family involvement, 109, 117–119
    identifying unfairness, 23, 38–40
    inclusion/collaboration among children, 23, 33–35
    problem solving, 23, 40–42
    and program planning, 24–29
    resources, 152–153
administrators, 144–145
adult relationships to activism
    adult dispositions, 117–119
    adult vs. children's agendas, 8, 15, 26, 51–52
    discomfort, ix, 1, 8, 66
    and observation, 74–75
    and teacher preparation, 14–15
affirmative action, 51–52
Alvarado, Cecelia, 2
Anti-Bias Curriculum: Tools for Empowering Young Children (Derman-Sparks & ABC Task Force), ix, xv, 1, 2, 11, 16
anti-bias curriculum, 1–6
    authors' personal experiences, xi–xvi
    and benevolence, ix
    four goals of, 2–6
    resources, 151–152
    and teacher preparation, 16
art activities, 31–32, 84–85

bathroom project, 61–62
Bell, Derrick, xiv
benevolence, ix
bias. *See* anti-bias curriculum; unfairness
Black Is Brown Is Tan (Adoff), 63
block catapult project, 25–26
Blue Angels project, 105–108
body size project, 49–50
books
    and comfort with differences, 33
    and empathy, 37
    and provocations, 50–51
    resources, 156–161
    and teaching strategies, 84
    See also literacy activities
bulletin boards, 80, 82, 116, 117

Carter, Margie, xi, 55
catapult project, 25–26
celebrations, 136–137
child-centered curriculum, xii
    and activist dispositions, 26
    and critical thinking, 10
    and family involvement, 118
    and project emergence, 45–48
    resources, 153
    and teacher preparation, 16–17
children as change-makers, x, 9, 41, 135, 137–138

children of color, xiv, 11–12. *See also* non-dominant–culture children
class differences, 13. *See also* homelessness; hunger project
classroom agreements, 26–27
classroom environment, 74, 76, 83
    and anti-bias goals, 4–5
    and comfort with differences, 4–5, 31–32, 33
    and continuing strategies, 129
    and identifying unfairness, 39
classroom visitors, 75, 87
    and comfort with differences, 33
    as continuing strategy, 130–131
    and provocations, 50
coaching
    and conflict negotiation, 27
    and empathy, 36–37
    and inclusion/collaboration among children, 34
    and problem solving, 41
collaboration among children. *See* inclusion/collaboration among children; problem solving
collaboration among teachers, 17
comfort with differences. *See* differences, comfort with
community attention, 141–143
community-building, 13–14, 95
concluding projects, 127–139
    continuing strategies, 129–131
    planning for, 135–139
    signs of waning interest, 128–129
    teacher intervention, 131–135
conferences, 147–148
conflict negotiation, 26–27, 152
construction, 72–76
continuing education, 143, 154
coteachers, 144–145
Council for Exceptional Children, 147
critical thinking, 10–11
    and anti-bias goals, 5
    and project emergence, 60–63, 67
    and questioning, 60, 87
Cronin, Sharon, 149
crosswalk project, 9, 10
cultural differences
    and concluding projects, 132–133
    and family involvement, 108–110, 122–123
    and support groups, 148
Culturally Relevant Anti-Bias Leadership Project, 148
Curtis, Deb, 55

Davidson, Fran, xiii–xv
demonstrating knowledge, 84–85
Derman-Sparks, Louise, ix, 1, 2, 11, 112, 148
developmental tasks, 2, 3, 113
dictating. *See* literacy activities
differences, children's awareness of, 2, 31
differences, comfort with, 9–10, 23
    and anti-bias goals, 5
    books about, 159–161
    and classroom environment, 4–5, 31–32, 33
    encouraging, 29–33
direct nature of children's activism, 7, 29, 138–139

disabilities, people with, 50–51. *See also* wheelchair ramp project

diverse books project, 12
Doctorow, E. L., 71
documentation, 78, 80–83
    child-made, 85–86
    and concluding projects, 136, 137
    as continuing strategy, 129
    and family involvement, 82–83, 116–117, 118, 119
    hunger project, 103
    and meetings, 90
    resources, 153
    stories, 84
    timeline example, 96–103
dominant-culture children, xii, xiii, 4, 12–13, 32
drama, 37
dramatic play. *See* play; *specific projects*

Edwards, Carolyn Pope, 3
electoral campaigns, 52
emergent curriculum. *See* child-centered curriculum
emotions. *See* feelings
empathy, 9–10, 13, 22, 23, 104
empowerment, x, 9, 41, 135, 137–138
enrollment forms, 109, 110–111
ERIC, 148, 150
Erikson, Erik, x
expert role, 67, 92–93, 117

family involvement, 13–14, 75, 105–124
    and activist dispositions, 109, 117–119
    barriers to, 119–124
    Blue Angels project, 105–108
    and comfort with differences, 32
    and concluding projects, 133, 135
    and cultural differences, 108–110, 122–123
    dialogue among parents, 113–115
    and documentation, 82–83, 116–117, 118, 119
    during projects, 115–117
    hunger project example, 99, 101, 102
    parent educators, 145–146
    and project management, 95
    and questioning, 80
    resources, 155
    sharing teachers' values, 111–113
    and support, 147
    teacher preparation, 17
fanciful nature of children's activism, 7
feelings
    calling attention to, 34
    and community attention, 142–143
    empathy, 22, 23, 35–37
    and project emergence, 57–60, 67
    songs, xviii, 37
    vocabulary for, 37
"Feelings and Faces" game, 37
fence-building project, 22–23
field trips, 75, 86–87, 130–131
Fjell, Judi, 140
flannelboard stories, 32
"Food Bank Rap" (Schimmel), 70
food banks, 6, 70, 98, 101, 102
Francisco, Kim, xi, xiii
friendships, 34, 35
Future Vision, Present Work (Cronin et al.), 149

gay and lesbian people, 45–46, 51
gender stereotypes, 2, 3
    classroom environment, 83
    field trips, 86–87
    observation, 27–28
    songs, 20
glass in the parking lot, 53–54
Gregory's brother project, 58
group discussions. *See* meetings
Gutiérrez, María, 112

health issues, 134
Helping Others Learn to Teach (Katz), 21
Hilltop Children's Center, xii–xiii
historical context, 31
homelessness projects
    acknowledging feelings, 59–60
    and activist dispositions, 29, 31
    community attention, 142–143
    concluding, 128, 136–137
    documentation, 80, 81
    family involvement, 119
    teacher input, 68, 91–92
    teaching strategies, 83–84
home visits, 110
homophobia, 45–46
hunger project
    and anti-bias goals, 6
    observation, 71–72
    songs, 70
    timeline, 96–103

identifying unfairness
    and activist dispositions, 23
    and anti-bias goals, 5
    encouraging, 38–40
    and family involvement, 113
    and value of activism, 8
inclusion/collaboration among children, 23, 33–35, 36
In Our Own Way (Alvarado et al.), 2
internalized bias, 11–12
Internet, 149–150

Johnson, Patty, 2
journals, 116

Katz, Lillian, 21
Katz, Phyllis, 2
Kids Like Us (Whitney), 88
Kozol, Jonathan, 12

The Last Free Bird, 52
lesbian and gay people, 45–46, 51
literacy activities, 85–86, 91–92, 116
logistical challenges, 120, 134–135

Madrona Cooperative Preschool, xiv–xv
Mama Zooms, 84
Mankiller, Wilma, 83
meetings, 90
    as continuing strategy, 130
    and project emergence, 60–63
    and waning interest, 128
miming games, 37
modeling, ix
"Moods and Emotions" game, 37
Mr. Beasley project, 9, 10–11, 12, 13
multicultural curriculum, xv, 1
My Teacher's in a Wheelchair, 84

National Association for the Education of Young Children (NAEYC), 147
National Black Child Development Institute (NBCDI), 147
National School-Age Care Alliance (NSACA), 147
negotiation, 26–27, 152. *See also* problem solving
non-dominant–culture children, xiv, 4, 11–12, 27
note taking, 55–57, 76, 78
NSACA (National School-Age Care Alliance), 147
observation, 71–72, 76, 78
    and activist dispositions, 27–29
    and adult relationships to activism, 74–75
    and family involvement, 109
    and project emergence, 55–57
    and teacher/parent educators, 146
older people. *See* Mr. Beasley project

pacing, 95–96
parent conferences, 117
parent educators, 145–146
parent meetings, 110, 117, 146
peacemaking, 152
Pelham, Ruth, 104
Pelo, Ann, xi–xiii
periodicals, 155
Persian Gulf War, 115
persona dolls, 32, 37, 74, 88–89
Phillips, Carol Brunson, 112
photos, 57, 78, 80
play
    and activist dispositions, 24–26, 27–29
    and cultural relevance, 109–110
    and empathy, 36
    entering in, 90–92
    and teacher preparation, 16–17
    and waning interest, 129
    See also observation; *specific projects*
play food example, 38
"Playing Winnie-the-Pooh" (Schimmel), 20
polls, 32
pollution, 52, 55–57
Prejudice: A Big Word for Little Kids, 2
privilege. *See* dominant-culture children
problem solving, 10–11, 23
    encouraging, 40–42
    and identifying unfairness, 39
    and inclusion/collaboration among children, 34
    and play, 25–26
program planning
    and activist dispositions, 24–29
    ongoing activities, 93–94
    project management, 94–96
    theme units, 3, 24
project emergence, 45–69
    acknowledging feelings, 57–60, 67
    appropriateness, 51–53
    critical thinking, 60–63, 67
    facilitating action, 63–66
    observation, 55–57
    sources, 45–51
    teacher responses, 66–69
project examples
    bathroom, 61–62
    Blue Angels project, 105–108
    body size, 49–50
    catapult project, 25–26
    crosswalk project, 9, 10
    diverse books, 12
    fence building, 22–23
    glass in the parking lot, 53–54
    Gregory's brother, 58
    homophobia, 45–46
    hunger project, 6, 70, 71–72, 96–103
    Mr. Beasley, 9, 10–11, 12, 13
    protecting the new trees, 65–66
    rocket building, 33–34
    saving the cedar tree, 44, 47–48
    saving the turtles, 46–47
    sidewalk project, 40–41
    skin color differences, 30–31, 62–63
    speeding cars project, 85–86
    stolen toys, 131–132
    timeline, 96–103
    violent puppet show, 63–64
    weapon play, 79–80
    wheelchair ramp, 72–76, 77, 80, 82, 87, 138
    Winnie-the-Pooh, 27–28
    See also homelessness projects
project management, 94–96
Promoting Social and Moral Development in Young Children (Edwards), 3
props, 129. *See also* classroom environment
protecting the new trees, 65–66

provocations, 48–51
publicity, 141–143
puppets, 4, 32, 37

questioning, 60, 78–80, 87–88

racism, 11–12, 30–31, 88–89. *See also* skin color differences
REACH, 148
receptive work, 71. *See also* teacher roles; teaching strategies
reflective questions
    observation, 55
    project appropriateness, 53
    teacher preparation, 15, 16, 17, 18
Reggio Emilia, xii, 48, 67
research. *See* observation
resources, 151–162
    activist dispositions, 152–153
    anti-bias curriculum, 151–152
    books, 156–161
    child-centered curriculum, 153
    conflict negotiation, 152
    documentation, 153
    parents, 155
    periodicals, 155
    songs, 161–162
Rethinking Schools, 155
"Ring Around the Cedar Tree" (Schimmel), 44
rocket-building example, 33–34
rules, 26–27

"Safe, Strong and Free" (Fjell), 140
safety issues, 133–134
Savage Inequalities: Children in America's Schools (Kozol), 12
saving the cedar tree project, 44, 47–48
saving the turtles project, 46–47
scheduling, 94–95
Schimmel, Nancy, xviii, 20, 44, 70, 126
scrapbooks, 80
self-esteem, 4–5, 8–9
sidewalk project, 40–41
skin color differences, 30–31, 62–63, 129
Skipping Stones, 155
social skills, 6
songs, xviii, 20, 37, 70, 104, 140
    resources, 161–162
"Speaking Up" (Schimmel), 126
speeding cars project, 85–86
standing up against unfairness
    and anti-bias goals, 6
    books about, 156–159
    children's school experiences, 45–46
    songs, 126
    See also identifying unfairness
Start Seeing Diversity (Wolpert), 2
stolen toys project, 131–132
storytelling, 84, 91–92
    and anti-bias goals, 4
    and concluding projects, 135
    as continuing strategy, 130
    and identifying unfairness, 39
    See also books; persona dolls
suggestions. *See* expert role
support, 141–150
    and community attention, 141–143
    coteachers and administrators, 144–145
    friends and partners, 144
    Internet, 149–150
    support groups, 148–149
    teacher/parent educators, 145–146
    teacher preparation, 17–18
    workshops and conferences, 147–148
support groups, 148–149

tape recordings, 57, 76, 78, 117
teacher educators, 145–146
teacher intervention, 13, 68, 91–92
    concluding projects, 131–135
teacher networks, 148–149
teacher preparation, 14–18
teacher roles
    authority, 121–122
    and compensation, 123–124
    expert role, 67, 92–93, 117
    gatekeeper, 122–123
    intervention, 13, 68, 91–92, 131–135
    modeling, ix
    observation, 55–57, 76
    provocation, 48–51
    responses to project emergence, 66–68
    See also teaching strategies
teaching strategies, 71–103
    classroom environment, 74, 76, 83
    classroom visitors, 87
    continuing, 129–131
    and demonstrating knowledge, 84–85
    entering in play, 90–92
    expert role, 92–93
    field trips, 86–87
    meetings, 60–63, 90
    persona dolls, 88–89
    questioning, 78–80, 87–88
    receptive vs. active roles, 71–76, 77
    storytelling, 83–84
    See also documentation; observation
Teaching Tolerance, 155
"Teaching Young Children to Resist Bias: What
    Parents Can Do" (Derman-Sparks, Gutiérrez,
    & Phillips), 112
telephone trees, 117
theme units, 3, 24
thinking games, 3–4, 37
timeline example, 96–103
The Trumpet of the Swan (White), 50–51
trust, x

understanding the issue, 47
unfairness
    and anti-bias goals, 3–4, 5
    early learning process, 2
    identifying, 5, 8, 23, 38–40, 112
    standing up against, 6, 45–46, 126, 156–159
updates, 116

value conflicts, 109–110
videotapes, 57, 117
violent puppet show, 63–64
visitors. *See* classroom visitors

war, 115
weapon play, 79–80
webs, 80, 81
What Color Are You?, 63
"What Do I Do?" (Pelham), 104
wheelchair ramp project, 72–76, 77, 80
    classroom visitors, 87
    concluding projects, 138
    documentation, 82
    persona dolls, 74, 88
    teacher roles, 77
"When I Feel Mad" (Schimmel), xviii
"When You're Happy and You Know It," 37
white children, 32. *See also* dominant-culture chil-
    dren
White, E. B., 50–51
Whitney, Trisha, 88
Why Does That Man Have Such a Big Nose?, 49
Winnie-the-Pooh (Milne), 20, 27–28
Wolpert, Ellen, 2
working parents, 123
workshops, 147–148

YMCA, 148
young children's activism
    characteristics of, 7–8, 15, 29, 138–139
    value of, 8–14

Other Resources from Redleaf Press

Big as Life: The Everyday Inclusive Curriculum, Volumes 1 & 2
By Stacey York
From the author of *Roots and Wings,* these two curriculum books explore the environment of a child's life and the connections that make life meaningful.

In Our Own Way: How Anti-Bias Work Shapes Our Lives
By Cecelia Alvarado, LaVita Burnley, Louise Derman-Sparks, Eric Hoffman, Linda Irene Jiménez, June Labyzon, Patricia Ramsey, Annette Unten, Beth Wallace & Barbara Yasui
Filled with the personal reflections of people who have worked in child care, each story shows how each came to think critically in his or her own life.

Future Vision, Present Work: Learning from the Culturally Relevant Anti-Bias Leadership Project
By Sharon Cronin, Louise Derman-Sparks, Sharon Henry, Cirecie Olatunji & Stacey York
Based on three leadership groups that performed cross-cultural advocacy work across the country, this book offers the latest information addressing anti-bias and cultural relevancy issues for your program.

Celebrate! An Anti-Bias Guide to Enjoying Holidays in Early Childhood Programs
By Julie Bisson
Filled with strategies for implementing holiday activities that are exciting, not biased, and developmentally appropriate.

Anti-Bias Books for Kids

Best Best Colors/Los mejores colores
By Eric Hoffman
The story of a boy with same-sex parents and the dilemma of choosing favorites—colors, friends, and even mamas.

Heroines and Heroes/Heroínas y héroes
By Eric Hoffman
The story about Kayla and Nate's wonderful play adventures and how leadership, bravery, and strength are not limited to gender.

No Fair to Tigers/No es justo para los tigres
By Eric Hoffman
The story of a girl and her stuffed tiger and how they ask for fair treatment and solutions to the problems they encounter.

Play Lady/La señora juguetona
By Eric Hoffman
A story about how children can cope with hate crime in their own neighborhood.

800-423-8309